Data Analysis
with
Excel

By

Manisha Nigam

FIRST EDITION 2019

ISBN: 978-93-88176-67-5

Distributors:

BPB PUBLICATIONS
20, Ansari Road, Darya Ganj
New Delhi-110002
Ph: 23254990/23254991

BPB BOOK CENTRE
376 Old Lajpat Rai Market,
Delhi-110006
Ph: 23861747

MICRO MEDIA
Shop No. 5, Mahendra Chambers,
150 DN Rd. Next to Capital Cinema,
V.T. (C.S.T.) Station, MUMBAI-400 001
Ph: 22078296/22078297

DECCAN AGENCIES
4-3-329, Bank Street,
Hyderabad-500195
Ph: 24756967/24756400

Published by Manish Jain for BPB Publications, 20, Ansari Road, Darya Ganj, New Delhi-110002 and Printed by Repro India Pvt Ltd, Mumbai

Preface

Brief Excel History

Microsoft Excel dates back to 1985 when the first version of Excel v1.0 was released on Macintosh and a Windows version 2.0 followed in 1987. Since then Excel has come a long way and now it is one of the most popular and vastly used spreadsheets. It has functions for calculations, graphing tools, pivot tables, data analysis tools, macro programming and also allows add-ins that enable more complex operations.

Version of Excel Referred in this Book

Excel has multiple versions, popular being Excel 2013, 2016 and is available on multiple platforms like Windows and Mac. There is also an Office 365 version of Excel that comes with the Microsoft Office 365 Suite. This book has been written for desktop version of Microsoft Excel 2016 for Windows only and not Mac. Excel 2013 & 2019 users may also find information in this book relevant and useful.

Also note that this book does not cover the touch screen gestures. In case you are working on a device that has touch screen enabled, then you will need to follow the touch screen commands instead of the keyboard and mouse actions given in this book. For example, 'Click' may be equivalent to 'Tap' in your touch screen.

Who can use this Book?

Anyone who wants to learn Excel and how it can help them to easily and quickly do the mundane tasks, complex calculations, analyze huge data from internal or external sources, take decisions based on predictions, do forecasting, create plans, charts, reporting dashboards for progress and status etc.

The intend of this book is to explain and simplify the usage of Excel features and functionalities, with help of examples. We hope that this book will enable users in working efficiently and will increase their workplace productivity. We assume that the users reading this book have basic knowledge of working with Excel like opening Excel, navigating around, enter data etc. Microsoft's official support website has been used as a reference for this book. For understanding a subject in depth, like the statistical or finance terms used in this book, we advise users to refer to subject related documentation or an expert.

How is the Book Organized?

Chapters 'Getting Started with Excel' and 'Performing functions with shortcut keys' will help you in getting started with Excel. You will learn about the basic components of Excel, the available menu options and tools, some customizations, working with multiple workbooks and worksheets, most frequently used and useful keyboard shortcuts.

Chapter 'Formulas and Functions' gives an initial understanding of what are formulas, functions, their components and in the later sections it goes on to explain important functions under different categories. Multiple examples have been used to explain the usage in real world scenario.

Chapters 'Data Visualization with new Charts types', 'Gantt and Milestone chart', 'SmartArt and Organization Chart' give details on the different chart types available in Excel and how best we can use them for creating different views of data, good graphics or visualizations for dashboards etc. Using Gantt and Milestone chart, you can plan and track your projects efficiently.

Chapters 'Putting Data in Perspective with Pivots', 'Complex data analysis using ToolPak' and 'Forecasting in Excel' help in learning the different ways and methods to consolidate data, do complex analysis and predict or forecast based on trends. These chapters are very helpful for people who require to do lot of data analysis and based on results or predictions make important decisions.

Chapters 'Mail Merge using Excel' and 'Macros in Excel' explain the Excel features that help in automating tasks. You will learn how to generate multiple documents automatically with customization and use of macros to do repeated task automatically.

And the last Chapter 'What's in Excel 2019' gives a list of new features introduced in the Microsoft Excel 2019.

References

Microsoft's official support website has been used as a reference for this book.

Thanks for selecting this book! Excel with EXCEL!!

Manisha Nigam (author)

About the Author

Manisha Nigam is a seasoned management professional with twenty plus years of information technology experience, working with multinationals across the globe. Her expertise in Excel comes from the vast experience she has in using and understanding the software over the years, that helped her in working efficiently and managing complex programs. A certified PMP (PMI - Project Management Professional), CSM (Scrum Alliance - Scrum Master), TOGAF 9.1 (The Open Group - Enterprise Architecture) and holds a post graduate degree in computer science and business management from prestigious universities in India.

Table of Content

CHAPTER 1
Getting Started with Excel

1.1 Workbook and Worksheets

When we talk about working in Excel, we basically work in a workbook, that is, the file that is created by Excel with the default extension ".**xlsx**". Each workbook contains one or more worksheets and by default, they are named as **Sheet1**, **Sheet2**, **Sheet3**, and so on, in the sequence in which they get created. The users can rename the worksheets by right-clicking on the sheet name and selecting **Rename** from the options, with a condition that each sheet name in a workbook is unique.

Sheets are structured as two-dimensional matrix with the columns named alphabetically (A-Z, AA-AZ, BA ..., ZZ, AAA, AAB, and so on) and the rows numerically (1 through 1048576). Each sheet contains individual cells which can contain number, text, or formula. The intersection of a row and a column is a single cell which is referenced using the column letter and row number. For example, the first cell in the worksheet is referenced as A1, that is, column A row 1. A worksheet also has an invisible drawing layer which holds charts, images, and diagrams. Objects on the drawing layer sit over the top of the cells, however, they are not inside the cells like a number or a formula.

An open Excel workbook screen looks like the following screenshot. It also shows the important and useful elements that are often used:

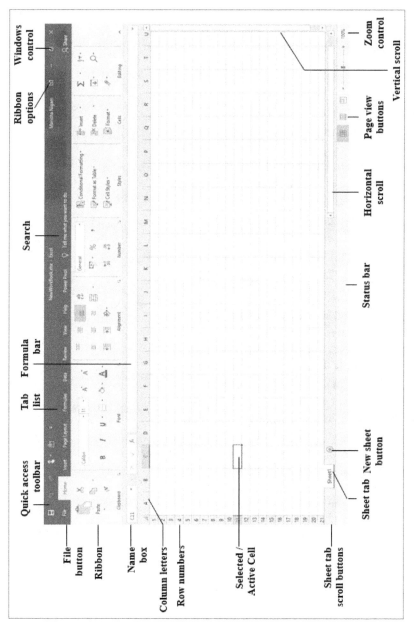

Figure 1.1 *Workbook Screen*

1.2 Navigation with Keyboard

Users are quite familiar with and find it easy to navigate through the cells using their mouse. But you can also use the standard navigation keys on the keyboard to move around the worksheet. For example, the down arrow moves the active cell down by one row, the right arrow moves it one column to the right, and so on, the *pgup* and *pgdn* keys move the active cell up or down by one full window. There are a lot of useful keyboard shortcuts available which are listed in Chapter 2 Perform Functions with Shortcut Keys.

1.3 Tabs and Ribbons

The user interface of Excel, like all other Microsoft products such as Word, PowerPoint, and so on, has Tabs and Ribbons. Each tab (**Home**, **Insert**, **Page Layout**, and so on) has an associated Ribbon with several group of buttons for working. For example, if you click the **Formulas** tab, you get a Ribbon with buttons that are useful for working with formulas. Also, when you hover the mouse pointer over a Ribbon button, it will show the description that contains the command's name along with a brief description.

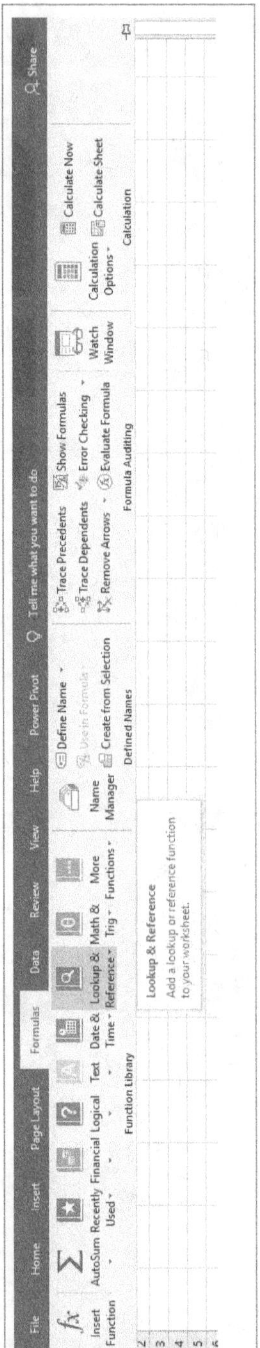

Figure 1.2 *Tabs and Ribbons*

1.3.1 Contextual Tabs

In addition to the standard tabs, Excel includes contextual tabs. Whenever an object (such as a chart, a table, or a SmartArt diagram) is selected, specific tools for working with that object are made available in the Ribbon. For example, when you select a chart, two tabs (Design and Format) become visible in the Chart Tools tab:

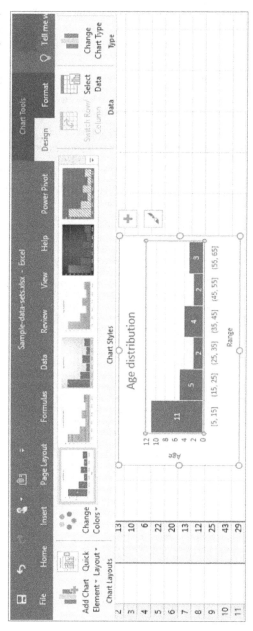

Figure 1.3 *Contextual Tabs and Ribbons*

1.3.2 Tab and Ribbon Visibility

If you need more space, you can right-click on any Ribbon and select **Collapse the Ribbon** button, you can then restore it in the same way. Also, note that depending on the width of the Excel window, some Ribbons might not show fully, however, everything is still available. To toggle the Ribbon's visibility, use the keyboard shortcut *CTRL + F1* (or double-click a tab at the top). You can also change the Tab and Ribbon visibility option using a control named **Ribbon Display Options** (next to the Minimize button) on the title bar. The control has three options: Auto-Hide Ribbon, Show Tabs, or Show Tabs and Commands.

There is also an option for customizing the Ribbons, you can right-click on any Ribbon and select **Customize the Ribbon**.

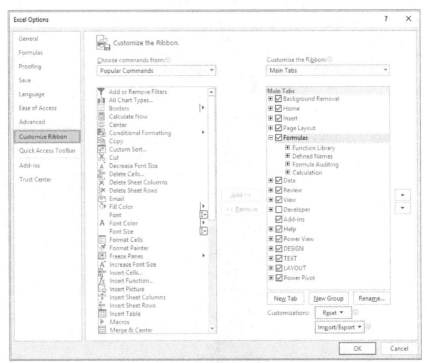

Figure 1.4 *Customizing Ribbons*

1.4 File Menu

The File menu takes you to the backstage view where you can perform file operations. You can also open the **Excel Options** dialog box from there. To go back and leave backstage view, simply click on the back arrow at the top-left.

Figure 1.5 *File Menu*

1.5 Quick Access Toolbar

There is a **Quick Access Toolbar (QAT)** at the top-left corner of the Excel window. You can put your favorite buttons on this toolbar so that they are always visible and available. The QAT comes with a few favorite buttons, however, you can add more. The QAT can be customized by clicking on the drop-down arrow to the right of your QAT. You will see a list to the right of the most commonly used buttons, which you can then check to add them to your QAT. You can also click on the **More Commands** item in this list to launch the dialog box which contains several other buttons that you can add to your QAT.

Figure 1.6 *Quick Access Toolbar*

1.6 Excel Options

Excel has many options for changing the software's behavior. Click on the **File** button in the upper-left corner of the screen and then on **Options** to see all the options. Options are grouped in categories: **General**, **Formulas**, and others. Though the option names are self-explanatory, for more details on what each option means, you can either click on the information icon or the help button on the upper-right corner of the screen.

For example, under the Advanced group, you will see many Editing options which you can change based on your style of working, such as using the *Enter* key to move the selection down, allowing Automatic flash fill, and so on.

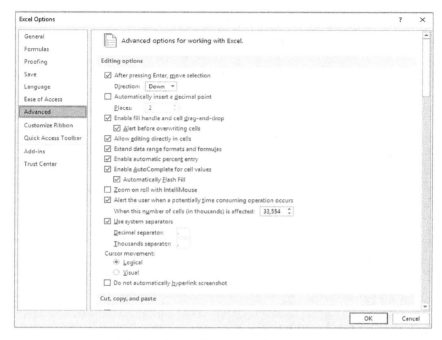

Figure 1.7 *Advance Editing options*

Most of the options are for Excel as a whole, not for any particular workbook or worksheet you might have opened. However, there are a few that are workbook-specific or worksheet-specific. For example, in the **Advanced** group, there are two sets of options, 'Display options for this workbook' and 'Display options for this worksheet' that can be varied from one workbook/worksheet to another.

Figure 1.8 *Advance Options at Worksheet & Workbook level*

1.7 Create a New Workbook, Print and Save

1.7.1 Create New File

You can create a new Excel file in your Window's explorer by going to the New option on the Home Tab or by right-clicking on any empty space in the explorer and choosing 'New ➔ Microsoft Excel Worksheet'. You can also launch Microsoft Excel application, which will show you multiple options to choose from a Blank Workbook or use an existing Template, take a Tour, and so on, as shown in the following screenshot. You can also use the shortcut key *CTRL+N*, to create a new workbook:

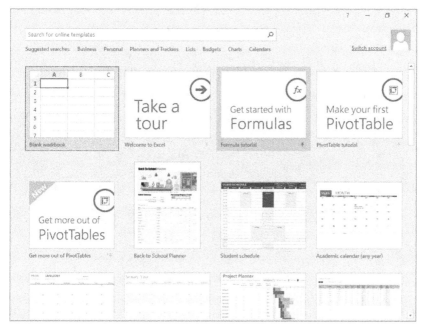

Figure 1.9 *Create New Excel file*

You can create as many worksheets required in a workbook and rename them as discussed earlier. There are very useful keyboard shortcuts for working in a worksheet, as detailed in *Chapter 2 Perform Functions with Shortcut Keys*. Working with data within the worksheet will be discussed in the later chapters of this book.

1.7.2 Print File

You can print the entire workbook, active sheets, or the selected area. The **Print** option is available on the **File** menu or you also can use the keyboard shortcut *CTRL + P* to launch the **Print** dialog box with all the print settings that can be configured, as in other Microsoft products.

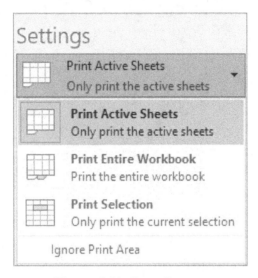

Figure 1.10 *Print Settings*

1.7.2.1 *Print Active Sheets*

Select the worksheets that you want to print. Click on the tab of the sheet for selecting a single worksheet or press the *SHIFT* key and click the tabs of the adjacent sheets for multiple sheets selection or in case you want to select multiple non-adjacent sheets then press the *CTRL* key and click on the sheet tabs.

Go to **File ➜ Print** menu or use the keyboard shortcut *CTRL + P* to launch the Print dialog box, select **Print Active Sheets** in **Settings** and then click on **Print**.

1.7.2.2 *Print Entire Workbook*

Open the workbook and go to **File ➜ Print**, select **Print Entire Workbook** and click on **Print**. In case you want to print multiple workbooks, in the File Explorer, select the file, right-click and select **Print** option.

You can also Print the workbook as a file, using the **Print to File** option in the Print dialog box under the **Printer** setting.

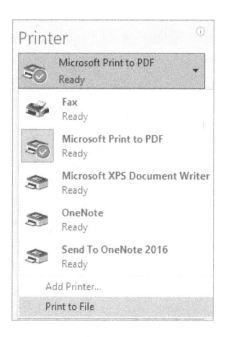

1.7.2.3 Print Selection

Open the worksheet and select the range of data that you want to print. Next, go to **File ➜ Print** menu, in the **Print** dialog box, select **Print Selection** and click on **Print**.

Print Selection with defined Print Area

Another way to print selection is by defining print area. A worksheet can have multiple print areas defined and each print area will print as a separate page. When the print areas are defined, only those are printed when you print the worksheet. You can add cells to expand the print area as needed, and you can clear the print area to print the entire worksheet.

Open the worksheet and select a single data range or multiple data ranges by pressing the *Ctrl* key. Go to the **Page Layout** tab, in the **Page Setup** group, select **Print Area** and click on **Set Print Area** to define the print area. Now, go to **File ➜ Print** to open the Print dialog box and select **Print Active Worksheet** which will print only the defined data ranges as the print area.

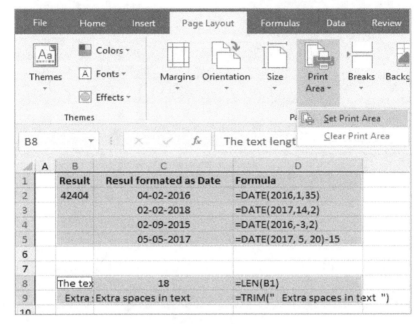

Figure 1.11 *Set / Clear Print Area*

Even if the file is closed and opened again, the defined print areas are saved and you do not need to do the selection again and define. Note that in order to remove the print area, you need to click on **Clear Print Area**.

Print Tables and Objects

When you select an Excel table in the worksheet and go to **File ➔ Print** menu, under **Settings** you will see a new option **Print Selected Table**.

Sometimes you may find that certain objects like text boxes, buttons, and arrows do not get printed. To correct that, right-click on any such object, select **Size** and **Properties**, and click on the **Properties** tab. This contains a **Print object** option that you can check or uncheck.

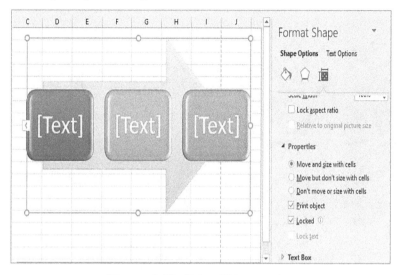

Figure 1.12 *Print Object option*

1.7.3 Save and Save As File

Saving the Excel file is as simple as printing and similar to what you see in other Microsoft products, with only difference that it shows the relevant file types. The first time you save an Excel workbook, Excel takes you to the Backstage screen that lets you choose the location for the file; online location or local computer and launches a **Save** dialog box. In the dialog box you can enter the Filename and the file type or extension you want to save the file in, click on **Save** button to save the file.

By default, Excel also saves a backup copy of your work automatically in every 10 minutes. AutoRecover setting can be changed, choose **File →Options** and click on the **Save** tab of the **Excel Options** dialog box.

The default file extension is **.xlsx**, however, it also gives other files type options as well, as given below. If want to save in a version compatible with older Excel version, then you can choose **Excel 97-2003 Workbook (*.xls)** or if you require a macro-enabled version, then choose **Excel Macro-Enabled Workbook (*.xlsm)** or a comma delimited files as **CSV UTF-8 (*.csv)**, and so on.

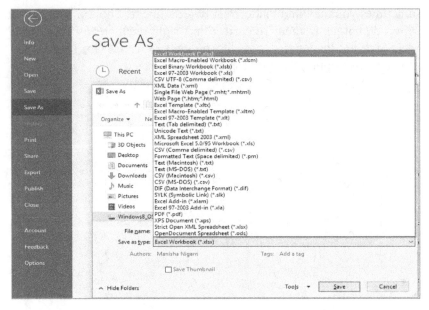

Figure 1.13 *Save As options*

1.8 Understanding Worksheet Basics

Worksheets are the playground for entering, editing, formatting, analyzing, and visualizing information or data. You can perform a lot of operations in the worksheet like renaming the sheet, adding/deleting a sheet, controlling the worksheet view, inserting/deleting rows and columns, grouping/ungrouping data, formatting data, and so on. In this section, we will learn the worksheet basics with the help of examples.

1.8.1 Commands for Entering/Editing Data

You can use mouse as well as keyboard to enter, modify, or delete data in the worksheet. There are many keyboard commands (*see Chapter 2 Perform Functions with Shortcut Keys*), but here, we will list only a few that are frequently used and will help you in your daily work with Excel and also in the following sections:

- **Edit a cell:** Select the cell, double-click with the mouse or press F2 on the keyboard

- **Insert a new line within a cell:** Press ALT+ENTER within the cell to insert a new line

- **Go to next cell**: Single click with mouse to select or use arrow keys or press the ENTER key

- **Cut/Copy/Paste/Paste Special in cell**: Select the source/destination cell, right-click with mouse for the desired options or press CTRL+X / CTRL+C / CTRL+V / CTRL+ALT+V on the keyboard

- **Add a new Table**: Press CTRL+T to add a new table

- **Insert/Delete in Table:** Press CTRL+'+' and CTRL+'- 'to insert or delete a table respectively

- **Copy same text in cells below**: Select the cell, press CTRL+C and then select the cells below where you want to paste the value and press CTRL+D

- **Undo/Redo change**: Press CTRL+Z to undo a change and CTRL+Y to redo a change

- **Flash fill cells** : Select the cell with mouse, click on the '+' sign at the lower-right corner and drag the mouse selecting the cells you want to fill with data

You can also change few settings like pressing the *enter* key will move the selection in the right side instead of down, using **File ➜ Options ➜ Advanced ➜ Edit Options**. In this book, we will assume the preceding commands hold true, unless specified.

1.8.2 Insert/Delete Cells

Excel gives options in the **Home** tab to insert new sheets, rows, columns, and even specific cells relative to the selection. Similarly, you can delete sheets, rows, columns, and cells.

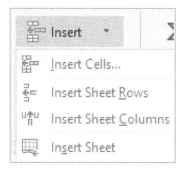

Figure 1.14 *Insert / Delete Rows & Columns menu options*

These options are also available on right-click of the mouse.

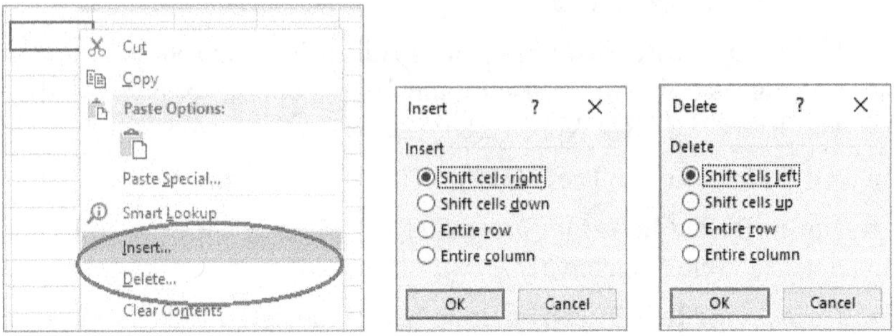

Figure 1.15 *Insert / Delete Rows & Columns options on right click*

1.8.2.1 Insert/Delete/Rename Sheet

Open the workbook in which you want to insert/delete worksheets. By default, it has one worksheet named **Sheet1**. Go to the **Home** tab, in the **Cells** group and click on **Insert Sheet**. The new sheet gets added on the left of the existing sheet with name **Sheet2**.

The sheet number (in the sheet name) depends on the number of sheets that were already created in the workbook. Assuming that your worksheet has **Sheet1**, **Sheet2**, and **Sheet3**, then the new sheet will be **Sheet4**. Now delete all the sheets except Sheet1 and again insert a new sheet. The new sheet in this case will be **Sheet5**, as Sheet4 was the last one that was created, even though you deleted it.

To delete a single sheet, select the sheet tab and click on **Delete Sheet**. In case you want to delete multiple sheets, press *CTRL* and select the sheet tabs (non-adjacent) or press *SHIFT* and select the sheet tabs (adjacent) and click on the **Delete Sheet** option. On delete, the sheets and its content are removed from the workbook.

You can rename the sheet, either by double-clicking on the sheet tab and typing the new name or right-clicking on the mouse and selecting the **Rename** option.

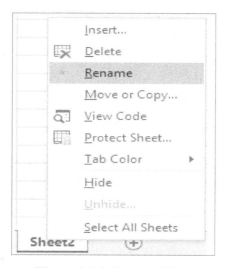

Figure 1.16 *Rename Sheet*

1.8.2.2 Insert/Delete Rows and Columns

The **Insert Sheet Rows** option inserts an empty row above the selected row. In case you selected multiple adjacent rows (by pressing *SHIFT* key), say 3 in number, then it will insert the same number of empty rows, that is, 3 above the row on top of the selection. In case you selected multiple non-adjacent rows (by pressing *CTRL* key), then it inserts a single empty row above each selected row. **Insert Sheet Columns** works in the same way; new columns are inserted on the left of the selected column.

To delete, select the rows/columns to delete (single or multiple) and click on **Delete Sheet Rows / Delete Sheet Columns**. Note that **Insert** and **Delete** options are also available by selecting the range through the keyboard and also through right-click (see *Figure 115*).

In the following example, we have entered some values in the cells, Row1...4 and Column 1...4. Select **Row 2** and **Row 4** (cells or entire rows) and click on insert rows, it will insert one empty row, each above **Row 2** and **Row 4**. Now select **Column 2** and **Column 3** (cells or entire columns C and D) and click on insert columns, it will insert two empty columns on the left of **Column 2**.

	A	B	C	D	E
1	Row 1	Column 1	Column 2	Column 3	Column 4
2	Row 2				
3	Row 3				
4	Row 4				
5					

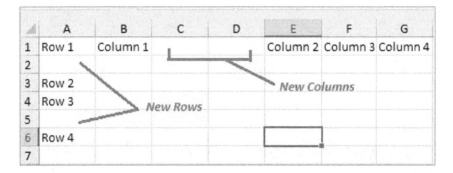

	A	B	C	D	E	F	G
1	Row 1	Column 1			Column 2	Column 3	Column 4
2							
3	Row 2						
4	Row 3		*New Rows*				
5							
6	Row 4						
7							

New Columns

1.8.2.3 Insert/Delete Cell range

The **Insert cells** option adds the cells to the left of the selected cells and **Delete Cells** deletes only the selected cells, unlike the Insert/Delete Rows and Columns that work on the entire Row and Column.

In the following example, we will see how inserting/deleting cells impact the other cells. Select the cells with values **V2**, **V6**, and **V10**, and insert cells by selecting the option to shift cells right. New cells are inserted to the left of the selected cells; the selected cells and all the cells beyond are moved by one column, that is, beyond **Column 4**. Also, note that since it works only on specific cells and not the entire column, the cells below, that is, values X2, X6, and X10 are not moved.

Now, select the cell with value **V1** and insert cell with option to shift cells down. New cell is inserted above **V1** and all cells below have moved by one place, while the other values in **Row 2** are not moved.

◢	A	B	C	D	E	F
1	Row 1	Column 1	Column 2	Column 3	Column 4	
2	Row 2			V2	V3	V4
3	Row 3	V1		V6	V7	V8
4	Row 4	V5		V10	V11	V12
5		V9				
6						
7	Row 5		Column 2	Column 3	Column 4	
8	Row 6	Column 1	X2	X3	X4	
9	Row 7	X1	X6	X7	X8	
10	Row 8	X5	X10	X11	X12	
11		X9				

Now we will revert what we did above, one-by-one, using the delete cell option. Select the cell above V1 and click to delete with an option to move cells up. It will move all the cells one place up. Now select the empty cells below **Column 2** and the left of cell values **V2**, **V6**, and **V10**, and delete the cells with the option to move cells to the left.

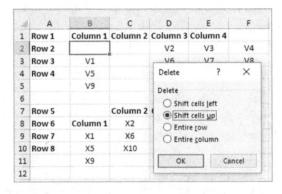

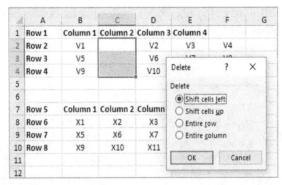

The data in the sheet comes back to the same state as we started.

1.8.3 Formatting Cells

Formatting in worksheet can be very helpful in understanding the purpose of the worksheet and help in preventing the data entry errors. The options are available on the **Home** tab in the **Font**, **Alignment**, **Number**, **Cell Styles**, and **Format Cells** groups.

These options can also be seen in the mini toolbar above the shortcut menu, when you right-click on the cells.

Most of the formatting can be done directly using these menu items, however, sometimes you need the **Format Cells** dialog box. The Format Cells dialog box contains six tabs; **Number**, **Alignment**, **Font**, **Border**, **Fill**, and **Protection**.

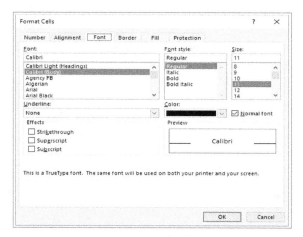

Figure 1.17 *Format Cells Dialog box*

The Format Cell dialog box can be launched from multiple places. Select the cell range to format and use any one of the following ways to launch the dialog box:

- Using the keyboard shortcut - Press *CTRL+1*.
- Click on the dialog box launcher in **Home → Font**, **Home → Alignment**, or **Home → Number**. The dialog box launcher is the small downward-pointing arrow icon displayed to the right of the group name in the Ribbon.
- Right-click on the selected cell or range and choose **Format Cells** from the shortcut menu.
- Click on the **More** command in some of the drop-down controls in the Ribbon. For example, in the Number group, clicking on the drop-down menu gives the **More Number Formats...** option.

1.8.3.1 Using fonts to format

You can use different fonts, font sizes, or text attributes in your worksheets to make various parts stand out, such as the headers for a table.

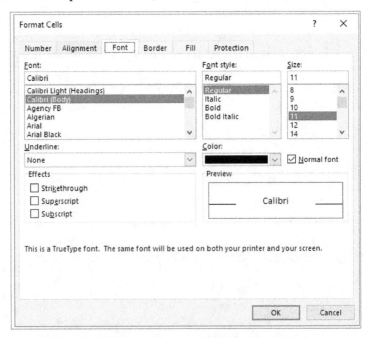

Figure 1.18 *Format Cells – Font*

You can select the font from the given list, make it bold or italics, select the size, color of the font, and effects such as strikethrough, superscript, and so on. You can see the preview of how your text will look in the preview section. You can also use the shortcut keys for changing the text, that is, *CTRL+B*: Bold, *CTRL+I*: Italic, *CTRL+U*: Underline, and *CTRL+5*: Strikethrough.

If a cell contains text, you can also apply formatting to individual characters in the cell by selecting the character and using the formatting options as described earlier.

1.8.3.2 Change Text Alignment

The contents of a cell can be aligned horizontally and vertically. By default, Excel aligns numbers to the right and text to the left. All the cells use bottom alignment by default. You can overwrite the defaults by using the **Alignment** tool.

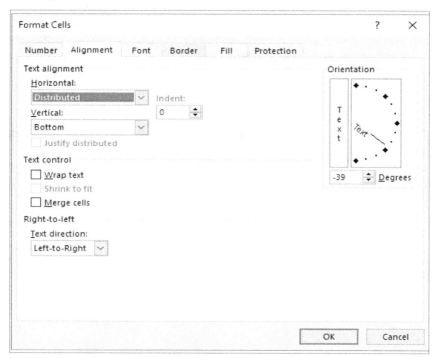

Figure 1.19 *Format Cells – Alignment*

The following are a few examples of how your text will look like with different alignments. You can try different styles and use whichever is more appropriate for your use.

	A	B	C	D	E
1	Text is aligned Top	Text is aligned Middle	Text is aligned Bottom	I am text in merged cells, cols D & E	
2	Text is aligned Left	Text is aligned Center	Text is aligned Right		I am wrap text
3	Text is Counterclockwise	Text is Clockwise	T h i s	I am example of how the distributed text looks like. I am distributed.	
4					

Note that for merging the cells, you need to select all the adjacent cells which you want to merge and then use the merge option. Merge will ask for confirmation before merging, sometimes it only keeps the text of the first cell selected and discards the text in other selected cells for merge. So, you need to be careful while merging text in cells. You can merge the cells before entering the text. Similar rule applies to unmerge, select all the merged cells and then click on the unmerge option.

1.8.3.3 Using Number Formatting

Numbers can be in different categories and there is a default setting in Excel for each category. For example, if you format the number in a cell say 42381 as **Date**, it will get converted to '12 January 2016' and if it is formatted as a **Number**, it will be converted as 42381.00. You can also make your own format by using the Custom option. There is some custom formatting already available, however, you can also create by typing a new one in the **Type** field. Type **mm-dd-yyyy** and click on **OK**. Instead of 12 January 2016, it will be converted to 01-12-2016.

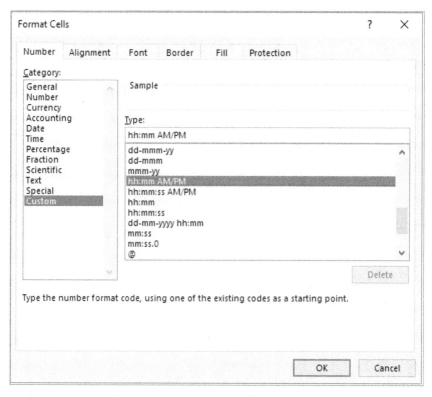

Figure 1.20 *Format Cells – Number*

Each category has different settings and you can use any based on your requirements. Category names are self-explanatory and hence easy to identify which category to use when:

Format	Description
General	This is the default number format that Excel applies when you type a number. For most part, numbers that are formatted with the General format are displayed just the way you type them. However, if the cell is not wide enough to show the entire number, the General format rounds the numbers with decimals. The General number format also uses scientific (exponential) notation for large numbers (12 or more digits).
Number	This is used for the general display of numbers. You can specify the number of decimal places that you want to use, whether you want to use a thousand separator, and how you want to display negative numbers.

Format	Description
Currency	This is used for general monetary values and displays the default currency symbol with numbers. You can specify the number of decimal places that you want to use, whether you want to use a thousand separator, and how you want to display negative numbers.
Accounting	This is also used for monetary values; however, it aligns the currency symbols and decimal points of numbers in a column.
Date	This displays date and time serial numbers as date values, according to the type and locale (location) that you specify.
Time	This displays date and time serial numbers as time values, according to the type and locale (location) that you specify.
Percentage	This multiplies the cell value by 100 and displays the result with a percent (%) symbol.
Fraction	This displays a number as a fraction, according to the type of fraction that you specify.
Scientific	This displays a number in an exponential notation, replacing a part of the number with E+n, where E (which stands for Exponent) multiplies the preceding number by 10 to the nth power.
Text	This treats the content of a cell as text and displays the content exactly as you type it, even when you type numbers.
Special	This displays a number as a postal code, ZIP Code, phone number, or Social Security number.
Custom	This allows you to modify a copy of an existing number format code. Use this format to create a custom number format that is added to the list of number format codes.

1.8.3.4 Changing Cell Styles

Excel has several built-in cell styles that you can apply or modify. You can also modify or duplicate a cell style to create a custom cell style. A cell style is a defined set of formatting characteristics, such as fonts and font sizes, number formats, cell borders, and cell shading. To prevent anyone from making changes to specific cells, you can also use a cell style that locks cells.

Good, Bad and Neutral					
Normal	Bad	Good	Neutral		

Data and Model

Calculation	Check Cell	Explanatory...	Followed Hy...	Hyperlink	Input
Linked Cell	Note	Output	Warning Text		

Titles and Headings

Heading 1	Heading 2	Heading 3	Heading 4	Title	Total

Themed Cell Styles

20% - Accent1	20% - Accent2	20% - Accent3	20% - Accent4	20% - Accent5	20% - Accent6
40% - Accent1	40% - Accent2	40% - Accent3	40% - Accent4	40% - Accent5	40% - Accent6
60% - Accent1	60% - Accent2	60% - Accent3	60% - Accent4	60% - Accent5	60% - Accent6
Accent1	Accent2	Accent3	Accent4	Accent5	Accent6

Number Format

Comma	Comma [0]	Currency	Currency [0]	Percent	

New Cell Style...
Merge Styles...

Figure 1.21   *Format Cells – Cell Styles*

In the following example, we have used **Heading 1** and **Ascent 6** cell styles to format the cells:

A	
4	
5	Scores ⇐ *Heading 1*
6	25
7	54
8	30 ⇐ *Ascent 6*
9	12
10	

In the **New Cell Style** dialog box, the settings are the default Excel settings for font, alignment, and so on. You can enter a name for your own style and by using the **Format** option, you can change the formatting for a **Number**, **Alignment**, **Font**, **Border**, shading, and so on as given in the following screenshot:

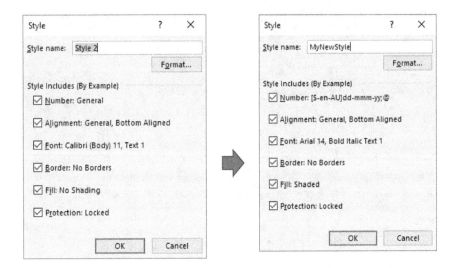

1.8.3.5 *Changing Borders and Lines*

Excel has another tool called Borders that you can add around the cells. There are 13 preset styles of borders in Excel, which are available under the **Home** tab, in the **Font** group's **Borders** drop-down list.

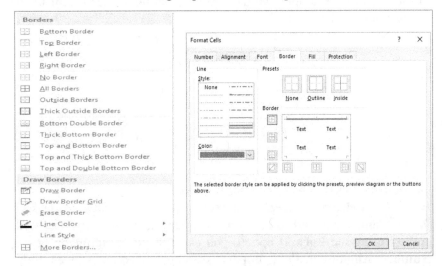

Figure 1.22 *Format Cells: Borders and Lines*

You can either select the existing styles or draw them yourself using the **Draw Borders** option.

1.8.4 Data Tools

1.8.4.1 Data Cleansing (Sort, Filter, Remove Duplicates)

Excel allows you to sort the data in ascending or descending order. You can also define a custom sort specific to your needs. It also lets you filter data so that only those items are visible that meet your filter criteria and all other items are hidden. The **Sort** and **Filter** options are available under the **Home** tab, in the **Editing** group and also under the **Data** tab, in the **Sort & Filter** group.

 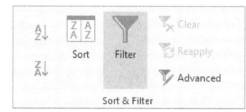

Figure 1.23 *Sort and Filter options in the 'Home' and 'Data' tabs*

Using these options, we will sort and filter our data, as shown in the following screenshot:

	A	B	C
1	Vendor 1	Apples	12
2	Vendor 2	Mangos	10
3	Vendor 3	Strawberries	6
4	Vendor 4	Banana	7
5	Vendor 5	Orange	3
6	Vendor 5	Apples	34
7	Vendor 1	Mangos	26
8	Vendor 2	Strawberries	75
9	Vendor 3	Banana	23
10	Vendor 4	Orange	11
11	Vendor 4	Apples	21
12	Vendor 5	Mangos	42
13	Vendor 1	Strawberries	8
14	Vendor 2	Banana	2
15	Vendor 3	Orange	9

Figure 1.24 *Sort and Filter – Example data*

We have data in three columns, A (Vendors list), B (Fruits list), and C (number of items).

Sorting

Select the data range from A1 to C15 and click on '*Sort A to Z*'. Excel will sort the data in ascending order, with reference to the first column in the selected range, that is, column A, where it will first put all Vendor 1 rows, followed by **Vendor 2** and so on. In case the '*Sort Z to A*' option was selected, it will put all the Vendor 5 rows first, followed by **Vendor 4,** and so on in descending order. Now, if we want to sort based on two columns that is, all Vendors in ascending order and for each Vendor, fruits sorted based on the number of items in descending order. Excel allows you to do that with the help of **Custom Sort**. Select the data range and go to custom sort. In the Sort dialog box, add the required levels for sorting by using **Add Level**. The resulting Sort criteria and results are as shown in the following screenshot:

	A	B	C
1	Vendor 1	Mangos	26
2	Vendor 1	Apples	12
3	Vendor 1	Strawberries	8
4	Vendor 2	Strawberries	[illegible]
5	Vendor 2	Mangos	10
6	Vendor 2	Banana	2
7	Vendor 3	Banana	23
8	Vendor 3	Orange	9
9	Vendor 3	Strawberries	6
10	Vendor 4	Apples	21
11	Vendor 4	Orange	11
12	Vendor 4	Banana	7
13	Vendor 5	Mangos	42
14	Vendor 5	Apples	34
15	Vendor 5	Orange	3

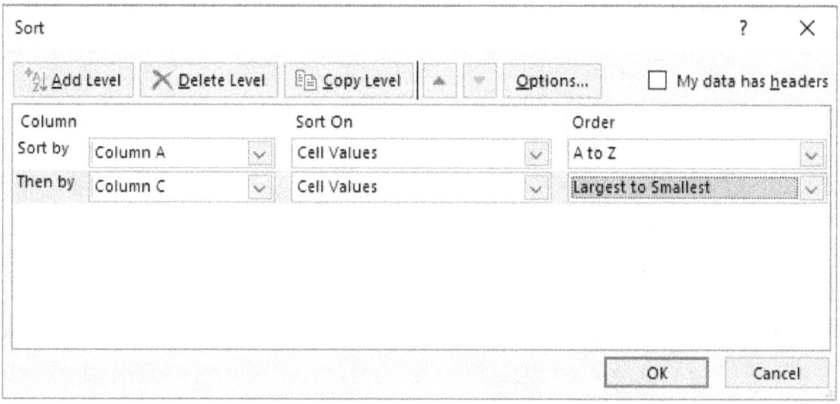

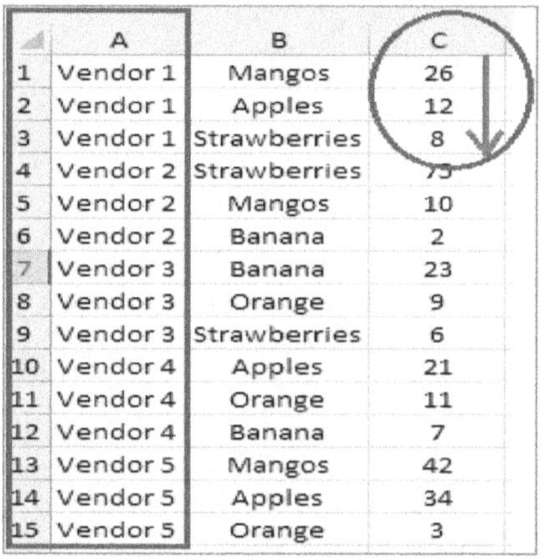

Since we wanted to sort Vendors first, the **Sort by** field shows **Column A** in ascending order that is, A-Z in the **Order** field. Next, we wanted to sort the data for each Vendor based on the number of items, hence in second level, we specified **Column C** and **Largest to Smallest** in the fields.

Filtering

Adding a filter to change the view of data is very simple in Excel. Select the data and go to the 'Filter' option (see *Figure 124*). It adds a little arrow in the first row of your data range. By clicking on the arrow, you get the options to add different filters based on the type of data in the column. In columns with text, it shows **Text Filters** and in columns with numbers it shows **Number Filters**:

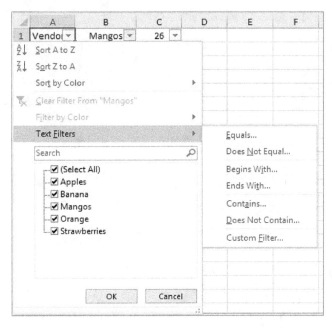

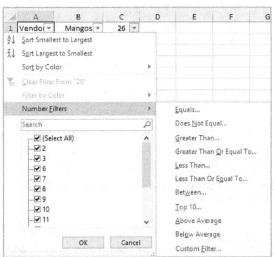

As in the preceding example, the filter lists all unique values for that column and allows you to select or deselect items by clicking on the checkbox. Based on your selection, the items are displayed in that column. Another way is to use one of the Text/Number filter options and add criterias like filter, if the text contains **berries** or number is greater than **10**.

Custom AutoFilter	? ×
Show rows where:	
Mangos	

contains ∨	berries ∨
◉ And ○ Or	
∨	∨

Use ? to represent any single character
Use * to represent any series of characters

| OK | Cancel |

Custom AutoFilter	? ×
Show rows where:	
26	

is greater than ∨	10 ∨
◉ And ○ Or	
∨	∨

Use ? to represent any single character
Use * to represent any series of characters

| OK | Cancel |

In the custom filter, you can add another critera and combine the two using the AND operator (for both criterias to be true) or the OR operator (any one of the criteria is true) connectors.

Clear & Reapply Filter

You can remove the filter by clicking on **Clear**. In case your data is changed in the filtered data, you can update the view by clicking on **Reapply**.

Using Advanced Fitering

If you want to filter the data based on complex criteria, then you can use the **Advanced** filter option. When you use the **Advanced Filter** option, you need to set up the criteria range. A criteria range is a designated range on a worksheet that conforms to certain requirements. Criteria range should have the same column headers as the dataset and you need to make sure there is at least one blank row between the criteria range and dataset. The fields in each row of the criteria range (except for the header row) are joined with an AND operator. If you enter more than one row in the criteria range, the rows of the criteria are joined with an OR operator.

In the following example, we have entered two criterias: first creates a filter to view only **Vendor 5** where the number of Apples is greater than 20 and second creates a filter to view only **Vendor 1** where it can be any fruit having number greater than 10. Click on **Advanced** and in the **Advanced Filter** dialog box enter the values as shown in the following screenshot:

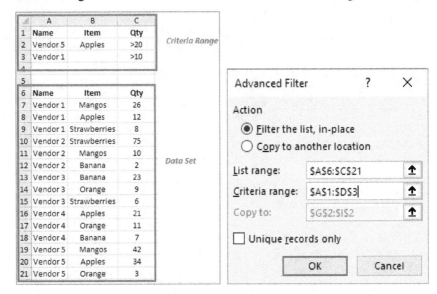

Specify the **List Range** and **Criteria Range** and select the option labeled 'Filter the List, In-Place'. Click on **OK**, and the list is filtered by the criteria that you specified.

	A	B	C
1	Name	Item	Qty
2	Vendor 5	Apples	>20
3	Vendor 1		>10
4			
5			
6	Name	Item	Qty
7	Vendor 1	Mangos	26
8	Vendor 1	Apples	12
20	Vendor 5	Apples	34

You can also copy your filtered dataset to another location by selecting the option **Copy to another location** and specifying the destination range in **Copy To**. In case your data contains duplicates and you want to see unique records only, select the **Unique records only** checkbox in the **Advanced Filter** dialog box.

Remove Duplicates

Remove Duplicates helps you to clean your data, the duplicate data will be permanently deleted. Hence, it is preferable to backup or copy the original data in another worksheet before removing duplicates so you don't accidentally lose any information.

Select the range of cells that has duplicate values you want to remove. Go to the **Data** tab in the **Data Tools** group and select **Remove Duplicates**. In the **Remove Duplicates** dialog box, under **Columns**, check or uncheck the columns where you want to remove the duplicates and click on **OK**.

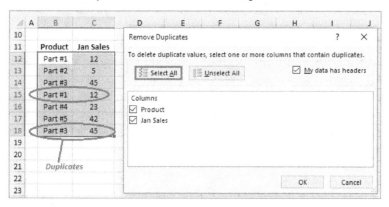

Excel will display a message with the number of duplicates removed and unique values remaining, and remove the duplicates from the data range.

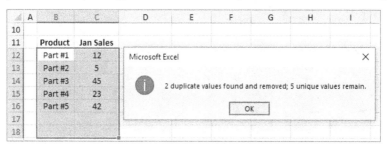

1.8.4.2 Data Grouping

You can group and summarize your list of data using the outline or grouping feature of Excel. You can create an outline of upto eight levels, one for each group. Each inner level, represented by a higher number in the outline symbols, displays detailed data for the preceding outer level, represented by a lower number in the outline symbols. You can also **Ungroup** once the grouping has been created. **Group** & **Ungroup** options are available under the **Data** tab in the **Outline** group.

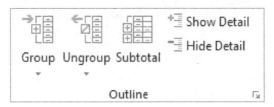

Figure 1.25 *Outline – Grouping*

Grouping/Ungrouping Rows and Columns

Select the rows you want to group, click on **Group** and select **Rows** in the **Group** dialog box. An outline is created and represented by a level number. Similarly, select the columns you want to group, click on **Group** and select **Columns** in the Group dialog box. Grouping can be removed by selecting the **Ungroup** option and selecting **Rows** or **Columns** in the Ungroup dialog box:

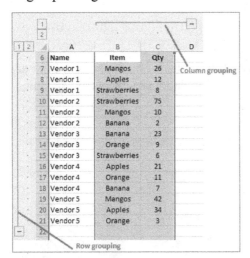

Show/Hide Details

To hide a group, click on the minus sign or select the **Hide Detail** option. To show a hidden group, click on the plus sign or select the **Show Detail** option in the **Data ➔ Outline** group.

Subtotal

Subtotal has been explained in a later chapter, see *section 3.10.7*, Example #2 (Figure 3-30).

1.8.4.3 Conditional Formatting

Conditional formatting helps you to apply cell formatting selectively and automatically to cells, rows, columns, or tables based on the cell value or based on another cell's value. Conditional formatting is more flexible than the usual cell formats in a sense that it allows you to format only the data that meets certain criteria or conditions. The **Conditional Formatting** option is available under the **Home** tab in the **Styles** group.

Select the cells and use one of the commands from the Conditional formatting drop-down menu to set, manage, or create new rules that will get applied based on selected cell content.

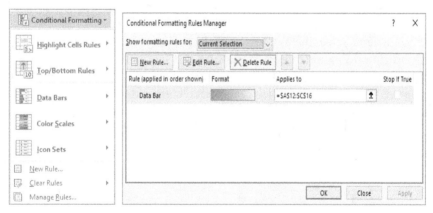

Choices	Description/Examples
Highlight Cells Rules	Highlighting cells that are greater than, less than, are between two values, equal to, contain a specific text string, contain a date occurring, or duplicated values.
Top/Bottom Rules	Highlighting the top/bottom 10 items, top/bottom 10% items, and the items that are above/below average.
Data Bars	Show graphic bars directly in the cells, proportional to the cell's value.

Choices	Description/Examples
Color Scales	Changes background color, proportional to the cell's value.
Icon Sets	Displays icons directly in the cells, depending on the cell's value.
New Rule	To add new conditional formatting rules, including rules based on a logical formula.
Clear Rules	Deletes all conditional formatting rules from the selected cells.
Manage Rules	Displays the Conditional Formatting Rules Manager dialog box in which you can create, edit, or delete conditional formatting rules

We will explain how to use conditional formatting using some examples. Not all rules can be covered, however, the method to do or apply others is the same as the following examples:

Example #1: In this example, we will use different conditional formatting that is, Data bars, Icons Sets, and Color Scales to indicate the trend in data. Select the **Total Sales** that is, cells H12 to H16 and then select **Conditional Formatting → Data Bars → Gradient Fill → Green Data Bar**. The longest data bar is for the highest number and all other bars are relative to that. Similarly, select the other cells and apply the conditional formatting styles that is, E12:E16 – Icon Sets: Shapes, B12:B16 – Color Scales and B17:G17, which is the Total for each month, is shown using Icons Set – Directional.

	A	B	C	D	E	F	G	H	
11	Product	Jan	Feb	Mar	Apr	May	Jun	Total Sales	
12	Part #1	12	21	15	13	3	10	74	Data Bars
13	Part #2	5	43	74	41	12	11	186	Gradient Fill
14	Part #3	2	23	34	12	43	23	137	
15	Part #4	23	16	23	45	34	66	207	
16	Part #5	42	29	54	32	44	43	244	
17	Total	84	132	200	143	136	153		Icons Set Directional

Colour Scales   Icon Sets - Shapes

Example #2: Highlight the Total Sales that are greater than 150. Select the cells H12:H16, go to **Conditional Formatting → Highlight Cell rules → Greater Than…** and specify the condition of 150 and highlight the text using green color.

	A	B	C	D	E	F	G	H	I	J	K	L	M	N	O	P
19																
20	Product	Jan	Feb	Mar	Apr	May	Jun	Total Sales								
21	Part #1	12	21	15	13	3	10	74								
22	Part #2	5	43	74	41	12	11	186								
23	Part #3	2	23	34	12	43	23	137								
24	Part #4	23	16	23	45	34	66	207								
25	Part #5	42	29	54	32	44	43	244								
26	Total	84	132	200	143	136	153									
27																

Greater Than dialog: "Format cells that are GREATER THAN:" value 150 with "Green Fill with Dark Green Text", OK / Cancel.

Example #3: Highlight all the sale values between 25 and 100. In this case, we will select the complete data range from B21:G25 and go to the **Conditional formatting → New Rule** option. In the **New Formatting Rule** dialog box, we will select one of the rule types, 'Format only cells that contain', and create the new rule where the cell contains values between 25-100 and fill those cells with light green color. Using the **Format** option, select Fill color.

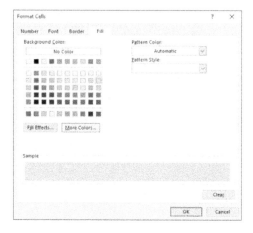

▲	A	B	C	D	E	F	G	H
19								
20	Product	Jan	Feb	Mar	Apr	May	Jun	Total Sales
21	Part #1	12	21	15	13	3	10	74
22	Part #2	5	43	74	41	12	11	186
23	Part #3	2	23	34	12	43	23	137
24	Part #4	23	16	23	45	34	66	207
25	Part #5	42	29	54	32	44	43	244
26	Total	84	132	200	143	136	153	
27								

Example #4: Highlight the low performing product, that is, the one with the lowest Total Sales. Using the Icons Set – Directional arrows we will show the least performing product. Select the **Total Sales** cell range H21:H25 and apply conditional formatting using the Icons Set -Directional indicators, that is, go to **Conditional Formatting** ➔**Icons Sets** ➔**Directional**. The arrows are shown for all cells, but we need to display only the least sales, that is, the down arrow.

▲	A	B	C	D	E	F	G	H
19								
20	Product	Jan	Feb	Mar	Apr	May	Jun	Total Sales
21	Part #1	12	21	15	13	3	10	⬇ 74
22	Part #2	5	43	74	41	12	11	⇨ 186
23	Part #3	45	23	34	12	43	23	⇨ 180
24	Part #4	23	16	23	45	34	66	⬆ 207
25	Part #5	42	29	54	32	44	43	⬆ 244
26	Total	127	132	200	143	136	153	
27								

Add a New Rule, if the cell value is greater than the average of all the selected cells, then don't add any formatting to the cells. That is, in the New Formatting Rule, select **Format only cells that contain** and add a condition that cell value is greater than =**AVERAGE(H21:H25)**. Do not add any formatting so that it displays **No Format set** and click on **OK**.

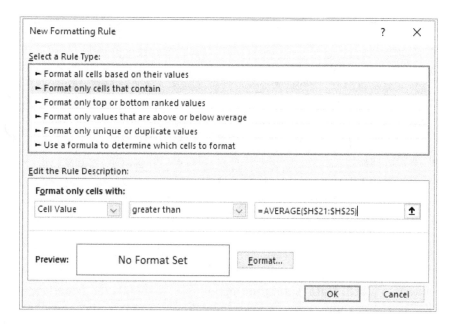

Now, go to **Conditional Formatting->Manage Rules…** and tick into the **Stop if True** checkbox which is next to the rule you have just created. Click on **OK**.

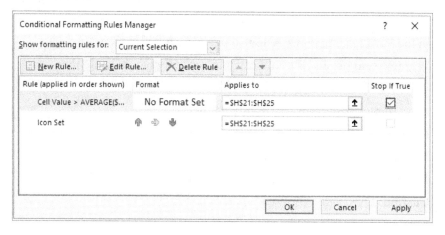

Now, only the down arrow is displayed in the cell that has the lowest sale. Since we ticked the checkbox **Stop if True**, as soon as the condition is found to be True, Excel stops processing the other rules and hence the Icon Set rule is not applied to cells that have values greater than average.

◢	A	B	C	D	E	F	G	H
19								
20	Product	Jan	Feb	Mar	Apr	May	Jun	Total Sales
21	Part #1	12	21	15	13	3	10	⬇ 74
22	Part #2	5	43	74	41	12	11	186
23	Part #3	45	23	34	12	43	23	180
24	Part #4	23	16	23	45	34	66	207
25	Part #5	42	29	54	32	44	43	244
26	Total	127	132	200	143	136	153	
27								

1.8.4.4 Data Validation

Data validation is helpful to restrict the type of data or the values that users enter into a cell. **Data Validation** option is available on the **Data** tab, in the **Data Tools** group. In the Data Validation dialog box, there are three tabs: **Settings, Input Message**, and **Error Alert**. In the Settings tab, there are two fields: **Validation criteria** and **Data** where you can set the specific conditions. In the Input Message, enter the message you want users to see on cell selection and in the Error Alert enter the message you want the users to see in case a wrong value is entered.

In the **Settings** tab, under **Allow**, the options available are:

Whole Number: To restrict the cell to accept only whole numbers

Decimal: To restrict the cell to accept only decimal numbers

List: To pick data from the drop-down list

Date: To restrict the cell to accept only date

Time: To restrict the cell to accept only time

Text Length: To restrict the length of the text

Custom: For custom formula

The conditions that can be set under Data are:

between, not between, equal to, not equal to

greater than, less than, greater than or equal to, less than or equal to

We will explain the use of data validation with the help of the following examples:

Example #1: We want to enter the sales data for multiple products and want to restrict users from entering zero or negative values. Select the cells you want to add data validation to. Open the Data Validation dialog box. In the **Settings** tab, under **Allow**, select the **Whole Numbers** option and in Data select **greater than** with Minimum value as 0.

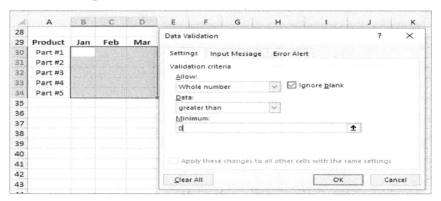

Figure 1.26 *Data Validation – Allow Whole Number*

Click on **OK** to apply data validation to the cells. Now try entering 0 or any negative number in any of the selected cells B30:D34, Excel shows a generic error message.

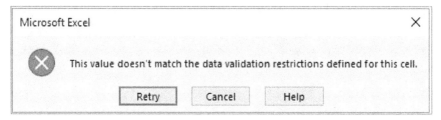

This does not help the user to know the exact restrictions on the cell. You can customize the Input message and the **Error Alert** to make it more helpful, as given in the following screenshot:

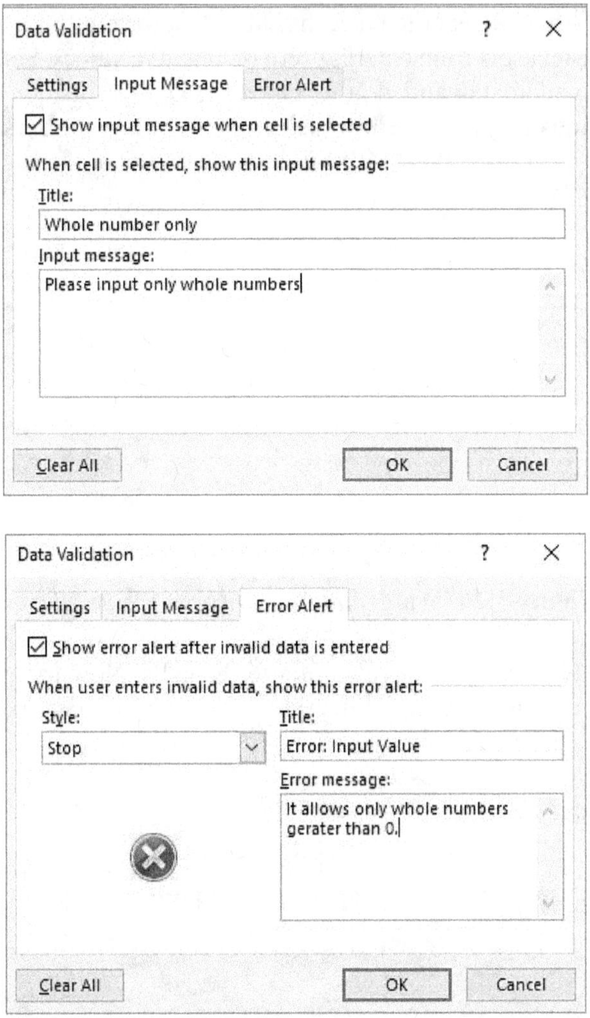

Figure 1.27 *Data Validation: Input Message and Error alert tabs*

Now select any cell in the data validation range of cells. You will see the message you added in the **Input Message** and on entering 0 in any of the cells you will see the error message you entered in the **Error Alert**.

	A	B	C	D	E	F	G	H	I	J
28										
29	Product	Jan	Feb	Mar		Error: Input Value				×
30	Part #1	0								
31	Part #2		Whole number only				It allows only whole numbers gerater than 0.			
32	Part #3		Please input only whole							
33	Part #4		numbers				Retry	Cancel	Help	
34	Part #5									
35										

Similarly, you can restrict using the other conditions of allowing only Decimals, Date, and so on.

Example #2: Set the data validation as in *Example #1, Figure 1.26,* however, in the Input Message and Error Alert tabs, *Figure 1.27,* remove the tick from the checkboxes that allow to *Show Input Message when a cell is selected* and *Show error alert after invalid data is entered.* Now enter 0 and -1 in cells within the data validation cell range that is, B30:D34. Select the data range, then go to **Data → Data Tools → Circle Invalid Data.** All the cells with 0 and -1 values will be circled as below.

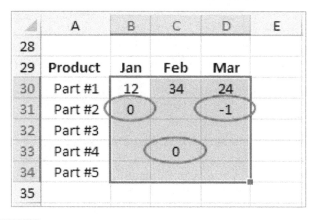

Example #3: In this example, we want to restrict the user to select only from the drop-down list provided in the cell. For each student, the teacher needs to select their class (**Class 1, Class 2,** or **Class 3**) and specify their attendance (Present or Absent) for the day. In order to provide drop-down for class and attendance, we will first make two lists; **List 1 & List 2,** separately in either the same sheet of a different sheet.

◢	A	B	C	D	E	F	G	H
37								
38	Name	Class	Attendance			List 1		List 2
39	Mike					Class 1		Present
40	Tom					Class 2		Absent
41	Gary					Class 3		
42	Neha							
43	Puja							

Select the cells B39:B43, go to **Data Validation** and in the **Settings** tab under **Allow**, select List. In **Source**, select the cell range (F39:F41) and click on **OK**. Similarly select the C39:C43 cells and in **Source** select the cell range (H39:H40) and click on **OK**. Select any one of the cells in the data validation range, they now have a drop-down list.

◢	A	B	C
37			
38	Name	Class	Attendance
39	Mike		
40	Tom		
41	Gary	Class 1	
42	Neha	Class 2	
43	Puja	Class 3	
44			

◢	A	B	C	[
37				
38	Name	Class	Attendance	
39	Mike			
40	Tom		Present	
41	Gary		Absent	
42	Neha			
43	Puja			

Creating the data validation list (like **List 1** and **List 2**) in the same sheet is not preferable as any deletion or addition of rows in the sheet may change the list and hence disrupt the data validation. A good practice is to keep all the lists to be used in the workbook in a separate sheet. Also using defined names or named ranges (see 3.3) is very helpful in this case.

In a new sheet, name it as List, copy **List 1**, and **List 2**. Using the **Name Manager**, define the lists names as **Class_List** (for cells B3 to B5) and **Attendance_List** (for cells D3 to D4). See *section 3.3* on how to create defined names.

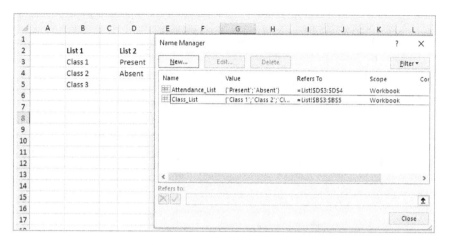

Now go back to the sheet where you want to add data validation. Select the cells B39:B43, go to **Data Validation** and in the **Settings** tab under **Allow**, select **List**. In **Source**, enter the corresponding list name that is, type =**Class_List** and click on **OK**. Similarly, select cells C39:C43 and in **Source**, enter the corresponding list name that is, type =**Attendance_List** and click on **OK**. Select any one of the cells in the data validation range, they now have a drop-down list.

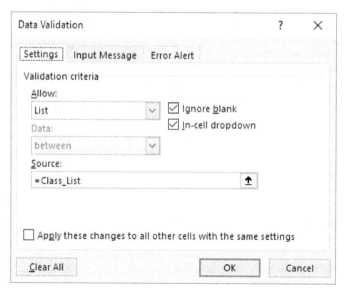

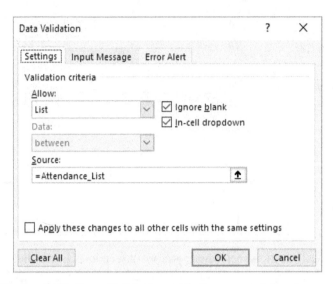

Figure 1.28 *Data Validation with Source as defined names*

An advantage of this method is that with any addition or deletion of rows or columns in the data sheet, the lists are not touched. Also, in case you want to add items to the list, you can do so without disrupting your validation. See *section 3.3.1* on defined names for details. One of the most common use of data validation is to create a drop-down list.

Example #4: Remove all data validations or validation circles added in the sheet. Select the cell ranges where data validation has been added. Go to the **Data** tab in the **Data Tools** group and select **Data Validation**. Excel will confirm if you want to erase, click on **OK** and then in the Data Validation dialog box click on **Clear All** button. All validations will be removed. To remove the validation circles, select the data range from where you want to erase and go to the **Data** tab, in the **Data Tools** group, select **Clear Validation Circles**. All the circles that were displayed on invalid cells will be removed.

1.8.5 Working with Excel tables

Excel table is a powerful feature that helps grouping of the data into rows and columns. When the data is designated as a table, Excel gives it special properties that enable quick and easy options to analyze the data and help prevent errors.

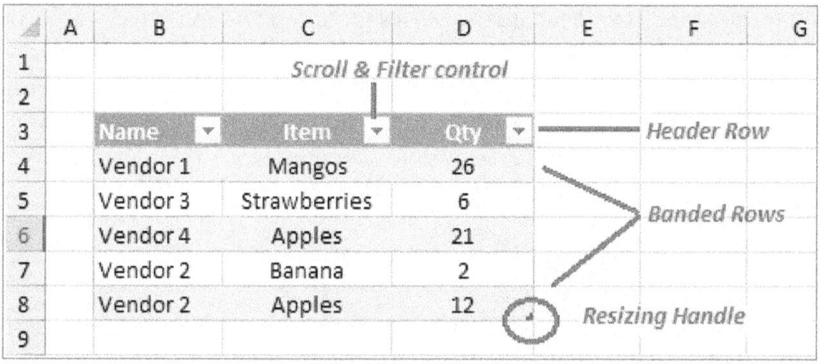

Figure 1.29 *Excel Table components*

Table can consist of a set of rows and columns in a sheet that are specifically designated as Excel tables using the create options. There can be multiple tables in a sheet. Table components are the following:

Header Row: It is the first row within the table that has names identifying the columns. Generally, the header row color would be different than other rows, also depends on the table style chosen. Excel automatically adds filter buttons and subtotals to the table that adapt as you filter your data.

Banded Rows or Data: One or more rows of data. By default, the rows are banded that is, formatted with alternating colors. When we add new data to the table, the existing formatting, formulas, conditional formatting, data validation, and so on, all get applied to the new data. This is a very big advantage of having tables.

Resizing Handle: It is at the bottom right of the last cell of the table. You can drag this handle to extend the table that is, can add empty rows as well as columns and the new cells inherit the same formatting, color and so on from the existing. You can also decrease the size of the table that is, less rows columns will be considered as part of the table. Decreasing the size does not delete the data in the removed cells but they are no longer considered as part of the table and will not get included in calculation, formulas, and so on.

1.8.5.1 Create a table

To convert data to a table, the first step is to identify the data range that you want to convert. The data range should not have any row or column that is completely blank for Excel to work correctly. Select any cell in the data range, go to the **Home** tab, in the **Styles** group select **Format as Table** and choose from the different styles for the table. Upon selection of the style, Excel automatically selects the adjoining cells and launches the **Format as Table** dialog box. Confirm the table settings, data range and tick the checkbox if your data has a header row and click on **OK**. Data range is converted into a table, with banded rows and sort & filter control.

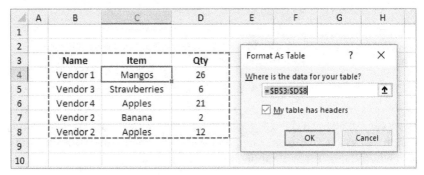

Figure 1.30 *Format as Table*

Another method to convert a range to table is by selecting any cell in the data range and pressing *CTRL+T* on the keyboard. A **Create Table** dialog box is launched where you can give the data range and specify if selection has a header row or not.

Figure 1.31 *Create Table*

Click on **OK** to create the table. You can change the table style from the **Table Tools | Design** tab, using the **Table Styles** group options.

Excel also allows you to create a table first, with empty rows and columns using the **Format as Table** and **Create Table** options, and then entering the data. By default, the column names are added as **Column1**, **Column2**, and so on. You can change the names of columns as required.

1.8.5.2 Use table styles

By clicking anywhere in the table, you can see a contextual '**Table Tools** → **Design** tab. Click on the **Table Styles** drop-down and select any one of the style thumbnails to apply the selected color scheme to your data.

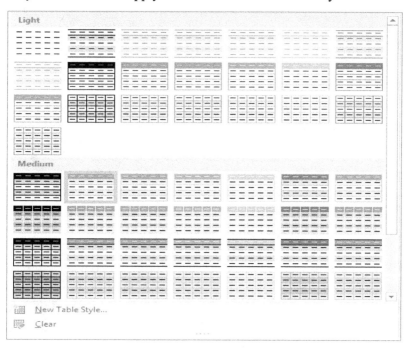

Figure 1.32 *Table Styles*

These quick styles make it easier and faster to change the look of your table and to make a good data representation.

1.8.5.3 Convert to Range

Excel allows you to convert a table to a data range. Upon conversion, all the special properties associated with the table are lost, the data remains as is. The **Convert to Range** option is available on the **Table Tools** → **Design** tab, in the **Tools** group and on mouse right click. Excel converts table to range only after getting confirmation.

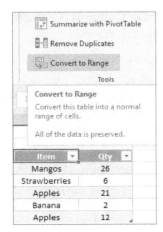

Figure 1.33 *Convert table to range*

After the table is converted to a range, all the table properties get removed but the row colors or bands may remain based on the style that was selected for the original table.

1.8.5.4 Add name to table

By default, the table names given by Excel are **Table1**, **Table2**, and so on. You can change the table name, which is preferable as it makes it easier to identify and reference the table data in formulas. To change the table name, go to the **Table Tools → Design** tab, in the **Properties** group on left-hand side of the ribbon and type the name in the **Table Name** field. Table name should be a single word that is, no spaces are allowed.

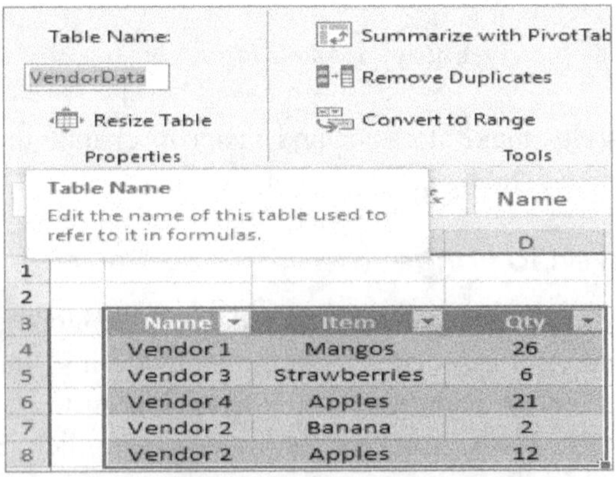

Figure 1.34 *Add table name*

Table name can be used in formulas as reference and when the table changes with new rows or columns, these references get updated as well.

1.8.5.5 Add or Delete data from table

You start typing text in the cell adjacent to the last row or column of the table and as you click *ENTER*, Excel automatically expands the table and applies all the formatting, formulas, data validations to the new added row or column.

Using the resizing handle also you can expand or reduce the table. Click on the resizing handle using the mouse and drag to add or delete rows or columns. Adding applies all formatting, formulas, and so on while deleting removes the cells from all special properties of the table.

You can also add or delete rows and columns in the table using the insert or delete menu options (see 1.8.2.2). You can also use the keyboard shortcuts CTRL+'+' and CTRL+'-'; click on any cell within the table and press the keyboard shortcuts.

There is also an option to **Resize Table** under the **Table Tools** ➔ **Design** ➔ **Properties** group. Select the new data range for the table and click **OK**. The new added columns will be given the default name as **Column1**, **Column2**, and so on.

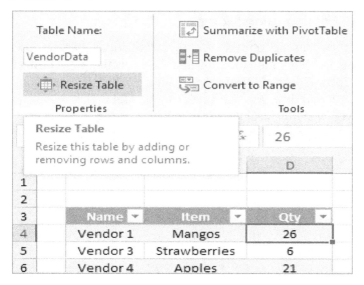

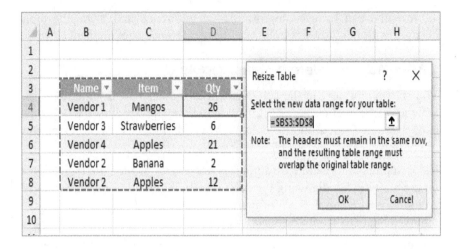

1.8.5.6 Sorting and Filtering Data

Sorting and Filtering of data in tables are similar to the normal range sort and filter. See *section 1.8.4.1*. Filtering makes it easy to copy a subset of a larger table and paste it to another location. Note that when you copy data from a filtered table, only the visible data is copied and the pasted data is a normal range, not a table.

1.8.5.7 Filtering using Slicers

Another way of filtering is, using slicers. Slicers can be inserted by selecting any cell within the table and then selecting **Insert Slicer** option in the **Table Tools** ➔ **Design** ➔ **Tools** group. Excel responds with a dialog box that displays each header in the table. Tick the checkbox for which you want to create the slicer and click on **OK**.

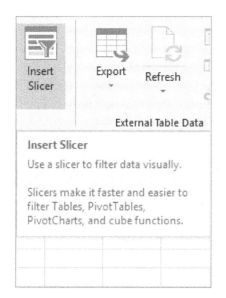

You can create a slicer for each column. To use a slicer, just click one of the buttons and the table displays only the rows that have a value that corresponds to the button. In case of more than one slicer, data is filtered by the selected buttons in each slicer. You can remove filtering for a particular slicer by clicking on the **Clear Filter** icon in the upper-right corner of the slicer.

1.8.5.8 Quick Analysis

Quick Analysis tools are very helpful, wherein you don't have to add formulas for calculating sum or averages however, you can add them quickly using the options. These work on the complete data designated as a table. Select any cell in the table and select the **Quick Analysis** option on mouse right-click menu options.

This allows you to add conditional **Formatting**, create Charts, add Totals, create Pivot Tables and create Sparklines. Here, we will discuss adding Totals in tables, all other options are discussed under different sections of Pivot Table, Charts, and so on.

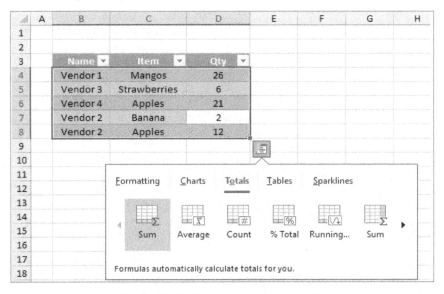

Figure 1.35 *Quick analysis on table*

In **Quick analysis**, click on **Totals**, move your cursor across the buttons to see the calculation results for your data, and then click on the button to apply the totals. For example, the row and column sums are shown by selecting the two sum options:

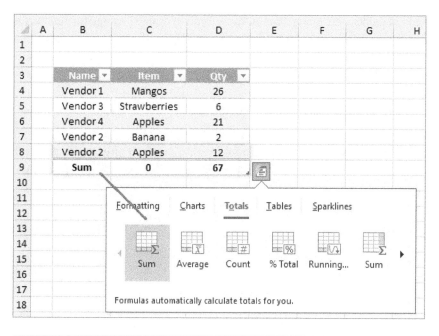

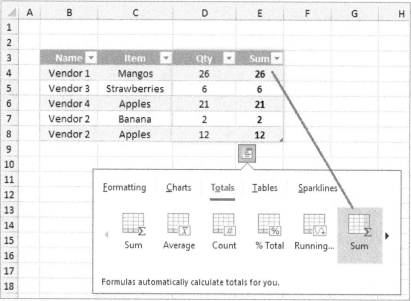

This is easier and faster than adding totals manually using formulas. The totals automatically apply to the complete data in the table. In case you add data in new rows or columns or delete from existing, the totals are updated automatically.

1.8.6 Controlling View of Worksheet

Excel includes a few options under the **View** tab that enables you to view multiple sheets at a time. The Zoom in and Zoom out options are available under the **Zoom** group. The **Split**, **Arrange All**, **Freeze Panes**, and more such options are available under the **Windows** group.

Figure 1.36 *Zoom and Windows options*

1.8.6.1 Zoom Options

By default, the view is displayed at 100%. You can change the zoom percentage and make it big with **Zoom In** or make it small with **Zoom Out**. These options do not change the font or picture size, the original content remains the same. Zoom factor of the active sheet can be changed either using the zoom slider on the status bar, by pressing *CTRL* and using the mouse wheel button, or using the options under the **Zoom** group in the **View** tab.

The **Zoom to Selection** option zooms in the selected cell range to a factor that fits in the Excel window. As the name suggests, the **100%** option displays the content in 100% mode. The **Zoom** option launches a dialog box where you can either select from the existing percentage or specify your own under the **Custom** option.

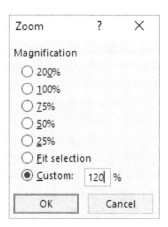

You can have different Zoom percentages for different worksheets and different windows (displaying the same worksheet).

1.8.6.2 Windows Options

New Window

A worksheet may have lots of information that is not easily visible and fits the screen for your analysis or you may want to see multiple sheets of the workbook simultaneously. Excel gives an option to launch a new window or multiple windows to the workbook using the **New Window** option (see *Figure 1.36*). In each of the new window, you can have a different view of the same worksheet or have different sheets opened. Changes made in any of the new windows and on saving the file gets reflected in all windows. As soon as a new window is launched, Excel changes the name of the original file by appending the number, '1', to the name. All the new workbooks will have the same name as the original file but with a number appended, based on the creation sequence. For example, if the workbook name is **Myfile.xlsx** and two new windows are launched then the original file will be renamed to **Myfile.xlsx:1** and the new ones as **MyFile.xlsx:2** and **MyFile.xlsx:3**.

Hide/Unhide

Open a new workbook named **MyFile.xlsx** and launch two new windows as explained in the preceding section. Go to each of the new workbooks— **MyFile.xlsx:2** and **MyFile.xlsx:3**—and click on the **Hide** option in the **Windows** group under **View** tab (see *Figure 1.36*), the workbooks are no longer visible. In order to make those workbooks visible, go to **Unhide** option in the workbook that is open. In the **Unhide** dialog box, the hidden workbooks are listed under **Unhide workbook**, select the workbook to unhide and click on **OK**.

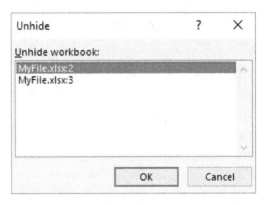

The workbook selected to unhide is now visible.

Arrange All

You can arrange all open windows in different ways, **Tiled**, **Horizontal**, **Vertical**, or **Cascade**. In any one of the open windows, go to the **View** tab, in the **Windows** group and select **Arrange All**, a dialog box is launched where you can select the arrangement style and click on **OK**.

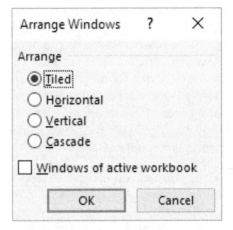

Split window

Split window is a very helpful feature, wherein you can split the active window into two or four panes and have different views of the same worksheet. Select the worksheet you want to split and then go to the **View** tab, in the **Windows** group and select **Split**. The worksheet will be divided into four panes, the split is done at the position of the active cell. You can drag the split lines and change the view size of the panes.

	A	B	C	D	E	N	O
1	Product ▾	Unit Pric ▾	Quantit ▾	Sales ▾	Pane 1	Pane 2	
2	Apple	120	2	240			
3	Banana	65	4	260			
4	Grapes	97	1	97			
5	Mango	154	5	770			
6	Orange	42	2	84			
7							
11						Pane 3	Pane 4
12			*Split Lines*				
13							

Freeze Panes

Freeze Panes option helps in keeping the column headers and row labels visible even when the user scrolls the worksheet up or down. For example, we have a sales data with column headers in the first row and the data goes beyond the rows that are currently visible in the window. In order to see the rows below, we will scroll down, and in this process the column header also scroll ups. To avoid this, go to the **View** tab, in the **Windows** group, select **Freeze Panes | Freeze Top Row**.

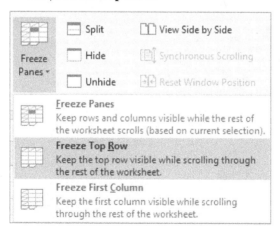

Now the top row is fixed and on scrolling down, the rows below move up, but the first header row is always visible. Similarly, if you select **Freeze First column**, then the first column is always visible even when the user scrolls to extreme right. In case of **Freeze Panes**, based on the cell that is selected, the rows and columns are fixed while rest of the worksheet scrolls.

View Side by Side and synchronous Scrolling

When you have multiple windows or workbooks open, you can tile them side-by-side for comparison using the **View Side by Side** option in the **View ➔ Window** group. The **Synchronous Scrolling** option gets enabled after you click on **View Side by Side**. Synchronous scrolling means that the scrolling happens at the same pace in both the open windows simultaneously.

1.9 Protecting Excel Workbook and Worksheet

You can protect your workbook to control the changes that can be made to the workbook, go to **File** menu and the first option on right-hand side pane is Protect Workbook. It has a drop-down menu, which gives options like opening the file in Read-only mode, **Encrypt with Password**, **Protect Current Sheet**, and Workbook Structure (which we will discuss in details later in this section), Restrict Access (using Azure Rights Management System), Add digital signatures (digitally signing the document using a Microsoft Partner) and last but not the least option is **Mark as Final**. The **Mark as Final** option is used to designate the workbook as **final**. The document is saved as a read-only file to prevent changes and useful to let others know that you're sharing a completed version of a workbook.

Figure 1.37 *Protect Workbook Options*

Excel gives multiple options for unprotecting and protecting your work, under the Protect section in the Review tab; Protect Sheet, Protect Workbook, Allow Edit Ranges, and Unshare Workbook.

1.9.1 Protect Workbook

Project Workbook opens the **Protect Structure and Windows** dialogue box. You can add your password and click on **OK** to save it. It will ask you to re-enter the password for confirmation and finally setting the same. Next time you try to open the workbook, Excel will ask for the password and if correctly entered, it will open the workbook else it will disallow. So, it is important to remember your password.

Figure 1.38 *Protect Workbook with Password*

1.9.2 Protect Sheet

Protect Sheet option can also be launched by selecting the sheet to protect and right-clicking. It launches a dialog box with different options you can protect a sheet and its contents with password and also set permissions for the user operations like selecting locked cells, changing format of cells, or allow inserting/deleting rows/columns, and so on. For example, if the **Select locked cells** were unchecked, users wouldn't even be allowed to select locked cells, so any formulas in these cells would be hidden. The Allow Users to Edit Ranges menu option allows you to add or modify the range of cells and set permissions for users to allow/disallow operations.

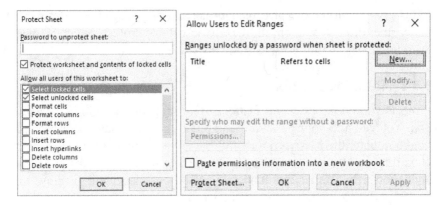

Figure 1.39 *Protect Sheet with Password / Edit Ranges*

1.10 Importing Data into Excel

Data you want to analyze may not always be in Excel format, it could be in a text file, website, in a database, or some other source. Excel allows you to import data using the **Get External Data** option under Data. More detailed information on importing data from other sources will be discussed later in the data analysis section of this book.

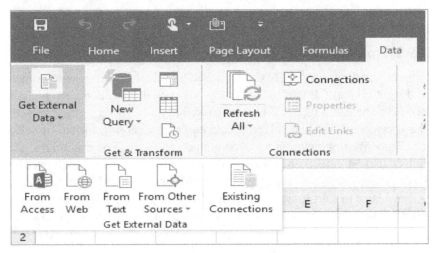

Figure 1.40 *Import External Data*

1.10.1 Importing from Text

Text files come in two varieties: fixed width and delimited. In a fixed width dataset, each variable starts in the same column. For example, Country name might be in columns 1-15, Capital name might be in columns 16-30, and so on. In contrast, in a delimited text file, as the name suggests, the data is separated by a delimiter character like a space, a tab, a comma, and a semicolon.

Importing from a text file takes you through a three-step wizard. In the first dialog box, you can see from the data in the first few rows that the data is not of a fixed width, so Delimited is the correct choice. You also have the option to start the import at a row other than the first row and specify if your data has headers and should be considered while importing. After all the selections are made, click on **Next** to go to the second screen.

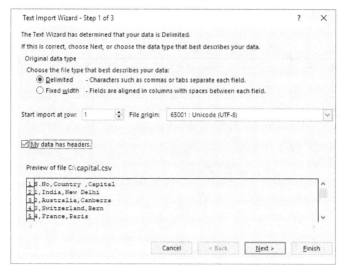

Figure 1.41 *Text Import Wizard – Step1*

In the second step, you can specify the delimiter to be used for aligning the data in columns and rows, in the following example, it is a comma. In case neither of the default delimiters work for you, you can specify the delimiter under **Other**. In case that also does not work then try opening the file in text editor and see if the columns align or they are ragged, so may need a fix in the original text file.

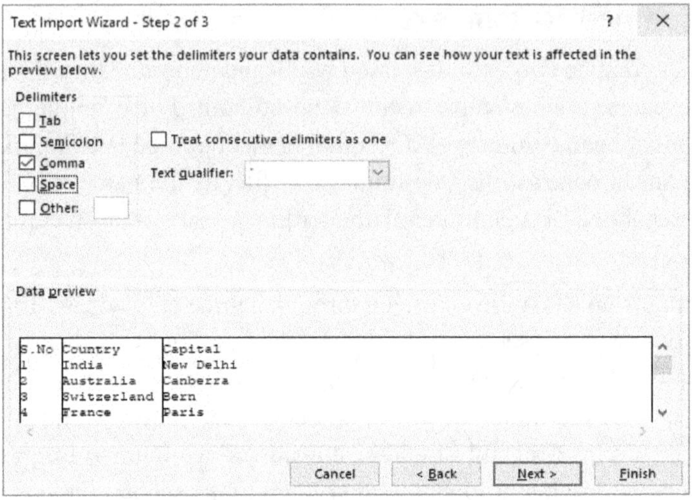

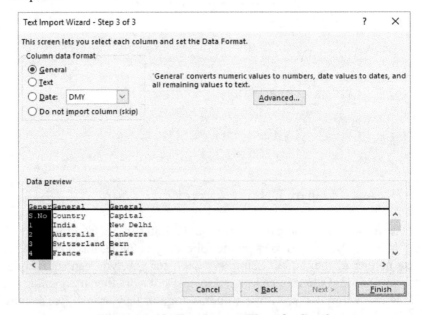

Figure 1.42 *Text Import Wizard – Step2*

In the third step, you can fine-tune the import or click on the **Finish** button. You can also fine tune the data later in the Excel file after the import is complete.

Figure 1.43 *Text Import Wizard – Step3*

When you click on **Finish**, Excel will ask you for the location from where you want to import the data in the worksheet:

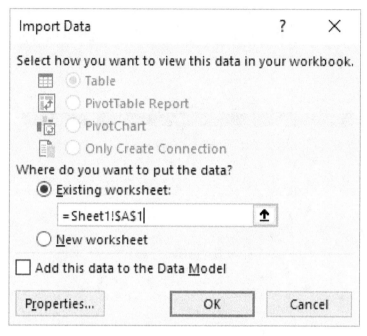

Figure 1.44 *Import data location*

1.10.2 Importing from Web

Importing from web could be a little tricky as sites can be designed in variety of ways and data may not be easily importable. You can try using the Excel Web query, which can import anything that is surrounded by table tags in the HTML page. Go to the Data tab and select From Web under the Get External Data option. In the Address, type or copy the URL from where you want to import data. To get the exact URL, open your web browser and go to the page from where you want to import data, see that it has tables, as that is what Excel identifies. For example, you can import weather forecast data. Click on Import and in the next dialog box specify the location for importing.

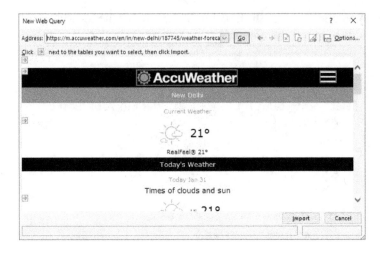

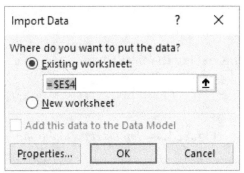

Figure 1.45 *New Web Query for Import*

1.10.3 Import from Database

Importing data from a database can be done from multiple sources like Microsoft Access (part of the Office suite) and many server-based systems such as Microsoft's SQL Server, Oracle RDMS, and so on. All of these store data in essentially the same way, as related tables and use essentially Structured Query Language, or SQL, to retrieve specific subsets of the data. For example, to import data from MS Access, use **From Access** from the **Get External Data** option under the **Data** tab. After you browse for an Access database file, you have the option to import one or more tables.

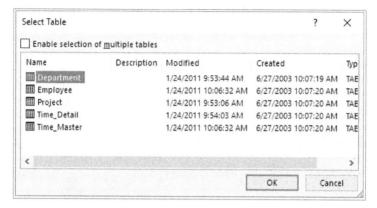

Figure 1.46 *Import from database – Select table*

Note that importing data From Other Sources have been discussed in later sections in context of data analysis using Pivots.

1.11 Exporting Data from Excel

1.11.1 Export to File

You can Export data from Excel in PDF format (Adobe Acrobat document) or different file types as given in the following screenshot. Go to **File** menu and select the **Export** option:

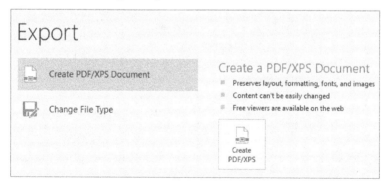

Click on **Create PDF/XPS document** for exporting the workbook in PDF format. A file Save dialog is launched. Using the **Options** setting in the Save dialog you can specify what to publish in the PDF from Excel like page numbers, entire workbook, the active sheet, or selection.

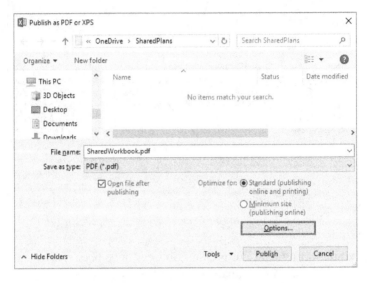

Click **OK** and on the Save dialog click on **Publish** to print the Excel in PDF format.

If you want to save the workbook in a different file type (excluding PDF), select the file type and click on **Save As** (see details 1.7.3).

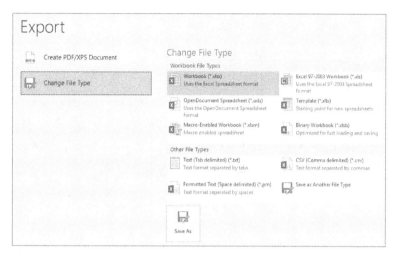

Figure 1.47 *Export from Excel*

1.11.2 Export table to SharePoint List

There is also an option to export an Excel table to a SharePoint List. When you export the list, Excel will create a new SharePoint list on the site for you to work. For doing this, you need a SharePoint site and the correct permissions.

Select the table in the sheet and from the **Table Tools → Design** tab, select **Export → Export Table to SharePoint List…**.

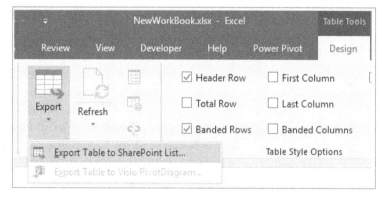

```
┌────────────────────────────────────────────────────────────────────┐
│  Export Table to SharePoint List - Step 1 of 2          ?      ✕    │
│                                                                      │
│  Where do you want to publish your table?                            │
│    A̲ddress:  ┌──────────────────────────────────────────────┬───┐  │
│             │ http://mysharepoint                            │ ∨ │  │
│             └──────────────────────────────────────────────┴───┘  │
│             ☐ C̲reate a read-only connection to the new SharePoint list│
│  Provide a name and description for your table.                      │
│    Na̲me:   ┌──────────────────────────────────────────────────┐    │
│           │ Vendor Products & Sales                            │    │
│           └──────────────────────────────────────────────────┘    │
│    D̲escription:  ┌───────────────────────────────────────────┐     │
│                  │ List of Vendor products, pricing and sales│     │
│                  │                                           │     │
│                  │                                           │     │
│                  │                                           │     │
│                  │                                           │     │
│                  │                                           │     │
│                  └───────────────────────────────────────────┘     │
│  ┌────────┐  ┌──────────┐  ┌──────────┐  ┌──────────┐  ┌─────────┐ │
│  │  Help  │  │  Cancel  │  │  B̲ack    │  │  N̲ext    │  │ F̲inish  │ │
│  └────────┘  └──────────┘  └──────────┘  └──────────┘  └─────────┘ │
└────────────────────────────────────────────────────────────────────┘
```

Figure 1.48 *Export to SharePoint List*

Specify the URL of the SharePoint site in **Address**, type the **Name** and **Description** and click on **Next** or **Finish**. When you click on **Next**, it might ask for Office credentials. Review the information given in Columns and Data Types and then click on Finish. Click on **OK** to complete. A message indicating that your table is published, along with the **Uniform Resource Locator (URL)** appears.

1.12 Sharing in Excel

You can share and collaborate in Excel using a new feature called **Co-authoring** that is, multiple people can open and work on the same shared Excel workbook and also see each other's changes quickly. In older versions of Excel, the feature was named **Shared Workbooks** that had many limitations and hence was replaced by co-authoring in newer versions. We will discuss Co-authoring and also see how to enable the old legacy features. Microsoft recommends using Co-authoring now.

1.12.1 Co-authoring (new)

Co-authoring is only available with Office 365 subscription and in a later version on Excel, including Excel 2016. If you're using a version of Excel that supports co-authoring, you can see the **Share** option in the upper-right corner.

Before sharing, we will save the Excel file in OneDrive (can also be done in SharePoint Online library). Note that you will need to have OneDrive software installed and correct permissions to copy on your system.

Open the workbook and go to **File → Share**, select **Share with People** or select the **Share** option in the upper-right corner of the Excel and click on **Save to Cloud**. This takes you to the **Save As** option, select the OneDrive location to save the file and click on **Save**. Now that your file is saved, again go to **File → Share** and select **Share with People** or click on **Share** option in the upper-right corner.

It will now give the option **Share with People**, click on it to open the Share pane in the worksheet. Type the email address in the **Invite People** field, set their permissions to either to edit or view, add a message and click on **Share**. Excel emails the invitation to share the workbook to each of the recipients entered in the **Invite People** textbox. The invitees are added in the **Share** pane.

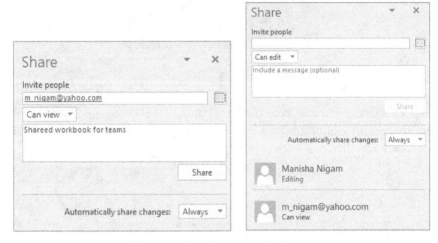

Figure 1.49 *Share on OneDrive*

All the recipients receive an email message containing a hyperlink to the workbook on your OneDrive. By clicking on the hyperlink, a copy of the workbook opens on a new page in their default web browser using the **Excel Online** Web app.

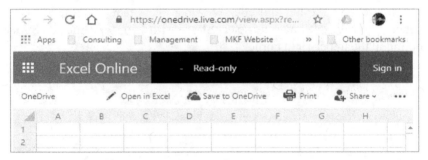

Instead of sending email invitations to individual recipients with links to the workbooks you want to share on your OneDrive, you can create hyperlinks to them and then make them available to all the people required. For creating a hyperlink, click on the **Get a sharing link** option at the bottom of the **Share** pane.

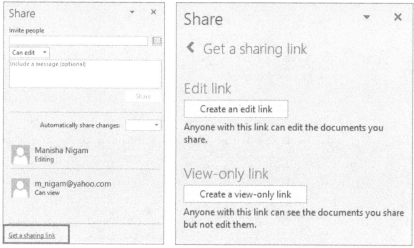

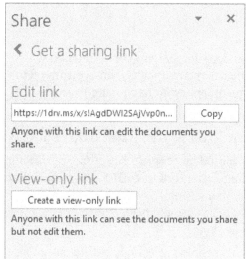

Click on **Create an edit link** to create a link that allows online editing and **Create a view-only link** to create a link that does not allow online editing.

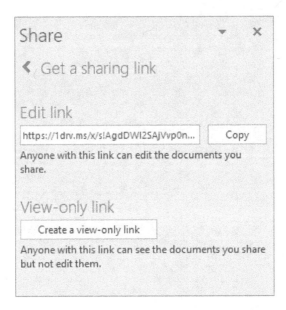

Click on **Copy** to copy the link on your clipboard which you can insert in a new email to the desired recipients. Now you are set to work on the same workbook with the people who have shared access.

Few things to know about Co-authoring that will be helpful:

- You can share Excel Workbooks in **.xlsx**, **.xlsm**, or **.xlsb** formats only.

- You might see other people's selections in different colors, only if they are using Excel for Office 365 subscribers, Excel Online, Excel for Android, Excel Mobile, or Excel for iOS. If they're using another version, you won't see their selections, but their changes will appear as they are working.

- If you see other people's selections in different colors, they'll show up as blue, purple, and so on. However, your selection will always be green.

- In case two people are making changes to the same thing then, the last change that is saved, either with the Save button or automatically with AutoSave, is the one that **wins**. It is recommended to assign areas to individuals in such cases to avoid conflicts.

- In order to view or restore previous version of the file in Excel for Office 365, go to **File ➔ Info ➔ View and restore previous versions**. Then find a past version in the list, and then click on Open version. The past version will open. If you want to restore it to the current version, wait until everyone is no longer co-authoring, and then click on **Restore**.

1.12.2 Shared Workbooks (legacy)

In latest versions of Excel like Excel 2016, the buttons related to the **Shared Workbook** feature are no longer available on the **Review** tab by default as this has been replaced by Co-authoring feature. Excel still gives an option to enable those.

1.12.2.1 Adding legacy features on QAT

We will enable the legacy features and add them to the Quick Access Toolbar. Go to **File → Options** and select **Quick Access Toolbar**.

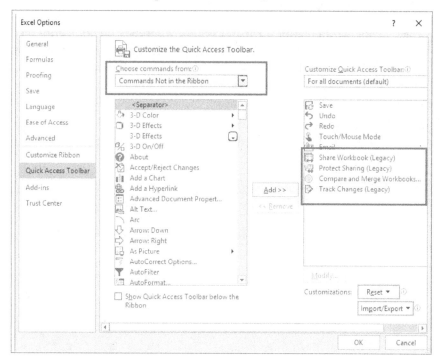

Figure 1.50 *Adding Shared Workbook legacy commands in QAT*

In **Choose commands from** select **Commands Not in the Ribbon**. This will display all commands in the list that are not currently seen in the **Ribbons** tab. Now select the Shared Workbook-related commands one-by-one that is, **Share Workbook (Legacy)**, **Track Changes (Legacy)**,

Protect Sharing (Legacy), **Compare and Merge Workbooks**, and add them to the right-hand side using the **Add>>** button. After you have added all the commands, click on **OK** to see the command buttons in the QAT.

Figure 1.51 *QAT with Shared workbook buttons*

Share Workbook button: 　　　　Protect and Share button:

Compare and Merge Workbooks button:

Track Changes button:

1.12.2.2 Share Workbook

Create a new workbook or open an existing workbook and upload it on a network location, similar to what we did in co-authoring example. From the **Quick Access Toolbar** (**QAT**), click on the **Share Workbook** button. There are two tabs in the **Share Workbook** dialog box: Editing and Advanced.

In the **Editing** tab, click on the checkbox to enable use of old features. In the Advanced tab, modify the settings as per your requirements and click on **OK** to save.

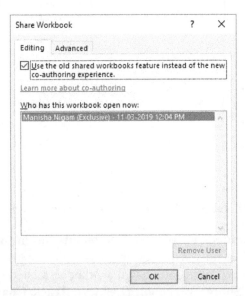

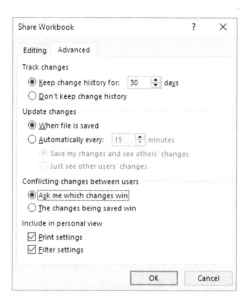

You can see that next to the file name, **Shared** is mentioned in brackets to indicate that now the file is in sharing mode.

As per the official Microsoft website, the following are the unsupported features and hence, it is advised to use the new feature Co-authoring.

Unsupported items	Unsupported actions
Creating or inserting tables	Inserting or deleting blocks of cells
Adding or changing conditional formats	Deleting worksheets
Adding or changing data validation	Merging cells or splitting merged cells
Creating or changing charts or PivotChart reports	Sorting or filtering by format
Inserting or changing pictures or other objects	Using drawing tools
Inserting or changing hyperlinks	Assigning, changing, or removing passwords
Creating, changing, or viewing scenarios	Protecting or unprotecting worksheets or the workbook

Inserting automatic subtotals	Grouping or outlining data
Creating data tables	Writing, recording, changing, viewing, or assigning macros
Creating or changing PivotTable reports	Changing or deleting array formulas
Creating or applying slicers	Adding, renaming, or deleting XML maps
Creating or modifying sparklines	Mapping cells to XML elements
Adding or changing Microsoft Excel 4 dialog sheets	Using the XML Source task pane, XML toolbar, or XML commands on the Data menu
	Using a data form to add new data
Adding threaded comments	Editing, or deleting threaded comments

1.12.2.3 Protect Shared Workbook

You can enable the option to prevent the change history to be removed by clicking on the **Sharing with track changes** checkbox in the **Protect Shared Workbook** dialog box.

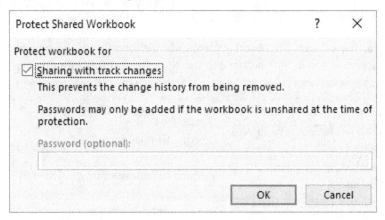

Figure 1.52 *Protect Shared Workbook*

1.12.2.4 Compare and Merge Workbooks

Open the Shared Workbook into which you want to merge changes. Click on the **Compare and Merge Workbooks** button on QAT, browse to select the copy of the workbook (can select multiple files) that contains the changes to merge and click on **OK**. The changes will be merged in the original shared workbook.

1.12.2.5 Track Changes

Track changes gives two options: **Highlight Changes** and Accept or Reject changes. You can change *When, Who,* and *Where* fields to selectively track the changes made by everyone or individuals or for specific cell ranges as selected in *Where.*

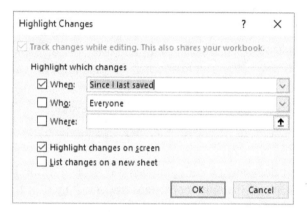

Figure 1.53 *Track changes in Shared Workbooks*

Again, a word of caution that the old features that is, these legacy features have some limitations and hence, it is advisable to use the new co-authoring feature to take full advantage of Excel.

CHAPTER 2

Perform Functions with Shortcut Keys

Excel provides many shortcut keys to help users perform major functions or operations on cells, columns, rows, or objects in worksheets and workbooks.

Benefits of Excel shortcut keys that are often overlooked:

- Faster operations that save time, increases productivity, and therefore saves money

- Reduced dependency on computer mouse that minimizes the hand movement and the number of steps or clicks to perform a function

- Improved work posture and prevents strain associated with repetitive strain injury

Excel has been a popular tool for many years and basic shortcuts for functions like copy, paste, and select all, are well known. In this section, we will discuss important shortcuts keys that are not very often used.

2.1 Keys for Menus

Show a shortcut menu	*SHIFT+F10*
Make the menu bar active	*F10* or *ALT*
Show the program icon menu (on the program title bar)	ALT+SPACEBAR
Select the next or previous command on the menu or submenu	DOWN/UP ARROW
Select the menu to the left or right, or, with a submenu visible, switch between the main menu and the submenu	LEFT/RIGHT ARROW

Select the first or last command on the menu or submenu	*HOME* or *END*
Close the visible menu and submenu at the same time	*ALT*

2.2 Move on a Worksheet or Workbook

Move to the first/last cell on the worksheet	*CTRL+ {HOME / END}*
Move up/down one screen	PAGE {UP / DOWN}
Move one screen to the right/left	*ALT* + PAGE {DOWN / UP}
Move to the next/previous sheet in the workbook	*CTRL*+PAGE {DOWN / UP}
Move to the next workbook or window	*CTRL+F6* or *CTRL+TAB*
Move to the previous workbook or window	*CTRL+SHIFT+F6*

2.3 Select Cells, Columns, Rows or Objects

Select the entire column/row	*{CTRL/ SHIFT}* + SPACEBAR
Select the entire worksheet	*CTRL+A*
Select the current region around the active cell (the current region is an area enclosed by blank rows and blank columns)	*CTRL+SHIFT*+* (ASTERISK)
Extend the selection by one cell	*SHIFT*+ ARROW KEY
Extend the selection to the last nonblank cell in the same column or row as the active cell	*CTRL+SHIFT*+ ARROW KEY
Extend the selection to the beginning of the row	*SHIFT+HOME*
Extend the selection to the first/last cell used on the worksheet (lower-right corner)	CTRL+SHIFT+ *{HOME / END}*

2.4 Select Cells with Special Characteristics

Select the current array, which is the array that the active cell belongs to	*CTRL+/*

Select all cells with comments	CTRL+*SHIFT*+O (the letter O)
Select cells whose content are different from the comparison cell in each row (for each row, the comparison cell is in the same column as the active cell)	*CTRL*+\
Select cells whose contents are different from the comparison cell in each column (for each column, the comparison cell is in the same row as the active cell)	*CTRL*+*SHIFT*+|
Select only cells that are directly referred to by formulas in the selection	*CTRL*+[
Select only cells with formulas that refer directly to the active cell	*CTRL*+]
Select all cells with formulas that refer directly or indirectly to the active cell	*CTRL*+*SHIFT*+}
Select only visible cells in the current selection	*ALT*+SEMICOLON
Format Data	
Display the Style command (Format menu)	*ALT*+' (APOSTROPHE)
Display the Cells command (Format menu)	*CTRL*+*1*
Apply bold style to all cells in the highlighted section	*CTRL*+*2*
Apply italics to all cells in the highlighted section	*CTRL*+*3*
Underline all cells in the highlighted section	*CTRL*+*4*
Apply or remove strikethrough formatting	*CTRL*+*5*
Apply the General number format	*CTRL*+*SHIFT*+~
Apply the Currency format with two decimal places (negative numbers appear in parentheses)	*CTRL*+*SHIFT*+$
Apply the Percentage format with no decimal places	*CTRL*+*SHIFT*+%
Apply the Exponential number format with two decimal places	*CTRL*+*SHIFT*+^
Apply the Date format with the day, month, and year	*CTRL*+*SHIFT*+#
Apply the Time format with the hour and minute, and indicate A.M. or P.M.	*CTRL*+*SHIFT*+@
Apply the Number format with two decimal places, 1000 separator, and – for negative values	*CTRL*+*SHIFT*+!
Hide rows	*CTRL*+*9*

Unhide rows	$CTRL+SHIFT+($
Hide columns	$CTRL+0$ (ZERO)
Unhide columns	$CTRL+SHIFT+)$
Changes between displaying cell values or formulas in the worksheet	$CTRL+\grave{}$
Filling data in cells	
Fill down. Fills the cell beneath with the contents of the selected cell. To fill more than one cell, select the source cell and press *Ctrl+Shift+Down* to select multiple cells. Then press *Ctrl+D* to fill them with the contents of the original cell.	$CTRL+D$
Fill right. Fills the cell to the right with the contents of the selected cell. To fill more than one cell, select the source cell and press *Ctrl+Shift+Right* to select multiple cells. Then press *Ctrl+R* to fill them with the contents of the original cell.	$CTRL+R$
Copies a formula from the cell above	$CTRL+'$
Copies value from cell above	$CTRL+SHIFT+"$
Working on Tables	
Creates table of selected cells	$CTRL+L / CTRL+T$
Insert, (Rows, Columns, or Cells) Depends on selection	$CTRL++ /$ $CTRL+SHIFT+=$
Delete, (Rows, Columns, or Cells) Depends on selection	$CTRL+-$
Apply the outline border	$CTRL+SHIFT+\&$
Remove all borders	$CTRL+SHIFT+\_$

CHAPTER 3

Formulas and Functions

3.1 Understanding Formulas

Formulas in Excel worksheets are very important and useful features of Excel that makes it so powerful. Formulas help to calculate results from the data stored in the worksheet. A formula consists of special code entered into a cell, performs calculations, and returns the result in the displayed cell. When data changes, the formulas calculate updated results dynamically. Formulas use a variety of operators and worksheet functions to work with values and text which can be located in other cells. The formula itself appears in the Formula bar when you select the cell.

A formula always begins with an equal sign and can contain any of these elements:

- Mathematical operators, such as + (for addition) and * (for multiplication)
- Cell references (including named cells and ranges)
- Values or Text
- Worksheet functions (such as SUM and COUNT)

3.2 Operators in Formula

Operators that are used in formulas are as given in the following table and also their precedence that is, when Excel calculates the value of a formula, it uses certain rules to determine the order in which the various parts of the formula are calculated. Note that the parentheses can be used to override Excel's built-in order of precedence. Expressions within parentheses are always evaluated first. You can also nest parentheses within formulas and Excel evaluates the most deeply nested expressions first and then works its way out.

Operator	Name	Precedence
^	Exponentiation	1
*	Multiplication	2
/	Division	2
+	Addition	3
–	Subtraction	3
&	Concatenation	4
=	Logical comparison (equal to)	5
>	Logical comparison (greater than)	5
<	Logical comparison (less than)	5
>=	Logical comparison (greater than or equal to)	5
<=	Logical comparison (less than or equal to)	5
<>	Logical comparison (not equal to)	5

Figure 3.1 *Operators & Precedence*

For example, in the following picture we have taken five values and are using different operators and parentheses to create multiple formulas, including nested parentheses to show how the result changes in each case. Note that the formula is displayed in the formula bar for the selected cell.

D2		▼	:	×	✓	*fx*	=B2-B3*B4+B5/B6	

⊿	A	B	C	D
1		Values	Formula	Result
2		10	=B2-B3*B4+B5/B6	-6
3		5	=(B2-B3)*B4+B5/B6	24
4		4	=((B2-B3)*(B4+B5))/B6	30
5		8	=((B2-B3)*(B4+B5/B6))	40
6		2	=(B2-(B3*(B4+B5)/B6))	-20
7				

Figure 3.2 *Operator precedence examples*

So, based on the precedence, Excel calculates the result for the above formulas. In first formula, that is, *=B2-B3*B4+B5/B6*, first the multiplication and division calculations will happen (result 20 and 4), then addition and subtractions (*=10-20+4*). In the last formula, we have nested parentheses, *=(B2-(B3*(B4+B5)/B6))*. Working from inner most parentheses, Excel first calculates *(B4+B5)* = 12, then 12/B6 = 6, *B3*6* = *30* and finally *B2-30 = -20*.

3.3 Defined Names

Excel gives an option of defined names where the user can define a descriptive name for a cell range, function, constant, or table. Defined name, range name, or named range refer to the same thing. Using named range in formulas, charts are easier to understand and maintain. Another benefit in using named range is that they do not change when the formula is copied to another location, so there is no chance of messing your formulas.

Note that the name cannot have spaces, however, you can use underscore or period. Excel will not allow names that conflict with the names it uses internally, it will show an error if it conflicts. There are multiple ways of defining a name that we will discuss in this chapter.

3.3.1 Create New, Delete, Edit Named Range

3.3.1.1 Directly typing name in Name box

Select the range of cells and type in the descriptive name that you want in the Name Box that is, on left corner above the first column A in the sheet. In the following example, we selected the cell range A2 to A6 and typed in the name *fruits* in the Name Box and hit *enter*.

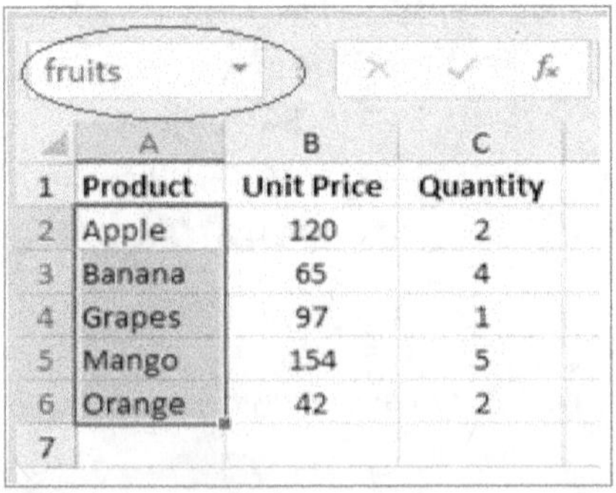

Figure 3.3 *Define name in Name Box*

Now, how do you confirm that this name you typed, has been added correctly? Go to menu **Formulas → Name Manger** under Defined Names group. This name should be displayed in the list of named ranges.

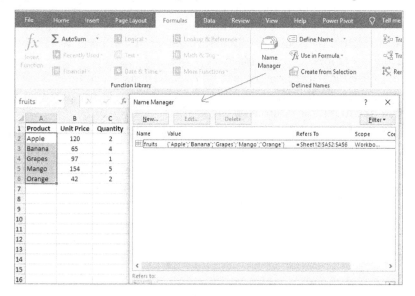

Figure 3.4 *Defined Names -Name Manager*

3.3.1.2 *Using Name Manager or Define Name*

You can also define a named range using the **Name Manager** or **Define Name** option under menu **Formulas → Defined Names** group. On clicking **Name Manager**, a window is displayed as given above in Figure 3.4. Click on New in the **Names Manager** window to launch the New Name dialog box. Same dialog box is launched if you select the **Define Name** option.

Figure 3.5 *Named Range: Define New Name*

In the **New Name** dialog box, you can specify the name like **fruits_sales** as in our preceding example, for the range of cells specified, that is, D2 to D6 in the **Refers to** field. You can define the range by clicking on the arrow button next to the field and selecting the cells. Click on **OK** in the **New Name** dialog box to save and return to the sheet. Note that additionally you can define the scope of the named range, it can be at workbook or specific sheet level. Workbook level is preferred as you would generally want to use the named ranges across sheets. There is a comments section also for describing the purpose of the named range or any text that you would like to put for future reference.

Name Manager can also be used for deleting the existing named range by selecting the named range in the Name Manager window and clicking on the *delete* button (see Figure *3.4*) and confirming by clicking on OK in the delete dialog box. It also allows us to Edit the existing named range that is, you can modify the name, comments, and the cell range.

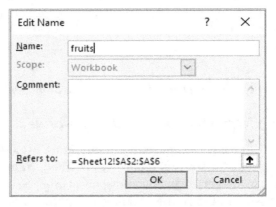

Figure 3.6 *Named Range: Edit*

3.3.1.3 Using Create from Selection

There is another option for creating names automatically from existing row or column labels. In the following example, we will create names from the column labels that is, **Unit Price, Quantity**, and **Sales** columns. Select the cells in range B1 to D6 and click on the **Create from Selection** option from the Formulas ribbon. In the **Create from Selection** dialog box, select the checkbox **Top Row** as we want to use the labels in top row of the selected range for defining the named ranges and click on **OK**.

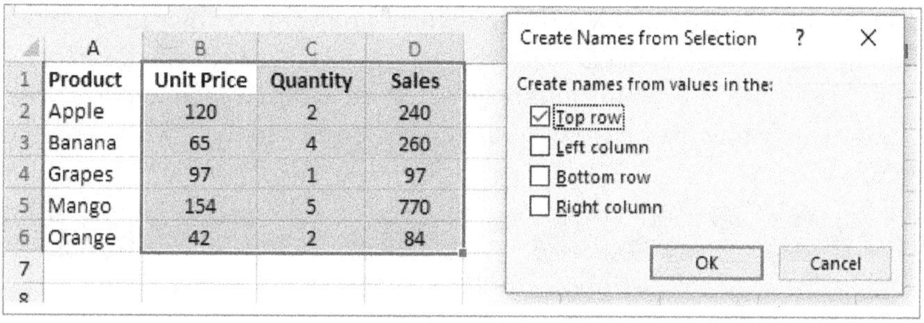

Figure 3.7 *Named Range: Create from Selection*

Now open the **Name Manager** window to view the named ranges created. Note that since column B had a space in the name that is, **Unit Price** and named ranges cannot have space, Excel has created the named range as **Unit_Price** that is, with an underscore.

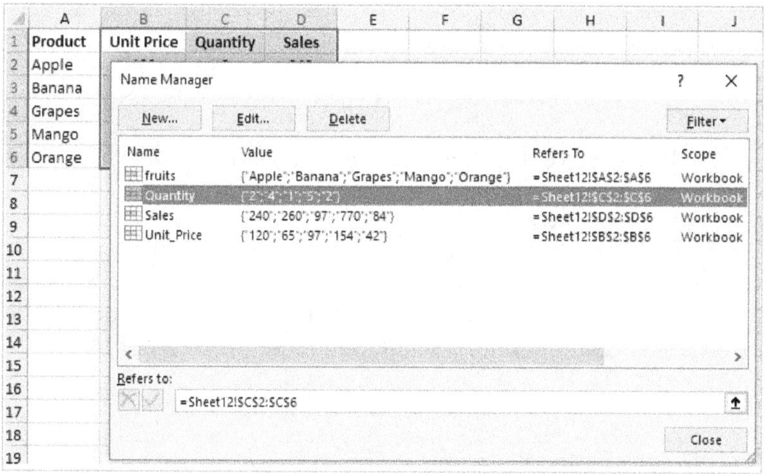

Figure 3.8 *Create from selection: New named ranges*

3.3.2 Using Named Range

We have seen how to create, edit, and delete named ranges. In this section, we will see how to use the named ranges in a formula and apply them.

3.3.2.1 Use in formula

Taking the same example as discussed before for creating named ranges, now we want to find the Total Sales and we will use **Sales** named range in the function SUM. Click on the cell where you want to enter the formula which is D7 in our case, and type '=SUM(' and then go to Formulas Ribbon and select 'Use in Formula' option to select the named range 'Sales', close the function bracket and press enter. The formula in cell will look like *=SUM(Sales)*.

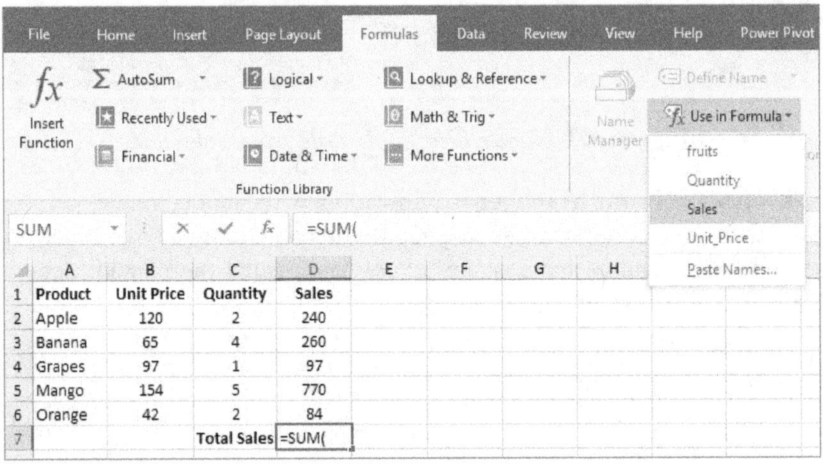

Figure 3.9 *Named Range: Use in formula*

3.3.2.2 Apply Name in formula

We can insert a named range into an existing formula. This is particularly helpful when you want to replace cell references with named ranges to make formulas easier to manage and look more user-friendly.

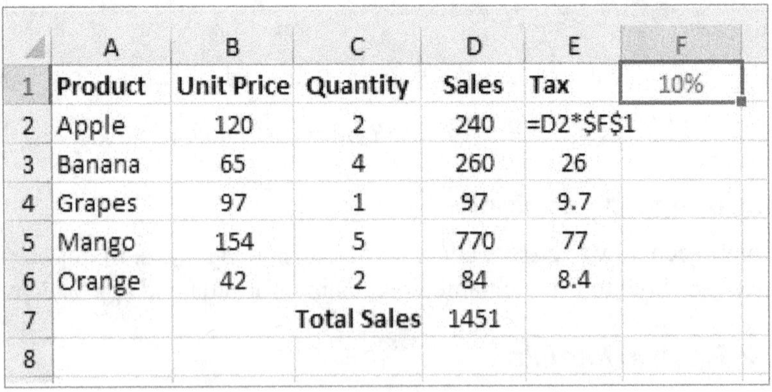

	A	B	C	D	E	F
1	Product	Unit Price	Quantity	Sales	Tax	10%
2	Apple	120	2	240	=D2*$F$1	
3	Banana	65	4	260	26	
4	Grapes	97	1	97	9.7	
5	Mango	154	5	770	77	
6	Orange	42	2	84	8.4	
7			Total Sales	1451		
8						

Figure 3.10 *Named Range: Apply Names*

In the preceding example, we are calculating the Tax amount on the Sales using the formula D2*F1, based on the Tax rate specified in cell F1. Now we will define name for the Tax rate in cell *F1* as *taxrate* and apply to the formula in cell range E2 to E6. Select the cell range E2 to E6 and from Formulas ribbon, click on Define Names ➔ Apply Names option, select named range 'taxrate' and click on OK.

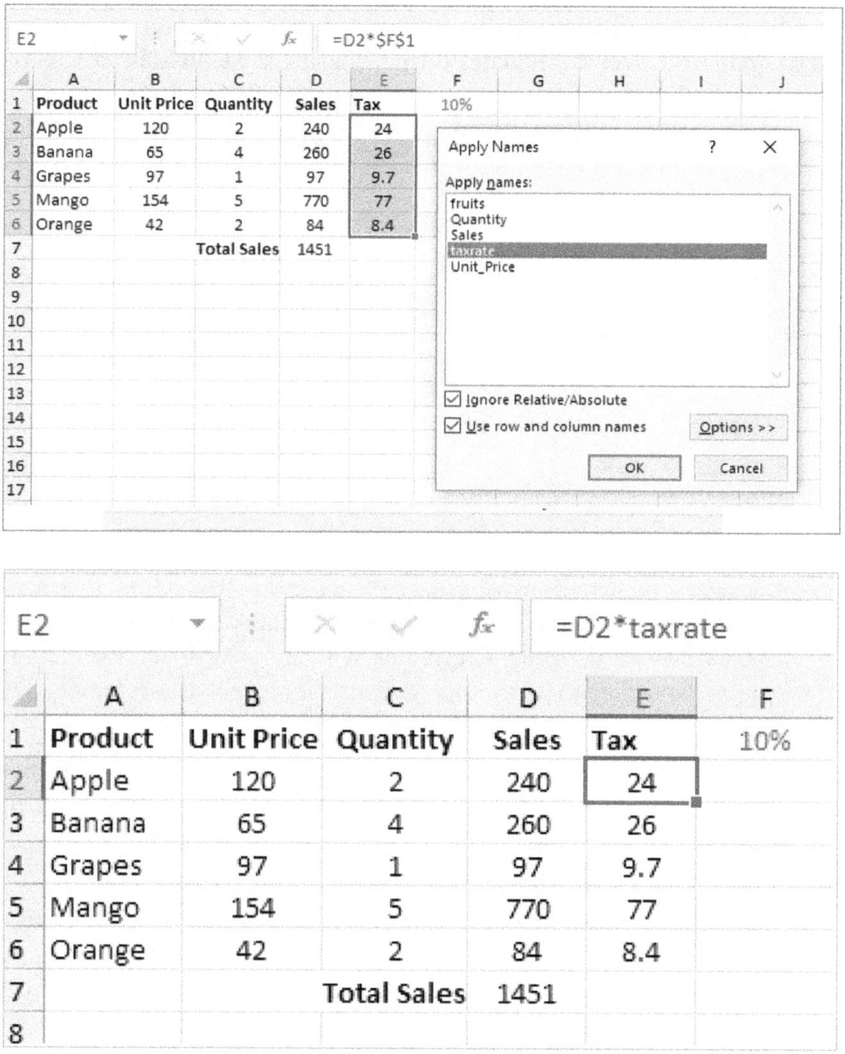

Figure 3.11 *Named Range: Apply names*

By clicking on **OK** in the **Apply Names** dialog box, Excel modifies the formula in the cell range E2 to E6 from *=D2*$F$1 to =D2*taxrate* respectively.

3.4 Calculations

By default, Excel automatically recalculates formulas only when the cells that the formula depends on, have changed. However, you can control when and how Excel recalculates formulas using the **Calculation** Ribbon option in the **Formulas** tab.

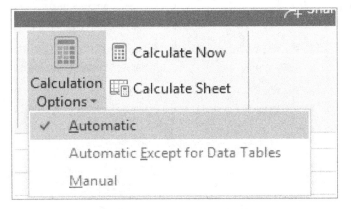

Figure 3.12 *Formulas: Calculations*

- **Calculation Options** → **Automatic** is the default setting. This means that all dependent formulas will be recalculated every time you make a change to a value, formula, or name that is referenced in the formula.

- **Calculation Options** → **Automatic Except for Data Tables** if set, then all dependent formulas, except the data tables, will be recalculated every time you make a change to a value, formula, or name that is referenced in the formula.

- **Calculation Options→Manual** if set, will turn off automatic recalculation and you will have to manually do it explicitly by pressing *F9* or clicking on **Calculate Now** (to recalculate) or **Calculate Sheet** options.

- **Calculate Now** recalculates all open worksheets, including data tables, and updates all open chart sheets.

- **Calculate Sheet** recalculates only the active worksheet, charts and any chart sheets linked to this worksheet.

3.5 Functions in Formula

Formulas also use Excel functions that enable users to perform complex calculations that are difficult to perform using just the operators or not otherwise possible, like finding tangent of an angle, which can easily be done using Excel TAN function. Excel has more than 400 built-in functions and you can use additional functions from third-party vendors or create custom formulas using **visual basic (VBA)**. On regular basis, we only use few of the functions and in the following section we will discuss those, how to find the correct function and their usage.

Excel functions are grouped into categories, including Math and Trig, Financial, Logical, Statistical, Web, and so on. In this chapter, we will look at some important functions that can be used separately or in combination, in order to do complex calculations/searches.

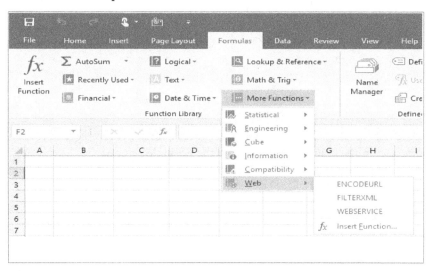

Figure 3.13 *Functions Categories*

Using the Insert function option from the Formula tab or the Formula bar, you can search a function, select a category to see all the relevant functions and also its corresponding help using the link Help On this Function.

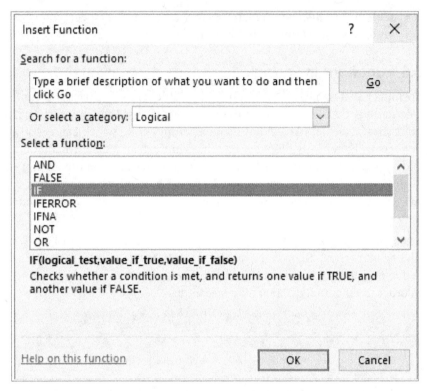

Figure 3.14 *Insert function*

Excel has an Auto Complete feature. As the user starts typing the formula/
function in the cell, Excel will show the possible options.

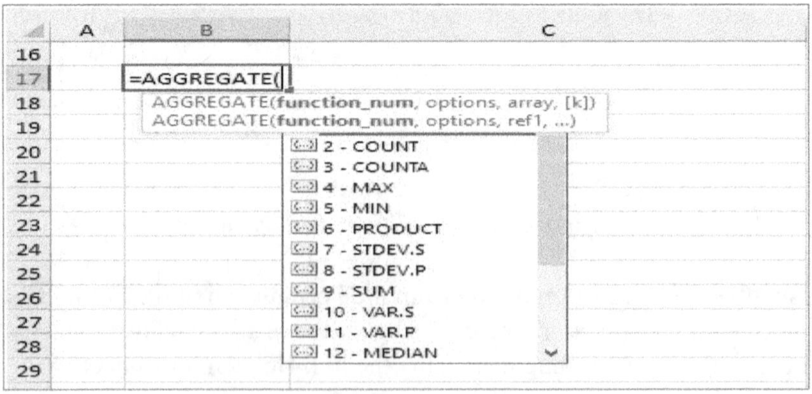

Figure 3.15 *Excel auto complete*

3.6 Relative and Absolute Addressing

Before we go ahead on discussing the different functions, we need to know about the Relative and Absolute addressing that is used quite often in functions. Absolute addressing is indicated in formula by dollar sign, which indicates that part of the formula to stay fixed and not change relative to the cell position. While Relative addressing lacks the dollar sign which indicates that part of the formula to change relative to the cell position.

E12			f_x	=C12*D12		

	A	B	C	D	E	F	G
7							
8							
9			Discount	10%			
10							
11		Product	Unit Price	Qty	Price	Discount	Discounted Price
12		P1	100	20	2000	200	1800
13		P2	80	10	800	80	720
14		P3	120	5	600	60	540
15							

F12			f_x	=E12*$D$9		

	A	B	C	D	E	F	G
7							
8							
9			Discount	10%			
10							
11		Product	Unit Price	Qty	Price	Discount	Discounted Price
12		P1	100	20	2000	200	1800
13		P2	80	10	800	80	720
14		P3	120	5	600	60	540
15							

Figure 3.16 *Relative & Absolute Addressing*

In the preceding example, the **Price** is calculated with relative addressing where the Price and Qty of each product is changing and if we enter the formula C12*D12 in first cell E12 and drag to fill or copy the formula in the cells below, it will change to C13*D13 and C14*D14. Now the

Discount (10%) is same for all and we want to use it to calculate the Discounted price. In cell *F12*, the formula we enter is E12*$D$9 and using the same technique if we drag to fill or copy the formula in cells below, it will change to E13*$D$9 and E14*$D$9. Note that here D9 does not change as we have dollar sign there before the row and column, making it fixed. In case the dollar sign was just before the column letter like $D9, then column is fixed but not the row. Hence, copying the formula in the cell below would have resulted in 0 as Excel would have copied it as E13*$D10. Based on what you want to be fixed, place the dollar sign before the row/column or both.

3.7 Referencing Cells Outside the Worksheet

Excel allows you to refer a cell in another worksheet in the same workbook. Format =**SheetName!CellAddress**" can be used in the formulas to refer the cell. For Example, =B2*'Sales Data'!A12. If the worksheet name in the reference includes one or more spaces, enclose SheetName in single quotation marks.

3.8 Referencing Cells Outside the Workbook

In order to add a reference to a cell in another workbook, use the format =*[WorkbookName]SheetName!CellAddress*. For Example, = B2*'[Financial Data]Sales Date'!A12.

3.9 Logical Functions

3.9.1 Using IF

This function tests a condition and if condition is met it is considered TRUE, else it is considered FALSE. We will understand its usage with the help of an example.

> Syntax is "=IF (Criteria, True, False)"

Example #1: The following table shows the Sales figures and Targets for sales reps. Using IF we will compare Sales with Targets and see who Achieved their targets and who did not.

⊿	A	B	C	D	E	F	G	H	I
1									
2									
3		Name	Sales	Target	Result				
4		Joey	1000	3000	Not Achieved	=IF(C4>=D4,"Achieved","Not Achieved")			
5		Ross	6000	5000	Achieved	=IF(C5>=D5,"Achieved","Not Achieved")			
6		Rachel	3000	4000	Not Achieved	=IF(C6>=D6,"Achieved","Not Achieved")			
7									

Figure 3.17 *Example using IF with values*

Let us understand the formula, in row 4 column F, the formula checks if C4 [1000] is greater than or equal to D4 [3000], since the result is *False*, the IF function will return the value given as third argument. And in row 5 column F the condition is *True*, hence the IF function returns the value given as second argument.

Example #2: Now we want to calculate the commission, it is 10% of Sales if the Sales are greater than or equal to the Target, else it is 5%.

⊿	A	B	C	D	E	F	G	H	I
8									
9		Name	Sales	Target	Commission				
10		Joey	1000	3000	50	=IF(C10>=D10,C10*10%,C10*5%)			
11		Ross	6000	5000	600	=IF(C11>=D11,C11*10%,C11*5%)			
12		Rachel	3000	4000	150	=IF(C12>=D12,C12*10%,C12*5%)			
13									

Figure 3.18 *Example using IF with reference*

Note that the you can have text or formula as values for the *True* and *False* parameters. In this example, the value returned for *True* condition is the multiplication of the Sales figures with 10% as the commission and 5% if *False*.

3.9.2 Using nested IF

Syntax is

"=IF(condition1,expression1,IF(condition2,expression2,expression3))"

Expressions can have nested IF functions. If condition1 is true, the relevant value is expression1. Otherwise, condition2 is checked. If it is true, the relevant value is expression2. Otherwise, the relevant value is expression3.

Example #1: For example, there might be three possibilities, depending on whether the value in cell A1 is negative, zero, or positive. A nested IF formula can then be used as follows:

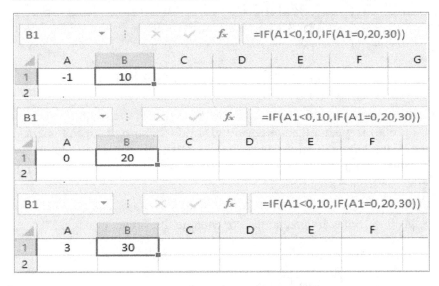

Figure 3.19 *Example using nested IF*

3.9.3 Writing Conditional Expressions: IF Combined with AND / OR

The IF function is many times used in combination of AND/OR, where we have multiple conditions to consider.

Example #1: In this example, we will see how to use IF() with AND() and OR(). A vendor gives 10% discount on certain product lines.

The discount is given in either of the two conditions:

i. Products are on Special Offer and the Order Value is 1000 or above
ii. Customer is eligible for Loyalty Bonus

◢	A	B	C	D	E	F	G	H	I	J	K	L
20												
21												
22			Loyalty	Special	Order							
23		Product	Bonus	Offer	Value	Discount	Total					
24		Wood	No	Yes	3,000.00	300.00	2,700.00					
25		Glass	Yes	No	2,000.00	200.00	1,800.00					
26		Cement	No	Yes	500.00	-	500.00					
27		Turf	Yes	Yes	2,000.00	200.00	1,800.00					
28						=IF(OR(AND(D26="Yes",E26>=1000) , C26="Yes"), E26*10% , 0)						

Condition #1   Condition #2

Figure 3.20 *Example of IF with AND / OR*

Condition #1: is a case of AND, where both conditions given in (i) have to be satisfied. If either of **Condition #1 or Condition #2** is satisfied, then 10% discount will be given.

3.10 Summarizing Functions

3.10.1 COUNT, COUNTA, COUNTBLANK

Commonly used functions for counting number of cells are COUNT (for counting cells that contain numbers), COUNTA (for counting non-blank cells), and COUNTBLANK (for counting empty cells).

Syntax is

"=COUNT (value1, [value2], ...)"

"=COUNTA (value1, [value2], ...)"

"=COUNTBLANK (value1, [value2], ...)"

Example #1: The following example shows how these functions work in case data is text and numbers. Note that you can count individual values, cell references or ranges or a mix of all three.

Since COUNT only counts cells with numbers, for **Student** column it returns 0, while for **Scores** column it returns the value 6, even though total cells considered are 7 from rows 18 to 24. Note that in column Scores, 0 is considered as non-blank cell and hence COUNTA returns 6.

	A	B	C	D
16				
17		Student	Scores	
18		Ankit	8	
19		Puja	10	
20		Ishan	9	
21		Arav	9	
22			0	
23				
24		Mani	6	
25		Total		
26		0	6	=COUNT(C18:C24)
27		5	6	=COUNTA(C18:C24)
28		2	1	=COUNTBLANK(C18:C24)
29				

Figure 3.21 *Example of COUNT, COUNTA, COUNTBALNK functions*

3.10.2 COUNTIF, COUNTIFS

These functions are used for counting number of cells that satisfy the given criteria(s) or conditions.

Syntax is

"=COUNTIF (Data Range, Criteria to be matched)"

"=COUNTIFS (Data Range1, Criteria1, [Data Range2, Criteria2] …)"

Example #2: Use of COUNTIF and COUNTIFS are explained with the help of the following data. In the **COUNTIFS ()** function, we can write multiple Range and Criteria pairs.

⊿	A	B	C	D	E	F	G	H	I	J	K
30											
31		Item	Date	Cost							
32		Brakes	Jan	80							
33		Tyres	May	50							
34		Brakes	Feb	80							
35		Mirror	Mar	150							
36		Mirror	Jan	300							
37		Window	Jun	50							
38		Tyres	Apr	200							
39		Tyres	Mar	100							
40		Clutch	May	250							
41											
42		How many Brakes Have been bought.				2	=COUNTIF(B32:B40,"Brakes")				
43		How many Tyres have been bought.				3	=COUNTIF(B32:B40,"Tyres")				
44		How many items cost 100 or above.				5	=COUNTIF(D32:D40,">=100")				
45											
46		Type the name of the item to count			mirror	2	=COUNTIF(B32:B40,E46)				
47											
48		How many Tyres have been bought that cost				2	=COUNTIFS(B32:B40,"Tyres",D32:D40,">=100")				
49											

Figure 3.22 *Example of COUNTIF & COUNTIFS functions*

In the preceding example, the rows #42, 43, 44, and 46, the COUNTIF(S) function uses a single criterion, specified directly and as a parameter for counting the number of cells. Note that the criteria can be a simple text or a formula as in row #44 or a reference to a cell like in row #46. In row #48, there are two criterions to be satisfied, one for Item and the other for Cost. The range of cells to look for are specified before each criterion.

3.10.3 SUM, AVERAGE, PRODUCT

The SUM function as the name suggests, sums all values in one or more ranges. The **AVERAGE** function calculates the average of all the numeric cells in a range and the **PRODUCT** function is similar to the **SUM** function, however, instead of adding it multiplies all the values in the range.

Syntax is

"=SUM (Data Range)"

"=AVERAGE (Data Range)"

"=PRODUCT (Data Range)"

Note that you can add individual values, cell references, or ranges, or a mix of all three as you can see in the following examples. In case of PRODUCT, since it only multiplies the values in the range, mentioning Absent in cell E35 will neither give an error, nor will the result change if Absent text is removed.

◢	A	B	C	D	E	F
31						
32		Student	Maths	Science	English	
33		Puja	8	7	10	
34		Ishan	10	9	8	
35		Ankit	0	6	Absent	
36						
37		Total Puja Score		25	=SUM(C33,D33,E33)	
38		Total Ishan Score		27	=SUM(C34:E34)	
39		Average Science Score		7.3	=AVERAGE(D33:D35)	
40		Product of English Score		80	=PRODUCT(E33,E34:E35)	
41		Product of Maths Score		0	=PRODUCT(C33:C35)	
42						

Figure 3.23 *Example of SUM, AVERAGE, PRODUCT functions*

3.10.4 SUMIF, SUMIFS

The SUM function is the most commonly and widely used function for adding all values in the given range. Although SUMIF and SUMIFS are not that popular, these functions are very helpful in complex situations where we only want to add values in a range based on given criteria(s).

> Syntax is
>
> "=SUMIF (Range, Criteria to Match, Sum Range)"
>
> "=SUMIFS (Sum Range, Criteria Range1, Criteria1, Criteria Range2, Criteria2 ...)"

Example #1: Use of **SUMIF** and **SUMIFS** are explained with the help of the following example:

	A	B	C	D	E	F	G	H	I	J	K
50											
51		Item	Date	Cost							
52		Brakes	Jan	80							
53		Tyres	May	50							
54		Brakes	Feb	80							
55		Mirror	Mar	150							
56		Mirror	Jan	300							
57		Window	Jun	50							
58		Tyres	Apr	200							
59		Tyres	Mar	100							
60		Clutch	May	250							
61											
62		Total cost of all Brakes bought.				160	=SUMIF(B52:B60,"Brakes",D52:D60)				
63		Total cost of all Tyres bought.				350	=SUMIF(B52:B60,"Tyres",D52:D60)				
64		Total of items costing 100 or above.				1000	=SUMIF(D52:D60,">=100")				
65											
66		Total of item typed in following cell.			mirror	450	=SUMIF(B52:B60,E66,D52:D60)				
67											
68		Total cost Tyres bought costing above 100				200	=SUMIFS(D52:D60,B52:B60,"Tyres",D52:D60,">100")				
69											

Figure 3.24 *Example of SUMIF, SUMIFS functions*

Similar to COUNTIF(S) function, instead of counting the number of cells, the formulas in the preceding example are adding the values based on the criteria(s) specified. Again, note that the criteria can be a simple text or a formula or a reference to a cell.

3.10.5 SUMPRODUCT

Multiplies corresponding components in the given arrays and returns the sum of those products.

Syntax is

=SUMPRODUCT (array1, [array2], [array3], ...)

Example #1: SUMPRODUCT is explained with the help of an example here:

	A	B	C	D	E	F	G	H
70								
71		Item	Sold	price				
72		Tyres	5	100				
73		Mirrors	2	10				
74		Bulbs	3	2				
75								
76		Total Sales Value :		526	=SUMPRODUCT(C72:C74,D72:D74)			
77								

Figure 3.25 *Example of SUMPRODUCT*

3.10.6 Calculations using SUM with OFFSET function

OFFSET together with the **SUM** function helps to create a dynamic function that can sum a variable number of cells. Limitation with the regular **SUM** formula is that it is a static calculation, but with **OFFSET** we can have the cell reference move around.

> Syntax is
>
> = OFFSET (Reference to base offset, no. of rows, no. of cols, [no of rows in returned reference], [no of columns in returned reference])

Note that the OFFSET function is also discussed in section 3.12.3.

Example #1: The following OFFSET function returns the 1 x 2 range, that is, 8 rows below from base offset B79 and 1 column to the right of cell B79. The SUM function calculates the sum of this range.

	A	B	C	D	E	F	G	H
78			Sales					
79		Region	North	South				
		Month						
80		Jan	100	1324				
81		Feb	506	789				
82		Mar	300	500				
83		Apr	928	1409		SUM of August Sales		
84		May	300	212		776		
85		Jun	815	983		=SUM(OFFSET(B79, 8, 1, 1, 2))		
86		Jul	919	1023				
87		Aug	241	535			1x 2 range	
88		Sep	1334	982				
89		Oct	452	645				
90		Nov	647	757				
91		Dec	322	346				

Figure 3.26 *Example of OFFSET with values*

Example #2: In this example, the table has data for five months and based on the value entered for the Start and End month, the OFFSET function is used for cell range reference to SUM.

	A	B	C	D	E	F	G	H	I	J
93										
94			Type in the Start month.		Feb-18					
95			Type in the End month.		Mar-18					
96										
97		Total			Jan-18	Feb-18	Mar-18	Apr-18	May-18	
98		900			10	400	500	600	700	
99										
100		1020			15	20	1000	2000	3000	
101										
102		13			5	3	10	800	900	
103		=SUM(OFFSET(C102, 0, MONTH($E$94)) : OFFSET(C102, 0, MONTH($E$95)))								
104					*Returns value 2*				*Returns value 3*	

Figure 3.27 *Example of OFFSET with reference*

In the preceding example, the Total value in cell B102 is calculated as 13 using the formula =SUM(OFFSET(C102,0,MONTH($E$94)) : OFFSET(C102,0,MONTH($E$95))).

3.10.7 SUBTOTAL

The **SUBTOTAL** function returns an aggregate result for supplied values. **SUBTOTAL** can return a **SUM**, **AVERAGE**, **COUNT**, **MAX**, and many others. When you type **SUBTOTAL** in a cell, Excel will show the complete list of functions, as given below.

SUM	▼	:	×	✓	*fx*	=SUBTOTAL(		SUM	▼	:	×	✓	*fx*	=SUBTOTAL(

	A	B	C	D	E				A	B	C	D	E
18								19					
19		=SUBTOTAL(						20		=SUBTOTAL(			
20		SUBTOTAL(function_num, ref1, ...)						21		SUBTOTAL(function_num, ref1, ...)			
21			1 - AVERAGE ⌃					22			11 - VAR.P ⌃		
22			2 - COUNT					23			101 - AVERAGE		
23			3 - COUNTA					24			102 - COUNT		
24			4 - MAX					25			103 - COUNTA		
25			5 - MIN					26			104 - MAX		
26			6 - PRODUCT					27			105 - MIN		
27			7 - STDEV.S					28			106 - PRODUCT		
28			8 - STDEV.P					29			107 - STDEV.S		
29			9 - SUM					30			108 - STDEV.P		
30			10 - VAR.S					31			109 - SUM		
			11 - VAR.P								110 - VAR.S		
30			101 - AVERAGE ⌄					32			111 - VAR.P ⌄		
31													

Figure 3.28 *SUBTOTAL functions argument*

As shown in the function list above, each function has been assigned a number that is used as the first argument in the **SUBTOTAL** function.

Syntax is

=SUBTOTAL(function number, range 1, [range 2],...)

If you choose function number between 1-11, all the manually hidden rows are included in the calculation, while 101-111 excludes them; filtered-out cells are always excluded. **SUBTOTAL** function is designed for columns of data, or vertical ranges. It is not designed for rows of data, or horizontal ranges.

Example #1:

	A	B	C
23			
24		2	
25		4	
26		6	
27		10	
28		8	
29		4	
30		6	
31		10	
32		2	
33	SUBTOTAL		
34	SUM	52	=SUBTOTAL(9,B24:B32)
35	COUNT	9	=SUBTOTAL(2,B24:B32)
36			

	A	B	C
23			
24		2	
25		4	
26		6	
30		6	
31		10	
32		2	
33	SUBTOTAL		
34	SUM	52	=SUBTOTAL(9,B24:B32)
35	COUNT	9	=SUBTOTAL(2,B24:B32)
36	SUM	30	=SUBTOTAL(109,B24:B32)
37	COUNT	6	=SUBTOTAL(102,B24:B32)
38			

Figure 3.29 *Example of SUBTOTAL function*

In the preceding example, see how the result changes when we used the different functions. In first case, the **SUBTOTAL** function returns 52 for function number 9 (SUM) and 9 for function number 2 (COUNT). In second case, we have hidden three rows, that is, rows 27, 28, and 29 are hidden. Now the **SUBTOTAL** function returns the same values for function numbers 9 and 2 but for function number 109 (SUM) it returns 30 versus 52 and for function number 102 (COUNT) it returns 6 versus 9.

Example #2: When we need data based on different categories, **SUBTOTALS** help us to get the totals of several columns of data broken down into various categories. An apparel owner wants to know how many items of different colors (**Red, Green, White, Blue, Orange**) and sizes (2, 4, 6, 8, 10) are in the inventory of the two outlets. The raw data received for the two outlets is as given here:

	A	B	C	D
1	Color	Size	No in Shop#1	No in Shop#2
2	Red	2	10	12
3	Green	4	30	23
4	White	6	50	70
5	Blue	10	12	24
6	Orange	8	57	85
7	Red	4	35	36
8	Green	6	75	36
9	White	10	43	28
10	Blue	2	56	30
11	Orange	8	12	89
12	Red	6	62	67
13	Green	10	17	64
14	White	2	24	98
15	Blue	8	84	24
16	Orange	8	25	56
17	Red	10	88	34
18	Green	2	34	33
19	White	8	13	76
20	Blue	6	10	45
21	Orange	4	30	40

Before we use the SUBTOTAL function, we will have to sort the data for which we want to find the subtotal. Then, we can use the SUBTOTAL option from 'Data → Outline.

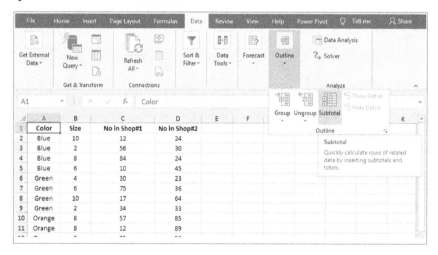

In the Subtotal dialog box, we selected SUM as the function and selected checkbox for No in Shop#1 and No in Shop#2 as we want to get the subtotal of the different color items in both outlets.

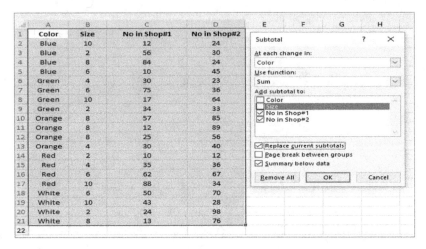

Figure 3.30 *SUBTOTAL with SUM example*

By clicking on OK, Excel will show the subtotals as shown in the following screenshot. Note that subtotals are added in a new row below each color and the worksheet is now divided into different levels, that is, 1, 2, and 3 as seen in the top-left corner. Depending on the information you wish to display in the worksheet, you can switch between these levels.

Color	Size	No in Shop#1	No in Shop#2
Color	Size	No in Shop#1	No in Shop#2
Blue	10	12	24
Blue	2	56	30
Blue	8	84	24
Blue	6	10	45
Blue Total		**162**	**123**
Green	4	30	23
Green	6	75	36
Green	10	17	64
Green	2	34	33
Green Total		**156**	**156**
Orange	8	57	85
Orange	8	12	89
Orange	8	25	56
Orange	4	30	40
Orange Total		**124**	**270**
Red	2	10	12
Red	4	35	36
Red	6	62	67
Red	10	88	34
Red Total		**195**	**149**
White	6	50	70

Figure 3.31 *SUBTOTAL with SUM result*

Now if owner wants to see the count of each size for the outlets, to make sure that all sizes are available in either of them, SUBTOTAL for Size with COUNT function can be used as shown here:

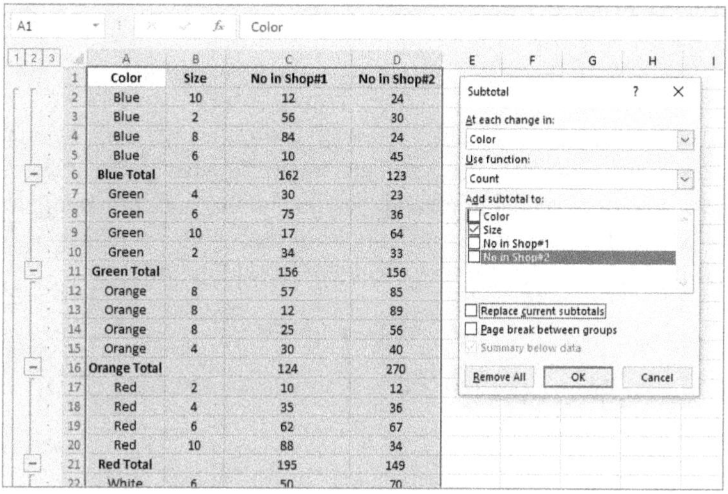

Figure 3.32 *SUBTOTAL with COUNT example*

Note that here we will uncheck the Replace current subtotals as we want to keep the previous subtotals.

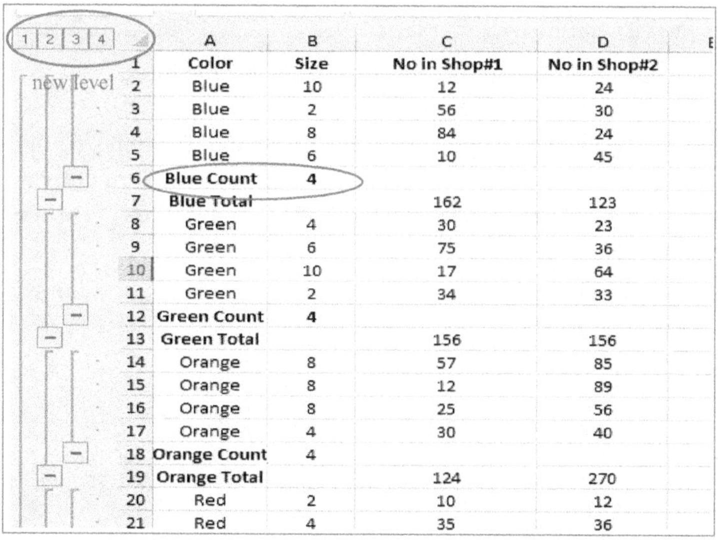

	Color	Size	No in Shop#1	No in Shop#2
1	Color	Size	No in Shop#1	No in Shop#2
2	Blue	10	12	24
3	Blue	2	56	30
4	Blue	8	84	24
5	Blue	6	10	45
6	Blue Count	4		
7	Blue Total		162	123
8	Green	4	30	23
9	Green	6	75	36
10	Green	10	17	64
11	Green	2	34	33
12	Green Count	4		
13	Green Total		156	156
14	Orange	8	57	85
15	Orange	8	12	89
16	Orange	8	25	56
17	Orange	4	30	40
18	Orange Count	4		
19	Orange Total		124	270
20	Red	2	10	12
21	Red	4	35	36

Figure 3.33 *SUBTOTAL with COUNT result*

Now, a new level has been added. You can switch between levels, click on the level for which you want to see data.

3.11 Text Functions

3.11.1 TEXT

This function lets you change the way a number appears by applying formatting to it with format codes. It can be useful when you want to display numbers in a more readable format, or you want to combine numbers with text or symbols. Remember that once the numbers are changed to text format; it will be difficult to refer to them in calculations.

Syntax is

=TEXT(Value to format, "Format code to apply")

	A	B	C
10			
11		1,234.57	=TEXT(1234.567,"#,##0.00")
12		1:04 PM	=TEXT(NOW(),"H:MM AM/PM")
13		02/04/18	=TEXT(TODAY(),"MM/DD/YY")
14		Sun	=TEXT(TODAY(),"DDD")
15		56.5%	=TEXT(0.565,"0.0%")
16			

Figure 3.34 *Example of TEXT function*

The preceding examples are some of the popular examples of the TEXT function usage. In the first one, it changes the number format by adding a thousand separator and two decimals. Note that it rounds the value to two decimal places in the process.

Another interesting use of the TEXT function is when you want to join the two strings, one being text and other, say a date.

	A	B	C	D	E
18		Text 1	Text 2	Result ⇩	Formula
19		Report on	02-05-2018	Report on : 43222	=B19&" : "&C19
20		Report on	02-05-2018	Report on : 05/02/18	=B20&" : "&TEXT(C20,"mm/dd/yy")
21					

Figure 3.35 *Example of TEXT function to join strings*

In the preceding example, result in row#19 shows a number instead of the date and in the next row by using the TEXT function we get the desired results.

3.11.2 FIND

This function returns the position of the first occurrence of a string of characters (which could be a single character) in a piece of text.

Syntax is =FIND(find text, within text, [start no. to start search])

In the following table, we will see how the return value of FIND function changes based on the input arguments.

⊿	A	B	C
1			
2		Albert Einstein	
3			
4		3	=FIND("bert",B2)
5		3	=FIND("b",B2)
6		4	=FIND("e",B2)
7		13	=FIND("e",B2,5)
8		8	=FIND("E",B2)

Figure 3.36 *Example of FIND function*

Note that the return value is same, that is, 3 for first two formulas, reason being that function returns the start of the first occurrence of the search string bert or character b. Similarly, it returns 4 for search string e and 13 only when the start number to search string was moved to 5. By default, the start number to search the string is 0. Also, it is case sensitive, hence, the return position of e and E is different, that is, 4 and 8 respectively.

3.11.3 LEN and TRIM

These functions are useful to know the length of your text and remove all spaces from the text except for single spaces between words.

Syntax is "=LEN (text)", "=TRIM(text)"

	A	B	C	D
1		The text length is	18	=LEN(B1)
2		Extra spaces in text	Extra spaces in text	=TRIM(" Extra spaces in text ")
3				

Figure 3.37 *Example of LEN & TRIM functions*

3.11.4 CONCATENATE

This text function is helpful to join two or more text strings into one string. You can also join strings using "&", the ampersand symbol. See the following example where we join text using both the methods.

Syntax is "=CONCATENATE (text1, [text2], ...)"

C7	▼	⋮	✕ ✓	*fx*	=CONCATENATE(A5,B5)	

	A	B	C	D	E
4			**Result**	**Formula used**	
5	Na	Mo	NaMo	=A5&B5	
6			Na,Mo	=A5&","&B5	
7			NaMo	=CONCATENATE(A5,B5)	
8			Na,Mo	=CONCATENATE(A5,",",B5)	
9					

Figure 3.38 *Example for CONCATENATE*

Ampersand symbol does the same thing but when you do complex operations, CONCATENATE function is much easier and clean.

3.11.5 LEFT, MID and RIGHT

These text functions are very helpful in extracting parts of the text:

- **LEFT** function: Returns text from the beginning of a cell (left to right)
- **MID** function: Returns text from any start point of the cell (left to right)

- **RIGHT** function: Returns text from the end of the cell (right to left)

Syntax is

=LEFT (text, [no. of chars])

=RIGHT (text, [no. of chars])

=MID (text, start no., no. of chars)

Example #1: In the following example, we want to extract the Product ID (numerical value) that is embedded in the Product Description (text value). It would have been simple if the number of digits was the same but that is not the case below, both the text length and number of digits are different.

Using MID and FIND

	A	B	C	D	E	F	G	H	I	J
105										
106	Description		Product ID#	=MID (text, start_num, num_chars)						
107	TyresMRF(7283629)INDDL		7283629	=MID(B107, FIND("(",B107)+1, FIND(")",B107)-FIND("(",B107)-1)						
108	BrakesWLLKJD(1000290288)INDGGN		1000290288							
109						start no. =10		no. of chars =7		
110										

Figure 3.39 *Example using MID and FIND*

Let us understand the preceding example so that the usage is clear. The first argument is B107, that is, the whole string TyresMRF(7283629)INDDL from which want to extract. The second argument "FIND("(",B107)+1", is used to find the start number to extract the string. The FIND function returns position number 9 for "(", but since we want the number between the brackets, we add 1 to get the start position as 10. The third argument is an arithmetic expression, FIND(")",B107) − FIND("(",B107)-1, for getting the number of characters (7) to extract from the start position (10). Now, FIND(")",B107) will return the position of ")", that is, 17. From 17, subtract 9 (return value of FIND("(",B107) function as seen before) and also 1 as we do not want the ")" that is, 17-9-1 =7.

Using MID, LEFT, and FIND

	A	B	C	D	E	F	G	H	I	J
113										
114	**Description**		**Product ID**	=LEFT (text, [no. of chars])						
115	TyresMRF(7283629)INDDL		7283629	=MID(LEFT(B115,FIND(")",B115)-1), FIND("(",B115)+1, LEN(B115))						
116	BrakesWLLKJD(1000290288)INDGGN		1000290288							
117						text = TyresMRF(7283629		start no.=10	no. of chars=22	
118										

Figure 3.40 *Example using MID, LEFT & FIND*

In order to see the values returned by functions within a function, select the cell in which the formula has been written. Then go to the insert function icon next to the formula and click on it, the Function Arguments window gets launched showing the values returned.

Figure 3.41 *View functions within functions*

Example #2: In the following example, we want to extract the Product Location (text after the numerical value) that is embedded in the Product Description (text value).

	A	B	C	D	E	F	G
120		**Description**	**Product Loc**	=RIGHT (text, [no. of chars])			
121		TyresMRF(7283629)INDDL	INDDL	=RIGHT(B121,LEN(B121)-FIND(")",B121))			
122		BrakesWLLKJD(1000290288)INDGGN	INDGGN				
123							

Figure 3.42 *Example of RIGHT function*

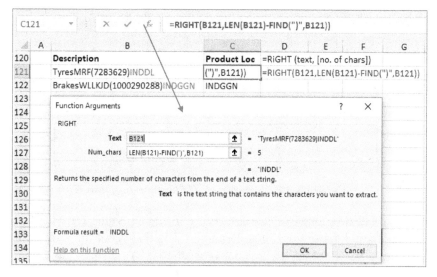

Figure 3.43 *View function return value*

3.12 Lookup and Reference functions

3.12.1 VLOOKUP, HLOOKUP

Use VLOOKUP when you need to find things in a table or a range by row. HLOOKUP searches for a value in the top row of a table or an array of values, and then returns a value in the same column from a row you specify in the table or array. VLOOKUP is more widely used function.

Syntax is

"=VLOOKUP (lookup value, table array,
column no in the range containing the return value,
Exact Match or Approximate Match – indicated as 0/FALSE or 1/TRUE)"

"= HLOOKUP (lookup value, table array, row index no., [range lookup])"

Example #1: In this example, we are trying to look up the value in third column/row for the month of Mar that is, 69. In both cases, the same value is looked up, however, the difference is in the function used for the same, which explains when to use VLOOKUP and HLOOKUP. Reason is because of the different data structure.

⊿	A	B	C	D	E	F	G	H	I	J
138										
139		Jan	15	20	50	34	60			
140		Feb	45	90	89	110	122			
141		Mar	90	**69**	50	51	80			
142										
143										
144				Specif month to look for :		Mar				
145				Which column to be picked :		3				
146										
147					Result is :	69				
148						=VLOOKUP(F144,B139:G141,F145,FALSE)				

Figure 3.44 *Example of VLOOKUP function*

In the preceding example, we are trying to lookup value for Mar from the table array starting B139 and ending G141 that is, all three rows and six columns. The third argument F145 (that is, 3) specifies the column from which we want the value to be returned corresponding to our lookup value, that is, Mar and FALSE indicates that we want an exact match to our lookup value that is, the value in column 1 should have text exactly as Mar. So now the 69 value is returned, which is in third column and row matching lookup value Mar in column 1.

Note that in order for VLOOKUP to work correctly, the lookup value (that is, Mar in the preceding example) should be in the first column (that is, column B above) of the table array to be searched (range B139:G141).

Similar logic applies to HLOOKUP as you will see in the following example. Based on the structure of the data, we make a choice between VLOOKUP (vertical lookup) and HLOOKUP (horizontal lookup). VLOOKUP is more popular than HLOOKUP.

⊿	A	B	C	D	E	F	G	H	I	J	K
125											
126		Jan	Feb	Mar							
127		15	45	90							
128		20	90	**69**							
129		50	89	50							
130		34	110	51							
131		60	122	80							
132											
133				Specify month to look for :		Mar					
134				Which row to be picked :		3					
135											
136				Result is :		69	=HLOOKUP(F133,B126:D131,F134,FALSE)				

Figure 3.45 *Example of HLOOKUP function*

3.12.2 MATCH, INDEX

Combination of the INDEX and MATCH functions is an advanced alternative to VLOOKUP or HLOOKUP, many times faster and more flexible.

Syntax is

=INDEX (cell range, row no. in array from which to return a value,

[column no. in array from which to return a value])

= MATCH (match value, cell range, [match type -1, 0, or 1])

where,

-1: smallest value that is greater than or equal to lookup value

0: first value that is exactly equal to lookup value

1 or omitted: largest value that is less than or equal to lookup value

Example #1: We have two tables below and correlating both, we want to find out if the student passed or failed as per the scores. We will use the combination of the INDEX and MATCH functions for getting the student grade.

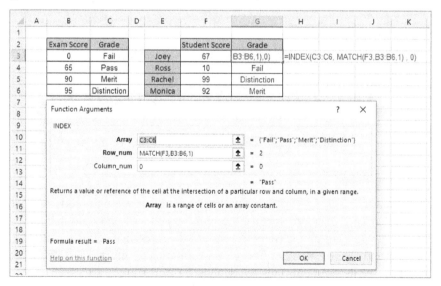

Figure 3.46 *Example of INDEX & MATCH*

In the preceding example, the first argument to the INDEX function is the cell range from where we want to return the value based on the match found, return of MATCH function (the row number) in second argument, and the column number 0 (column C) that is specified as the third argument. The MATCH function matches the student score (that is, 67) to the exam scores given in column B, and since we specified 1 as match type, it returns the row number as 2 because "65" is the largest value that is less than or equal to the lookup value.

In case you want to see the details of the MATCH function, select the cell in which formula is entered in column Grade, highlight the MATCH function and click the function icon on the menu bar.

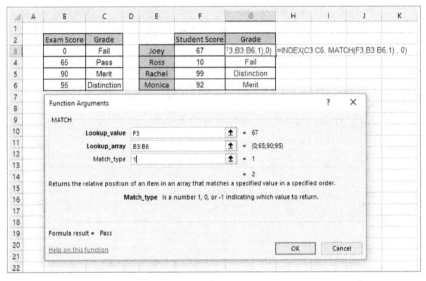

Figure 3.47 *Details of MATCH function*

3.12.3 OFFSET

This function allows you to reference a range (or a single cell) relative to another cell. You can specify the number of rows and columns below (positive value) or above (negative value) the reference cell that you want to refer and also the number of rows and columns to return. By default, the number of rows and columns returned is 1.

Syntax is

"OFFSET(reference to base the offset, rows, cols, [no of rows to return], [no of columns to return])"

In the following example, you can see how the values are returned based on the arguments, where a positive value of rows refers to a cell below the base offset and a negative value refers to a cell above the base offset.

◢	A	B	C
1			
2		Hello	Everyone
3		Bye	Good bye
4		Good	Morning
5		Lovely	Evening
6			
7		=OFFSET(B3,1,1)	Morning
8		=OFFSET(B3,-1,1)	Everyone

Figure 3.48 *Example of OFFSET*

The OFFSET function can also be used in combination with summarizing functions like SUM, as discussed in section 3.10.6.

3.12.4 INDIRECT

The INDIRECT function returns the reference specified by a text string. This function converts a plain text which looks like a cell address, either on the same worksheet or on a different worksheet, into a usable cell reference. INDIRECT's usage is when you want to change the reference to a cell without changing the formula itself.

Syntax is

"= INDIRECT (reference text, [type of reference text])"

where,

type of reference text if,

TRUE or omitted: reference text is interpreted as an A1-style reference

FALSE: reference text is interpreted as an R1C1-style reference

Example #1: In the following table, we have scores in column B and reference text in column D that is used in the INDIRECT function to get the value of the cell. First reference text, D10, is A1 style where it is a direct reference to the cell containing the value. In the next two, D12 and D14, the reference text is R1C1 style (a row number followed by a column number).

	A	B	C	D	E	F	G	H
8								
9		Scores		Ref Text	Return Value	Formula Used	Ref Type	
10		67		B12	99	=INDIRECT(D10)	A1 style	
11		10						
12		99		R12C2	99	=INDIRECT(D12, FALSE)	R1C1 style	
13		23						
14		92		R12C	99	=INDIRECT(D14, FALSE)	R1C1 style	
15								

row 12 in same column

Figure 3.49 *Example of INDIRECT with values*

Example #2: In the following example, we will see how to create indirect references from cell value and text.

	A	B	C	D	E	F	G
8							
9		Scores		Ref Text	Return Value	Formula Used	Ref Type
10		67		B12	99	=INDIRECT(D10)	A1 style
11		10					
12		99		R12C2	99	=INDIRECT(D12, FALSE)	R1C1 style
13		23					
14		92		R12C	99	=INDIRECT(D14, FALSE)	R1C1 style
15							
16		12	99	=INDIRECT("B"&B16)		Creating indirect reference from Text & Cell value	
17							

Figure 3.50 *Example of INDIRECT using indirect reference to cell*

In preceding example, the value in cell C16 is displayed using formula =INDIRECT("B"&B16) that is, in the INDIRECT function the text 'B' is concatenated with the value in cell B16 (12) resulting in =INDIRECT(B12).

Example #3: In the following example, we will see the use of the INDRIECT function with named ranges:

named range B21:B29

| Age ▾ | | | | f_x | 12 | |

▲	A	B	C	D	E	F	G
19							
20		Age	Height				
21		12	5		Range Name	age	
22		34	2.5		Total :	410	=SUM(INDIRECT($F$21))
23		67	6.1		Average:	45.56	=AVERAGE(INDIRECT($F$21))
24		23	4.1		Max:	96	=MAX(INDIRECT($F$21))
25		96	3		Min:	6	=MIN(INDIRECT($F$21))
26		85	5.1				
27		77	4.2				
28		6	2.8				
29		10	4				
30							

named range C21:C29

| height ▾ | | | | f_x | 5 | |

▲	A	B	C	D	E	F	G
19							
20		Age	Height				
21		12	5		Range Name	height	
22		34	2.5		Total :	36.8	=SUM(INDIRECT($F$21))
23		67	6.1		Average:	4.09	=AVERAGE(INDIRECT($F$21))
24		23	4.1		Max:	6	=MAX(INDIRECT($F$21))
25		96	3		Min:	3	=MIN(INDIRECT($F$21))
26		85	5.1				
27		77	4.2				
28		6	2.8				
29		10	4				
30							

Figure 3.51 *Example of INDIRECT using Named Ranges*

Example #4: In the following example, we will see the use of the INDRIECT function to dynamically refer to another worksheet. Using the same example as the previous one, now assume that the height data is in another sheet named Student Details and we want to copy the list in sheet that has student age list also.

Syntax is

"= INDIRECT ("" & Sheet's name & "!" & Cell to get data from)"

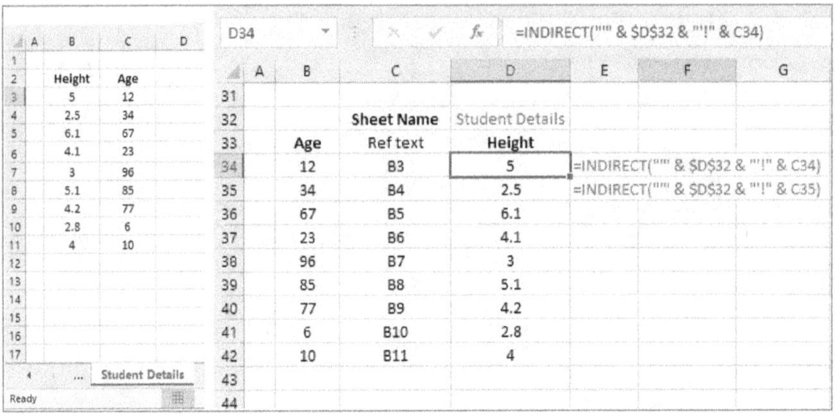

Figure 3.52 *Example of INDIRECT referring another worksheet*

In the preceding example, INDIRECT(""" & $D$32 & "'!" & C34) gets the sheet name, that is, Student Details from cell D32, which is concatenated with C34 (of current sheet) that has the reference of the cell containing the actual data, that is, B3 of the other worksheet (Student Details). If we substitute the values, the above formula will result in INDIRECT ("'Students Details'!B3"), which returns the value 5.

3.13 Date and Time Functions

Date and Time functions are very frequently used in formulas, but their calculation is sometimes tricky as Excel interprets according to the date system used by the local computer. We will try to cover different scenarios to help you in using these correctly in your formulas.

3.13.1 TIME

The TIME function returns the decimal number for a particular time.

> Syntax is "=TIME(hour, minute, second)"

For example, 12:00 PM is represented as 0.5 because it is half of a day, that is, =TIME(12,0,0)

3.13.2 DATE

The DATE function in Excel is categorized under the Date/Time Functions, returns the sequential serial number that represents a particular date.

Syntax is "=DATE(year,month,day)"

By default, Microsoft Excel for Windows uses the 1900 date system, which means the first date is January 1, 1900. January 1, 1900 is serial number 1, and January 1, 2008 is serial number 39448 because it is 39,447 days after January 1, 1900. Following are a few examples to help you see how results get calculated:

	A	B	C	D
1		Result	Resul formated as Date	Formula
2		42404	04-02-2016	=DATE(2016,1,35)
3			02-02-2018	=DATE(2017,14,2)
4			02-09-2015	=DATE(2016,-3,2)
5			05-05-2017	=DATE(2017, 5, 20)-15

Figure 3.53 *Example for DATE function*

In row#2 as mentioned earlier, the date function returns the sequential serial number 42404 (in cell B2) corresponding to the year, month, and day mentioned as given in D2 that is '=DATE(2016,1,35)'. When day is greater than the number of days in the specified month (1 to 31), day adds that number of days to the first day of the month. For example, DATE (2016,1,35) returns the serial number representing February 4, 2016 in C2, where the cell value is formatted as Date

Formula in D3 returns in cell C3 the serial number representing February 2, 2018. In case the month is greater than the number of months Excel takes as argument, that is, 1 to 12, then Excel will add the number of months to the first month of the specified year.

When the month is less than or equal to zero, like in D4, Excel will subtract the absolute value of month, plus 1, from the first month of the specified year. Hence in C4, Excel returns the serial number representing September 2, 2015.

In the last example, in cell C5, Excel returns the serial number representing May 5, 2017, that is, by Subtracting 15 days from May 20, 2017.

3.13.2.1 Same Date Format for Different Locale

As we mentioned earlier, Excel interprets date according to the date system used by the local computer. This becomes a problem when you have dates of different regions in the same worksheet, for example you have dates in US format i.e., mm/dd/yyyy and UK format i.e., dd/mm/yyyy. We will see how to work around this issue so that all dates are in consistent format.

	A	B	C	D	E	F	G	H	I	J	K	L
34												
35		Dates	Existing format	Converted format								
36		12/02/2018	dd/mm/yyyy	2018-02-12	=TEXT(YEAR(B36),"0000")&"-"&TEXT(MONTH(B36),"00")&"-"&TEXT(DAY(B36),"00")							
37		02/12/2018	mm/dd/yyyy	2018-02-12								
38												
39												

Figure 3.54 *Example of DATE formats in different locale*

In the preceding example, we have dates in two formats: US and UK and with our formula we have converted into the same format representing the date 12 Feb, 2018. We have already discussed the TEXT function in earlier section (3.11.1) so we will not discuss those in details here. But to see what each function returns, YEAR, MONTH, and DAY, you can click on the cell with the formula, select the function you want to view and click on the insert function icon to launch the dialog as given here:

A	B	C	D	E	F	G	H	I	J	K	L
	Dates	Existing format	Converted format								
	12/02/2018	dd/mm/yyyy	=TEXT(YEAR(B36),"0	=TEXT(YEAR(B36),"0000")&"-"&TEXT(MONTH(B36),"00")&"-"&TEXT(DAY(B36),"00")							
	02/12/2018	mm/dd/yyyy	2018-02-12								

Function Arguments   ? ✕

YEAR

Serial_number   B36   ↑   = 43143

                         = 2018

Returns the year of a date, an integer in the range 1900 - 9999.

             Serial_number is a number in the date-time code used by Microsoft Excel.

Formula result = 2018-02-12

Help on this function   OK   Cancel

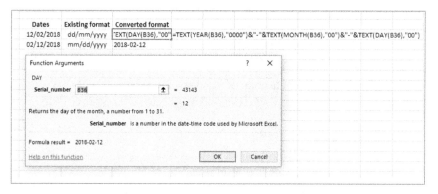

Now that we have the concept of the date function, we will look at other related and commonly used functions.

3.13.3 TODAY

Syntax is "=TODAY()"

The TODAY function returns the serial number of the current date. For example, if it is 26th day of the month of January of year 2011, then "=TODAY()" will return 26-01-2011.

3.13.4 EOMONTH

Syntax is "=EOMONTH((start date, months)"

The EOMONTH function returns the serial number for the last day of the month that is the indicated number of months before or after start date. EOMONTH is most often used in financial calculations.

For example, "=EOMONTH("26-01-2011",1) will return 28-02-2011, that is, date of the last day of the month, which is one month after 26-01-2011. And if it was "=EOMONTH("26-01-2011",3), result would have been 30-04-2011.

3.13.5 NETWORKDAYS

Syntax is

"=NETWORKDAYS (start date, end date, [holidays])"

The NETWORKDAYS function returns the number of whole working days between start date and end date. Working days exclude weekends and any dates identified in holidays.

For example, "=NETWORKDAYS("04-02-2019", "31-03-2019","14-02-2019")" will return the number of days as 39, where 04-02-2019 is the start date, 31-03-2019 the end date, and 14-02-2019 a holiday.

3.13.6 YEARFRAC

Syntax is

"=YEARFRAC (start date, end date, basis)"

The YEARFRAC function calculates the fraction of the year represented by the number of whole days between two dates (the start date and the end date). It also has an optional argument which specifies the type of day count basis to be used, that is, options 0,1,2,3, and 4 as given in the following table:

	A	B	C	D	E
	Start date	End date	Result	Formula	Day count basis
1	Start date	End date	Result	Formula	Day count basis
2	01-01-2012	30-07-2012	0.580555556	=YEARFRAC(A2,B2,0)	US (NASD) 30/360
3	01-01-2012	30-07-2012	0.576502732	=YEARFRAC(A3,B3,1)	Actual/actual
4	01-01-2012	30-07-2012	0.586111111	=YEARFRAC(A4,B4,2)	Actual/360
5	01-01-2012	30-07-2012	0.578082192	=YEARFRAC(A5,B5,3)	Actual/365
6	01-01-2012	30-07-2012	0.580555556	=YEARFRAC(A6,B6,4)	European 30/360
7					

As you see in the preceding screenshot, fraction between the same dates that is using the Actual/Actual day count basis, the result is the least because 2012 is a Leap year, it has a 366-day basis.

3.14 Math Functions

In the previous section (3.10), we already discussed few mathematical functions like SUM, SUMIF, SUMIFS, and SUMPRODUCT. In this section, we will cover other useful and commonly used mathematical functions.

3.14.1 INT

This is a very simple function that rounds a number down to the nearest integer.

Syntax is

"=INT (real number to round down to integer)"

Example #1:   In the following table, we will see how the real numbers are rounded by the function and their results.

◢	A	B	C	D	E
1	Real Number	-4.3	1.82	10	-7
2	INT result	-5	1	10	-7

Figure 3.55 *Example of INT function*

In this example, note that the negative number is rounded down away from 0, hence INT(-4.3) results in -5 and INT(1.82) is 1 as the function rounds down and does not round up to 2. Since the other two are integers, the same value is returned.

We will discuss the other functions in the subsequent sections that round up the numbers.

3.14.2 ROUND, ROUNDDOWN, ROUNDUP, MROUND

These functions round the numbers to the specified number of digits. We will see their usage using examples.

Syntax is

"=ROUND(number, number of digits to which you want to round)"

"=ROUNDDOWN(number, number of digits to which you want to round down)"

"=ROUNDUP(number, number of digits to which you want to round up)"

"=MROUND(number, multiple to which you want to round number)"

Example #1:

	A	B	C
3	**Number**	**Result**	**Function**
4	3.15	3.2	=ROUND(A4,1)
5	3.15	3	=ROUND(A5,0)
6	3.149	3.1	=ROUND(A5,1)
7	-1.481	-1.48	=ROUND(A6,2)
8	21.5	20	=ROUND(A7,-1)

Figure 3.56 *Example of ROUND*

In the preceding example, 3.15 is rounded to 3.2 because if the number of digits is greater than 0 (zero), then the ROUND function rounds the number to the specified number of decimal places. If the number of digits is 0, then the number is rounded to the nearest integer, that is, ROUND(3.15,0) which results in 3. If the number of digits is less than 0, the number is rounded to the left of the decimal point, that is, ROUND(21.5,-1) which results in 20, and ROUND(121.5,-2) which results in 100.

In case you want to always round up (away from zero) a number, ROUNDUP function should be used and similarly to always round down (toward zero), use the ROUNDDOWN function. In case you want to round a number to a specific multiple, use the MROUND function. We will see their usage in following examples.

Example #2: In the following table, we have numbers and two sets of results, first if the numbers are rounded up and second if the numbers are rounded down. See how the results change based on the function used.

	A	B	C	D	E	F
10	Number	Result 1	Function ROUNDUP		Result 2	Function ROUNDDOWN
11	3.15	3.2	=ROUNDUP(A11,1)		3.1	=ROUNDDOWN(A11,1)
12	3.15	4	=ROUNDUP(A12,0)		3	=ROUNDDOWN(A12,0)
13	3.149	3.2	=ROUNDUP(A13,1)		3.1	=ROUNDDOWN(A13,1)
14	-1.481	-1.49	=ROUNDUP(A14,2)		-1.48	=ROUNDDOWN(A14,2)
15	21.5	30	=ROUNDUP(A15,-1)		20	=ROUNDDOWN(A15,-1)
16						

Figure 3.57 *Example of ROUNDUP and ROUNDDOWN functions*

Example #3: MROUND(10,3) rounds 10 to the nearest multiple of 3, resulting in 9. Similarly, MROUND(8,3) results in 9 while MROUND(7,3) results in 6 as it rounds to the nearest multiple. MROUND(1.5, 0.2) will round 1.5 to the nearest multiple of 0.2, that is, 1.6 and MROUND(-1.5, -0.2) will result in -1.6. But MROUND(1.5, -0.2) will result in an error as the number and the multiple arguments must have the same sign.

3.14.3 CEILING, FLOOR

The CEILING function returns number rounded up, away from zero, to the nearest multiple of significance.

Syntax is

"=CEILING(number, significance or multiple to which you want to round)"

Example #1: CEILING is a similar function to MROUND with a difference that CEILING always rounds up the number while MROUND finds the nearest multiple. In the following table, for the same arguments, the results differ for both the functions.

	A	B	C	D	E
17	Number	Result CEILING		Result MROUND	
18	3.15	4	=CEILING(A18,1)	3	=MROUND(A18,1)
19	3.149	3.2	=CEILING(A19,0.1)	3.1	=MROUND(A19,0.1)
20					

Figure 3.58 *Example of CEILING function*

FLOOR is similar to the CEILING function but with a difference that it always rounds number down, towards zero, to the nearest multiple of significance.

Syntax is

"=FLOOR(number, significance or multiple to which you want to round)"

Example #2: In the following table, the results of the FLOOR function are given along with CEILING and MROUND to show how the results change for the same number and the given multiple.

	A	B	C	D	E
17	Number	Result CEILING		Result FLOOR / MROUND	
18	3.15	4	=CEILING(A18,1)	3	=FLOOR(A18,1)
19	3.149	3.2	=CEILING(A19,0.1)	3.1	=FLOOR(A19,0.1)
20	1.58	2	=CEILING(A20,2)	0	=FLOOR(A20,2)
21				2	=MROUND(A20,2)
22	2.58	4	=CEILING(A22,2)	2	=FLOOR(A22,2)
23				2	=MROUND(A22,2)
24					

Figure 3.59 *Example of FLOOR function*

Interesting results are of number 1.58 and 2.58. Since CEILING rounds up 1.58 to the multiple of 2, hence it returns 2 while FLOOR rounds down so returns 0 and MROUND finds the nearest multiple of 2 so returns 2. Now, in case of number 2.58, CEILING returns 4 while both FLOOR and MROUND return 2.

3.14.4 ABS, SQRT, SUMSQ

ABS return the absolute value of the number. SQRT returns the positive square root of the number and SUMSQ returns the sum of the squares of the arguments.

Syntax is

"=ABS(real number of which you want the absolute value)"

"=SQRT(number for which you want the square root)"

"=SUMSQ(number1, [number2], ...)"

Note that the arguments can either be numbers, names, arrays, or references that contain numbers.

Example #1:

ABS function returns 2 for both ABS(2) and ABS(-2)

SQRT function returns 4 in both cases SQRT(16) and SQRT(ABS(-16)). Not that it returns error in case the number is negative.

SUMSQ function returns 25 for SUMSQ(3,4) that is, sum of squares of 3 (that is, 9) and 4 (that is, 16).

3.14.5 EXP, LN

The EXP function returns 'e' raised to the power of number. The constant e equals 2.71828182845904, the base of the natural logarithm. LN is the inverse of the EXP function that returns the natural logarithm of a number.

Syntax is

"=EXP(number i.e., exponent applied to the base e)"

"=LN(positive real number for which you want the natural logarithm)"

These functions are often used in working with non-linear trend lines or graphs and in many statistical calculations.

Example #1: Assuming, we have a population data of three regions for the year 2014, and the rate of growth of population in the given areas for five years was approximately 0.13%. Now, in order to know the latest population of the regions after five years, we can use the EXP function.

C26	▼	:	×	✓	f_x	=B26*EXP($F$25*$F$26)

▲	A	B	C	D	E	F
25	Area	2014	2019		Rate of Growth	0.13
26	R / North	4340	8313	=B26*EXP($F$25*$F$26)	Time (yrs)	5
27	R / Central	10321	19770	=B27*EXP($F$25*$F$26)		
28	R / South	1892	3624	=B28*EXP($F$25*$F$26)		
29						

Figure 3.60 *Example of EXP function*

Example #2: LN function, LN(2.7182818) return 1 as the number is the value of the constant e. And LN(EXP(3)) returns 3, as LN is inverse of EXP.

3.14.6 RAND, RANDBETWEEN

RAND returns an evenly distributed random real number which is greater than or equal to 0 and less than 1. A new random real number is returned every time the worksheet is calculated.

RANDBETWEEN is similar to RAND with a difference that it returns a random integer number between the numbers specified.

Syntax is

"=RAND()"

"=RANDBETWEEN(bottom, top)"

Example #1: RAND and RANDBETWEEN returns a different number each time worksheet is recalculated by entering a formula or data in a different cell, or by manually recalculating (press F9).

▲	A	B	C
29			
30		0.8513784	=RAND()
31		1	=RANDBETWEEN(1,3)
32			
33		0.1600491	=RAND()
34		3	=RANDBETWEEN(1,3)
35			

Figure 3.61 *Example of RAND and RANDBETWEEN*

3.15 Statistical Functions

In the previous section (3.10), we have already discussed few functions like AVERAGE, COUNT, COUTIF, and so on, that are categorized under statistical functions in Excel. In this section, we will discuss other functions that are frequently used and are helpful in calculations.

3.15.1 MIN, MAX

The MIN function returns the smallest number in a set of values and the MAX function returns the largest number in a set of values.

Syntax is

"=MIN(number1, [number2], ...)"

"=MAX(number1, [number2], ...)"

Example #1: In the following example, we have a list of customers loyalty program scores and we want to find the minimum and maximum achieved.

A	B	G	H	I
39	Scores			
40	23	Lowest Score	3	=MIN(B40:B55)
41	45	Highest Score	121	=MAX(B40:B55)
42	3			
43	12			
44	56			
45	121			
46	78			
47	6			
48	33			
49	3			
50	41			
51	53			
52	10			
53	5			
54	27			
55	67			

Figure 3.62 *Example of MIN and MAX*

3.15.2 RANK.EQ, RANK.AVG

The RANK.EQ and RANK.AVG functions, both return the rank of a number in a list of numbers with a difference that if more than one value has the same rank, RANK.EQ returns the top rank of that set of values while RANK.AVG returns the average rank. Its size is relative to other values in the list.

Syntax is

"=RANK.EQ(number whose rank you want to find, list of numbers/ref, [order])"

"=RANK.AVG(number whose rank you want to find, list of numbers/ref, [order])"

where,

order: 0 or omitted is descending & non-zero is ascending order

Example #1: Using the same example of customer loyalty program scores, we now want to rank the customers based on the scores, without changing the sequence or data structure.

▲ A	B	C	D	E	F
39	Scores	RANK.EQ		RANK.AVG	
40	23	10	=RANK.EQ(B40, $B$40:$B$55)	10	=RANK.AVG(B40, $B$40:$B$55)
41	45	6		6	
42	3	15		15.5	
43	12	11		11	
44	56	4		4	
45	121	1		1	
46	78	2		2	
47	6	13		13	
48	33	8		8	
49	3	15		15.5	
50	41	7		7	
51	53	5		5	
52	10	12		12	
53	5	14		14	
54	27	9		9	
55	67	3		3	

Figure 3.63 *Example of RANK.EQ and RANK.AVG (descending order)*

Note that the highest number, 121, is given a rank of 1 because we did not specify the order. When the value for argument 'order' is omitted or specified as 0, it is descending order.

Example #2: In this example, the rank is specified in ascending order as we specified a non-zero value, that is, 1 for argument 'order'. In this case, the lowest number, 3, is given a rank of 1 while 121 is the last rank.

◢ A	B	C	D	E	F
39	Scores	RANK.EQ		RANK.AVG	
40	23	7	=RANK.EQ(B40, $B$40:$B$55,1)	7	=RANK.AVG(B40, $B$40:$B$55,1)
41	45	11		11	
42	3	1		1.5	
43	12	6		6	
44	56	13		13	
45	121	16		16	
46	78	15		15	
47	6	4		4	
48	33	9		9	
49	3	1		1.5	
50	41	10		10	
51	53	12		12	
52	10	5		5	
53	5	3		3	
54	27	8		8	
55	67	14		14	

Figure 3.64 *Example of RANK.EQ and RANK.AVG function (ascending order)*

3.15.3 MEDIAN, MODE.SNGL, MODE.MUTL

In statistics, the commonly used measures of central tendency are the mean, median, and mode. Mean, that is, the AVERAGE function in Excel, has been discussed in section 3.10. In this section, we will discuss median and mode. Median is the number in the middle of a set of numbers and Mode is the most frequently occurring, or repetitive value. For a small set of values, we can find the median and mode manually also but for huge complex data it becomes difficult. Excel has the MEDIAN and MODE functions that do it easily for us.

Syntax is

"=MEDIAN(number1, [number2], ...)"

"=MODE.SNGL(number1,[number2],...)"

"=MODE.MULT((number1,[number2],...)"

Excel defines two functions for mode, MODE.SNGL and MODE.MULT. MODE.SNGL returns the lowest mode value in case there are multiple repetitive values and MODE.MULT returns an array of the most frequently occurring or repetitive values. We will see their usage with an example in the following example:

Example #1: For the given scores, the median is 30. Median is the middle number of the given set of numbers, that is, half the numbers are greater than the median, and half the numbers are less than the median.

⊿	A	B	C	D	E	F	G	H	I	J	K	L	M	N	O	P	Q	R	
56																			
57		Scores	23	45	3	6	56	121	78	6	33	3	41	53	10	5	27	67	
58																			
59		Median	30	=MEDIAN(C57:R57)															

Figure 3.65 *Example of Median function*

Example #2: For the given scores, MODE.SNGL returns 3, as it returns the lowest mode in case of multiple repetitive numbers. MODE.MULT returns both the repetitive numbers 3 and 6.

⊿	A	B	C	D	E	F	G	H	I	J	K	L	M	N	O	P	Q	R
60																		
61		Scores	23	45	3	6	56	121	78	6	33	3	41	53	10	5	27	67
62		Single Mode	3	=MODE.SNGL(C61:R61)														
63																		
64		Multi Mode	3															
65			6		{=MODE.MULT(C61:R61)}													
66			#N/A															
67			#N/A															
68																		
69		Multi Mode	3	6	#N/A	#N/A												
70			{=TRANSPOSE(MODE.MULT(C61:R61))}															

Figure 3.66 *Example of MODE function*

Note that MODE.MULT returns an array of values, hence it must be entered as an array formula. If the formula was not entered as an array formula, the single result would have been 3, same result as using the MODE.SNGL function.

Array formula is entered by selecting the vertical range of cells, that is, C64 to C67, enter the formula =MODE.MULT(C61:R61) and confirm by pressing Ctrl + Shift + Enter. In each selected cell, the function returns the mode value, if any. Since there are only two values and we selected four cells in range, it returns 3 and 6 in C64 and C65 cells and #N/A in C66 and C67 as there are no more mode values.

MODE.MULT returns result in a vertical array. In case we want to return the results in horizontal array then we will use the TRANSPOSE function of Excel along with MODE.MULT. In this case, the array formula will be entered by selecting the horizontal range of cells, that is, C69 to F69, enter the same formula as before but inside the TRANSPOSE function =TRANPOSE(MODE.MULT(C61:R61)) and confirm by pressing Ctrl + Shift + Enter.

3.15.4 QUARTILE.INC(/.EXC), PERCENTILE.INC(/.EXC)

Quartiles in statistics are values that divide your data into quarters, that is, into four segments according to where the numbers fall on the number line; the lowest 25% of numbers, next lowest 25% of numbers (up to the median), second highest 25% of numbers (above the median), and the highest 25% of numbers. A percentile is a measure used in statistics indicating the value below which a given percentage of observations in a group of observations falls. Median is the 50th percentile, that is, the point in the data where 50% of the data fall below that point, and 50% fall above it.

Excel defines two functions each for quartile and percentile, QUARTILE. INC and PERCENTILE.INC, meaning inclusive and QUARTILE.EXC and PERCENTILE.EXC meaning exclusive.

Syntax is

"=QUARTILE.INC(numeric values for which you want the quartile value, quart)"

where,

quart value is 0 means minimum value, 1 is first quartile i.e., 25th percentile, 2 is median value i.e., 50th percentile, 3 is third quartile i.e., 75th percentile and 4 is maximum value

"=QUARTILE.EXC(numeric values for which you want the quartile value, quart)"

where,

quart value 1 is first quartile i.e., 25th percentile, 2 is median value i.e., 50th percentile, 3 is third quartile i.e., 75th percentile

"=PERCENTILE.INC(range of data that defines relative standing, percentile value)"

"=PERCENTILE.EXC(range of data that defines relative standing, percentile value)"

Example #1: Using the same Scores data, we will find the quartiles. Note that the median calculated in the previous example (Figure 3.65) was 30, which is returned by the QUARTILE.INC(B1:Q1,2) function.

	A	B	C	D	E	F	G	H	I	J	K	L	M	N	O	P	Q
1	Scores	23	45	3	6	56	121	78	6	33	3	41	53	10	5	27	67
2																	
3	Quartile Inclusive	3	=QUARTILE.INC(B1:Q1,0)														
4		6	=QUARTILE.INC(B1:Q1,1)														
5		30	=QUARTILE.INC(B1:Q1,2)														
6		54	=QUARTILE.INC(B1:Q1,3)														
7		121	=QUARTILE.INC(B1:Q1,4)														
8																	
9	Quartile Exclusive	6	=QUARTILE.EXC(B1:Q1,1)														
10		30	=QUARTILE.EXC(B1:Q1,2)														
11		55	=QUARTILE.EXC(B1:Q1,3)														

Figure 3.67 *Example of Quartile function*

QUARTILE.INC is similar to the older version of the QUARTILE function. QUARTILE.EXC has a slightly different algorithm for calculation, hence, the difference in the results for the 3rd quartile is 55 instead of 54 as returned by QUARTILE.INC.

Example #2: In the following example, PERCENTILE. INC(B13:Q13,0.25) returns 6, which means that value 6 occupies the 25th percentile of the given set of scores. Similarly, 4 occupies the 10th percentile, returned by the PERCENTILE.INC(B13:Q13,10%) function. As there is a little difference in how PERCENTILE.EXC calculates the percentile, you see the difference in results for the same dataset and 10th percentile, PERCENTILE.EXC(B13:Q13,0.1), returns 3.

	A	B	C	D	E	F	G	H	I	J	K	L	M	N	O	P	Q
13	Scores	23	45	3	6	56	121	78	6	33	3	41	53	10	5	27	67
14																	
15	Percentile Inclusive	6	=PERCENTILE.INC(B13:Q13,0.25)														
16		4	=PERCENTILE.INC(B13:Q13,10%)														
17																	
18	Percentile Exclusive	3	=PERCENTILE.EXC(B13:Q13,0.1)														
19																	

Figure 3.68 *Example of Percentile function*

PERCENTILE.INC is similar to the older version of the PERCENTILE function, a slightly less accurate algorithm and works for percentile value between 0 and 1. On the other hand, PERCENTILE.EXE works for percentile value between $1/n$ and $1-1/n$, where n is the number of elements in the dataset or array.

Percentile is commonly used in salary surveys and also by human resource department to compare employees' salary and see how they match to market compensation.

3.15.5 PERCENTRANK.INC, PERCENTRANK.EXC

PERCENTRANK.INC and PERCENTRANK.EXC return the percentile that a given data value has in relation to a set of data values. Basically, they are inverse functions of PERCENTILE.INC and PERCENTILE.EXC.

Syntax is

"=PERCENTRANK.INC(range of data that defines relative standing,
value for which you want to know the rank, [significance])"

"=PERCENTRANK.EXC(range of data that defines relative standing,
value for which you want to know the rank, [significance])"

where,

*significance: number of significant digits for the returned percentage
value, default is three digits (0.xxx).*

Example #1: In the following example, for each of the cases the
percentile is the 30th percentile.

	A	B	C	D	E	F	G	H	I	J	K
19											
20	1		3.6	=PERCENTILE.INC(A20:A24,0.3)							
21	3		0.3	=PERCENTRANK.INC(A20:A24,3.6)							
22	6										
23	12		2.6	=PERCENTILE.EXC(A20:A24,0.3)							
24	15		0.3	=PERCENTRANK.EXC(A20:A24,2.6)							
25											

Figure 3.69 *Example of PERCENTRANK function*

3.15.6 STDEV.P(/.S), VAR.P(./S)

Variance is a statistical measure that tells us how measured data vary from
the average value of the set of data. Standard deviation is the square root
of the variance. A low standard deviation indicates that the data points tend
to be close to the mean of the set, while a high standard deviation indicates
that the data points are spread out over a wider range of values.

Excel has two functions each for variance and standard deviation,
indicating measure across the whole population, that is, STDEV.P, VAR.P
and a sample, that is, STDEV.S, VAR.S of population respectively.

Syntax is

"=STDEV.P(number1, [number2],...)"

"=STDEV.S(number1, [number2],...)"

"=VAR.P(number1, [number2],...)"

"=VAR.S(number1, [number2],...)"

Example #1: For two groups Group 1 and Group 2 we have heights and we want to find the variance and standard deviation. Note that in case of sample, we have taken limited values for calculations and for population we have taken all values in consideration.

	A	B	C	D	E	F	G
26		Height (feet inches)					
27		Group 1	Group 2				
28		4.30	3.90		Population Variance	1.331	=VAR.P(B28:B32,C28:C32)
29		3.00	4.11		Standard Deviation	1.154	=STDEV.P(B28:B32,C28:C32)
30		5.20	5.12				
31		5.50	6.15		Sample Variance	0.331	=VAR.S(B28:B29,C28:C29)
32		6.10	7.00		Standard Devation	0.575	=STDEV.S(B28:B29,C28:C29)

Figure 3.70 *Example of Variance and Standard deviation functions*

3.15.7 CORREL, COVARIANCE.P(/.S)

Correlation and covariance are two statistical concepts that are used to determine the relationship of two random variables.

Covariance measures the total variation of two random variables from their expected values, help to gauge the direction of the relationship, that is, whether the variables tend to move in tandem (positive covariance) or show an inverse (negative covariance) relationship.

On the other hand, correlation measures the strength of the relationship between variables, how change in one impacts the other. A correlation of +1 indicates that random variables have a direct and strong relationship, -1 indicates that there is a strong inverse relationship and an increase in one variable will lead to an equal and opposite decrease in the other variable and 0 indicates that the two numbers are independent.

Excel has two functions, COVARIANCE.P and COVARIANCE.S, for covariance of the whole population and a sample of the population, similar to variance and standard deviation functions.

Syntax is

"=CORREL(cell range of values, second cell range of values)"

"=COVARIANCE.P(first cell range of integers, second cell range of integers)"

"=COVARIANCE.S(first cell range of integers, second cell range of integers)"

Example #1: We want to find correlation between the temperature and ice cream sales. From the following results, we can deduce that the temperature and ice cream sales are directly and strongly correlated as the correlation is 0.9. And the positive covariance of population and sample indicate that as the temperature increases/decreases, so does the ice creams sales increase/decrease, that is, they move in the same direction.

	A	B	C	D	E	F	G
34		Temp (C)	Ice Cream Sales				
35		22	420				
36		15	309		Correlation	0.9531	=CORREL(B35:B45,C35:C45)
37		26	432				
38		31	445		Covariance Population	1711.46	=COVARIANCE.P(B35:B45,C35:C45)
39		32	450		Covariance Sample	1084.00	=COVARIANCE.S(B35:B40,C35:C40)
40		10	101				
41		8	30				
42		29	445				
43		4	15				
44		17	312				
45		6	16				

Figure 3.71 *Example of Covariance and Correlation function*

3.16 Financial Functions

Excel formulas and functions are very helpful in performing financial analysis and building faster and efficient financial models. In the preceding sections, the functions discussed are generic, not very specific to a domain and are also used very often in financial analysis. Along with those, in this section we will discuss some useful functions that are more specific to financial analysis like calculating interest rates, monthly payments, or finding future value of investments.

3.16.1 PV and FV

PV function calculates the present value and FV function calculates the future value of a loan or an investment, based on a constant interest rate.

Syntax is

"=PV(rate, nper, pmt, [fv], [type])"

"=FV(rate, nper, pmt, [pv], [type])"

where,

> *rate – interest rate*
> *nper – total no of payment periods*
> *pmt – payment paid each period*
> *fv – future value or cash balance you want to attain*
> *pv – present value*
> *type – when payment is due i.e., 0 = at the end & 1=at beginning*

Example #1:   We want to calculate the present value of an annuity that pays 1,000 per month for a period of three years (3*12=36 months) at interest rate of 6% per year (that is, 0.50% per month) and each payment is made at the end of the month.

◢	A	B	C	D
1		Interest Rate (6% pa) = 6%/12	0.50%	
2		No of payment periods (3yrs) =3*12)	36	
3		Payment per month	1000	
4				
5		**Present Value (PV)**	-32871.02	=PV(C1, C2, C3)
6				

Figure 3.72 *Example of PV function*

In the preceding example, the future value is omitted and hence it is considered as 0. Argument payment due has also not been specified, which by default is 0 meaning it is due at end of the period. If 1 is specified, it is considered that payment is due at the beginning of the period. Both of these are optional arguments. Note that since the unit for calculation is monthly, we have divided the interest rate by 12 to get rate per month 0.50% and multiplied by 12 to get number of payment periods as 36.

Example #2: In this example, for an investment of 10,000 in 2017, paid yearly for interest rate of 10%, we want to know the future value of the investment in 2020, that is, after 3 years.

▲	A	B	C	D
8		Interest Rate 10%pa	10%	
9		No of payment periods 3yrs (2017-20)	3	
10		Present Value	10,000.00	
11		Type	1	
12				
13		**Future Value (FV)**	-13310.00	=FV(C8,C9,,C10,C11)
14				

Figure 3.73 *Example of FV function*

In the preceding example, the payment for each period is omitted, hence it is mandatory to specify the present value, that is, the lumpsum amount paid. Also, we have specified the type as 1, that is, the payments are due at the beginning of the period.

For both PV and FV functions to work correctly, you should be consistent about the units (yearly, monthly, weekly, and so on) you use for specifying rate and the total number of payment periods (nper).

Note that, in line with the general cash flow sign convention, cash outflows are represented by negative numbers and cash inflows are represented by positive numbers. Hence, the result in the preceding examples is negative, that is, cash outflow.

3.16.2 PMT, IPMT and PPMT

PMT function calculates the constant periodic payment required to pay off a loan or investment, with a constant interest rate, over a specified period.

Syntax is

"=PMT(rate, nper, pv, [fv], [type])"

where,

rate – interest rate
nper – total no of payment periods
fv – future value or cash balance you want to attain
pv – present value
type – when payment is due i.e., 0 = at the end & 1=at beginning

Example #1: The following example returns the annual payment on loan of 10,00,000 at an annual rate of 10%. The loan term is 20 years and all payments are made at the end of the period.

	A	B	C	D
15		Interest Rate 10%pa	10%	
16		No of payment periods 20yrs	20	
17		Amount of Loan / Present Value	10,00,000.00	
18		Type	0	
19				
20		PMT	-1,17,459.62 =PMT(C15,C16,C17,0,C18)	
21				

Figure 3.74 *Example of PMT function – annual payment*

If for the same example, we had to calculate the monthly payment, following will be the result:

	A	B	C	D
15		Interest Rate 10%pa	10%	
16		No of payment periods 20yrs	20	
17		Amount of Loan / Present Value	10,00,000.00	
18		Type	0	
19				
20		PMT (annual)	-1,17,459.62 =PMT(C15,C16,C17,0,C18)	
21				
22		PMT (monthly)	-9,650.22 =PMT(C15/12,C16*12,C17,0,C18)	

Figure 3.75 *Example of PMT function – monthly payment*

Note that, in line with the general cash flow sign convention, cash outflows are represented by negative numbers and cash inflows are represented by positive numbers.

Loan or Investment Payment has two components: Principal and the Interest Payment. PPMT and IPMT functions are related to these two components. IPMT and PPMT are similar functions to PMT with a difference that IPMT returns the interest payment for an investment while PPMT returns the payment on the principal amount for a given period for an investment based on periodic, constant payments, and a constant interest rate.

Syntax is

"=IPMT(rate, per, nper, pv, [fv], [type])"

"=PPMT(rate, per, nper, pv, [fv], [type])"

where,

   rate – interest rate
   per - period to calculate interest for
   nper – total no of payment periods
   fv – future value or cash balance you want to attain
   pv – present value
   type – when payment is due i.e., 0 = at the end & 1=at beginning

Example #2: In this example, we want to know the interest and principal payments for the 4th year on a loan amount of 10,00,000 at an annual rate of 10%. The loan term is 20 years and all payments are made at the end of the period.

◢	A	B	C	D
24		Interest Rate 10%pa	10%	
25		Period (4th year)	4	
26		No of payment periods 20yrs	20	
27		Amount of Loan / Present Value	10,00,000.00	
28		Type	0	
29				
30		**IPMT**	-94,220.86	=IPMT(C24,C25,C26,C27,0,C28)
31		**PPMT**	-23,238.76	=PPMT(C24,C25,C26,C27,0,C28)
32				

Figure 3.76 *Example for PPMT and IPMT functions*

3.16.3 NPV and XNPV

NPV calculates the net present value of an investment by using a discount rate (also called rate) and a series of future payments (negative values) and income (positive values). Basically, it is the difference between the present value of cash inflows and the present value of cash outflows over a period of time.

Example #1: For example, the PV for 10,000 cash received after 5 years at a rate of 10% annual return compounded annually is 6,209. Now, if we want to calculate the NPV for an investment of 5,000 today that will result in 10,000 cash at the end of 5 years, at the rate of 10% annual return compounded annually, it will be the result of the present value of the cash inflow, that is, 6,209 minus the present value of the 5,000 cash outflow, 1,209. Note that 5,000 cash outflows occurred at the present time, its present value is 5,000.

The difference between NPV and PV (as discussed in section 3.16.1) is that NPV formula accounts for the initial investment required to fund, making it a net figure, while the PV calculation only accounts for cash inflows.

Now we will see how Excel function NPV works.

Syntax is

"=NPV(rate,value1,[value2],...)"

where,

rate: rate of discount over the length of one period

value1, [value2], ... : payments and income equally spaced in time, in chronological order, occurring at end of each period

Note that the negative payments represent outgoing payments and positive payments represent incoming payments.

Example #2: In the following example, we will be calculating NPV with 10% rate of discount and the cash flow as given in the screenshot. If NPV is greater than zero, the series of cash flows returns something greater than 10%. If it's less than zero, the return is less than 10%.

	A	B	C	D
45		Rate	10%	
46		Period	Cash Flow	
47		0	-1000	Out-flow
48		1	200	In-flow
49		2	300	
50		3	400	
51		4	500	
52		5	600	
53				
54		NPV	444.34	=NPV(C45,C48:C52)+C47

Figure 3.77 *Example of NPV function*

Note that if the first cash flow occurs at the start of the first period, the first value must be added to the NPV result, not included in the values arguments.

Calculation can also be done manually which returns the same results using the following formula, however, we can see it is complex while Excel makes it very simple.

=C48/(1+0.1)^1+C49/(1+0.1)^2+C50/(1+0.1)^3+C51/(1+0.1)^4+C52/(1+0.1)^5 + C47

Instead of (1+0.1)^2 and (1+0.1)^3 we could use Excel POWER function also, that is, POWER(1+0.1,2) and POWER(1+0.1,3) respectively.

			C56	▾	:	×	✓	*fx*	=(C48/(1+0.1))+(C49/POWER(1+0.1,2)) +(C50/POWER(1+0.1,3))+(C51/POWER(1+0.1,4))+(C52/POWER(1+0.1,5))+C47

	A	B	C	D	E	F
45		Rate	10%			
46		Period	Cash Flow			
47		0	-1000	Out-flow		
48		1	200	In-flow		
49		2	300			
50		3	400			
51		4	500			
52		5	600			
53						
54		NPV	444.34	=NPV(C45,C48:C52)+C47		
55						
56			444.34			
57						

Figure 3.78 *Example of NPV – Manual calculation*

In comparison, XNVP returns the net present value for a schedule of cash flows that is not necessarily periodic.

Syntax is

"=XNPV(rate,values,dates)"

where,

rate: rate of discount to apply to the cash flows

values: series of cash flows that corresponds to a schedule of payments in dates

dates: schedule of payment dates that corresponds to the cash flow payments

Example #3: In the following example, we will calculate the XNPV and also the NPV values to see the difference. The discount rate is 10%, start date is Jun 2008, and the first cash flow happens after 6 months. Subsequent cash flows are received on the corresponding dates as follows:

	A	B	C	D
58		Rate	10%	
59		Period	Cash Flow	
60		30-06-2008	0	
61		31-12-2008	200	
62		01-02-2009	300	
63		01-05-2009	400	
64		03-01-2010	500	
65		04-03-2011	600	
66				
67		XNPV	1741.32	=XNPV(C58,C60:C65,B60:B65)
68		NPV	1313.03	=NPV(C58,C60:C65)
69				

Figure 3.79 *Example of XNPV function*

In the preceding example for the same data, XNPV and NPV results are different. The reason being that XNPV takes the exact dates into consideration, NPV assumes that cash flow happens at the end of each period.

3.16.4 IRR and XIRR

The internal rate of return (IRR) is the interest rate received for an investment consisting of payments (negative values) and income (positive values) that occur at regular periods. The cash flows must occur at regular intervals, such as monthly or annually. XIRR returns the interest rate for an investment or cash flows occurring at irregular intervals.

Syntax is

"=IRR(values, [guess])"

"=XIRR(values, dates, [guess])"

where,

value: stream of cash flows

dates: schedule of payment dates that corresponds to the cash flow payments

guess: an initial guess at what the IRR might be. This is an optional argument, which, if omitted, takes on the default value of 0.1 (=10%).

Note that values must contain at least one positive value and one negative value to calculate the internal rate of return. Function works by calculating the present value of each cash flow based on the guessed rate (if given or default 10%). If the sum of those is greater than zero, it reduces the rate and tries again. Excel keeps iterating through rates and summing present values until the sum is zero. Once the present values sum to zero, it returns that rate.

Example #1 The following example shows the difference between IRR and XIRR. The cash flow is the same in both cases but for IRR it assumes at regular interval while XIRR takes into account the actual dates at which the payments were made.

◢	A	B	C	D	E	F	G	H	I
70									
71		Period	1	2	3	4	5	6	
72		Cash Flow	-1000	200	300	400	500	600	
73									
74		IRR	23%	=IRR(C72:H72)					
75									
76		Dates	30-06-2008	31-12-2008	01-02-2009	01-05-2009	03-01-2010	04-03-2011	
77		Cash Flow	-1000	200	300	400	500	600	
78									
79		XIRR	70%	=XIRR(C77:H77,C76:H76)					
80									

Internal rate of return, both IRR and XIRR are good tools to evaluate the attractiveness of a project or investment using a percentage value. Helpful to compare the potential profitability of multiple prospective projects, and if the cost of investment is equal for all the projects, then the project with the highest IRR/XIRR would be considered to be the most attractive for investment.

NPV and XNVP can also be used as investment indicators, they use the actual money value for comparison while IRR and XIRR uses percentage value, which is more preferable.

3.17 Error Handling

In case the formula has an error, Excel returns a value starting hash mark (#). There are different error values #N/A, #VALUE, #REF, #DIV/0!, #NUM, #NAME?, and #NULL!, which we will explain in this section and how to handle these errors.

To avoid errors, you should carefully review, check your data and values in the Excel sheet. Many times, the return value of functions is used in another formula or calculation and error values will mess those calculations. Excel has some built-in functions for error handling, under the Information and Logical function categories, such as ISERR, ISERROR, ISNA, ERROR. TYPE, IFERROR, and IFNA.

3.17.1 Error Types

3.17.1.1 #N/A

This error is returned when the function is unable to find the value it has been asked to look for or when the numbers you are referring to in your formula cannot be found. Simple example is when we try to see the exact match 'A' in array {B,C,D} using formula =MATCH("A",{"B","C","D"},0). Another example could be if you are trying to look up a value using VLOOKUP/HLOOKUP and there are no matching values in the array, as shown here:

◢	A	B	C	D	E	F	G	H
1								
2		Group Name	Score					
3		Red	23		=VLOOKUP("White",B3:C6,2,FALSE)			
4		Green	56					
5		Yellow	41					
6		Blue	66					
7								

Figure 3.80   *Example of #N/A error*

We can also handle this error using the ISNA (see 3.17.2.2) or IFNA (see 3.17.2.4) functions, so that instead of returning error #N/A, we return something meaningful that does not disrupt further calculations or just a message informing user of the error.

3.17.1.2 #VALUE!

This error is very general and can occur whenever the data type of a given function doesn't match what it is expecting or something is wrong with the way the formula is typed or there is something wrong with cells being referred to in formula.

For example, the '="A"+1' formula returns the #VALUE! as it is expecting number to calculate.

3.17.1.3 #REF!

Excel usually displays #REF! when a formula references a cell that is not valid.

For example, in the following example, we are adding numbers in columns NUM1, NUM2, and NUM3. Now what will happen if we delete column NUM2. Excel gives #REF! error in Total column.

	A	B	C	D	E
1	Num1	Num2	Num3	Total	
2	1	5	3	9	=SUM(A2,B2,C2)
3	2	9	2	13	=SUM(A3,B3,C3)
4	3	7	1	11	=SUM(A4,B4,C4)
5	4	8	6	18	=SUM(A5,B5,C5)

C2	▾	:	✕ ✓	f_x	=SUM(A2,#REF!,B2)

	A	B	C	D	E	F
1	Num1	Num3	Total			
2	1	!	#REF!	=SUM(A2,B2,C2)		
3	2	2	#REF!	=SUM(A3,B3,C3)		
4	3	1	#REF!	=SUM(A4,B4,C4)		
5	4	6	#REF!	=SUM(A5,B5,C5)		
6						

3.17.1.4 #DIV/0!

This error occurs when you are asking Excel to divide a formula by zero or an empty cell.

For example, '=4/0', it types in the cell will return #DIV/0! Error.

3.17.1.5 #NUM!

Excel shows this error when a formula or function contains numeric values that aren't valid.

For example, '=SQRT(-9)' returns the #NUM! error as we entered a negative number.

3.17.1.6 #NAME?

The #NAME? error signifies that something needs to be corrected in the syntax.

For example, '=INT(a)' returns the #NAME? error as the INT function expects a number as value.

3.17.1.7 #NULL!

This error is shown when you use an incorrect range operator in a formula, or when you use an intersection operator (space character) between range references to specify an intersection of two ranges that don't intersect.

D2	▼ : × ✓ *fx*	=SUM(A2 C2)

▲	A	B	C	D	E
1	Num1	Num2	Num3	Total	
2	1	5	!	#NULL!	=SUM(A2 C2)
3	2	9	2		
4	3	7	1		
5	4	8	6		
6					

3.17.2 Error Handling Functions

3.17.2.1 ISERR and ISERROR

> Syntax is
>
> "=ISERR(value to test except #N/A)"
>
> "=ISERROR(value to test for any error value)"

The ISERR and ISERROR functions, checks the specified value and returns TRUE or FALSE depending on the outcome.

▲	A	B	C	D	E	F	G
13		Value	Result 1			Result 2	
14		#N/A	FALSE	=ISERR(B14)		TRUE	=ISERROR(B14)
15		#REF!	TRUE	=ISERR(B15)		TRUE	=ISERROR(B15)
16		0	FALSE	=ISERR(B16)		FALSE	=ISERROR(B16)
17							

Figure 3.81 *Example of ISERR & ISERROR function*

3.17.2.2 ISNA

ISNA function checks the value and returns TRUE if it is #N/A and FALSE otherwise.

Syntax is

"=ISNA(value to test for #N/A)"

As discussed in the example for error type #N/A in section 3.17.1.1, we will work further on that example to see how ISNA function helps in error handling and returning a meaningful information.

Example #1 We have two schools participating in a competition and each school has four groups representing them. The scorer wanted to find the score of the White group of School #2 but entered incorrect data range of School #1, hence, #N/A value was returned by the =VLOOKUP(C8,B3:C6,2,FALSE) formula. On correcting the data range in the =VLOOKUP(C8,E3:F6,2,FALSE) formula, correct value was returned, that is, 45. This is a tedious way to find scores by entering the correct data range. We can instead use the ISNA function to use the correct data range and get the correct value as given here:

	A	B	C	D	E	F	G	H
2		School #1	Group Score		School #2	Group Score		
3		Red	23		White	45		
4		Green	56		Orange	50		
5		Yellow	41		Pink	32		
6		Blue	66		Black	18		
7								
8		Score of Group	White		#N/A	=VLOOKUP(C8,B3:C6,2,FALSE)		
9					45	=VLOOKUP(C8,E3:F6,2,FALSE)		
10								
11		Generic formula with Error Handling	White		45	=IF(ISNA(VLOOKUP(C11,$B$3:$C$6,2,FALSE)), VLOOKUP(C11,$E$3:$F$6,2,FALSE), VLOOKUP(C11,$B$3:$C$6,2,FALSE))		
12			Red		23	=IF(ISNA(VLOOKUP(C11,$B$3:$C$6,2,FALSE)), VLOOKUP(C11,$E$3:$F$6,2,FALSE), VLOOKUP(C11,$B$3:$C$6,2,FALSE))		

Figure 3.82 *Example of ISNA function*

Conditional function IF is used with ISNA in the preceding formula. The ISNA function has been first used to check if error is returned, that is, TRUE if VLOOKUP returns #N/A and FALSE otherwise. If TRUE, then the IF function returns the value of the second argument, VLOOKUP(C11,$E$3:$F$6,2,FALSE), else the value of the third argument, VLOOKUP(C11,$B$3:$C$6,2,FALSE), in case of row#11.

3.17.2.3 IFERROR

Syntax is

"=IFERROR(value to test, value to return if the formula evaluates to an error)"

The IFERROR function returns the value specified if the value to test, returns error, else returns the result of the formula.

For example, the formula =IFERROR(MATCH("A",{"B","C","D"},0),"No Match") returns 'No Match' as the MATCH function returns #N/A. On the other hand, the =IFERROR(MATCH("C",{"B","C","D"},0),"No Match") formula returns 2 as a match for C is found at the 2nd position in array {B,C,D}.

3.17.2.4 IFNA

The IFNA function tests if the value returns error #N/A and returns the value specified as the second argument value.

Syntax is

"=IFNA(value to test,

value to return if the formula evaluates to the #N/A error value)"

Example #1 In the following example, we are trying to lookup the score of the 'white' group using the VLOOKUP function. But since it does not exist, VLOOKUP will return error #N/A (see error description in section 3.17.1.1) and hence IFNA will return the text Not Found, which was specified as second argument in the function.

⊿ A	B	C	D	J	K	L	M	N	O	P
1										
2	School #1	Group Score								
3	Red	23		Not Found	=IFNA(VLOOKUP("White",B3:C6,2,FALSE),"Not Found")					
4	Green	56								
5	Yellow	41								
6	Blue	66								

Figure 3.83 *Example of IFNA function*

3.17.2.5 ERROR.TYPE

Returns a number corresponding to one of the error values in Microsoft Excel or returns its own #N/A error if no error exists, that is, returns a number from 1 through 8 that corresponds to the type of error in its input cell reference.

Syntax is

"=ERROR.TYPE(error value whose identifying number you want to find)"

If error value is	ERROR.TYPE returns
#NULL!	1
#DIV/0!	2
#VALUE!	3
#REF!	4
#NAME?	5
#NUM!	6
#N/A	7
#GETTING_DATA	8
Anything else	#N/A

As per the preceding table, the '=ERROR.TYPE(#NULL!)' formula will return 1 and '=ERROR.TYPE(MATCH("A",{"B","C"},0))' returns 7 as the MATCH function returns error #N/A.

3.18 Formula Auditing

Formula auditing in Excel allows you to display the relationship between formulas and cells. It gives the options to Trace Precedents, Trace Dependents, Show or display Formulas in the sheet, Error checking and

Tracing Errors, Watch window to see change in cell values and Evaluate formula option to stepping in the formula.

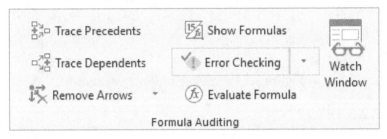

Figure 3.84 *Formula Auditing*

3.18.1 Show Formulas

The Formula Auditing ➜ Show Formulas option can be used for displaying the formulas in the sheet rather than the results of the formulas.

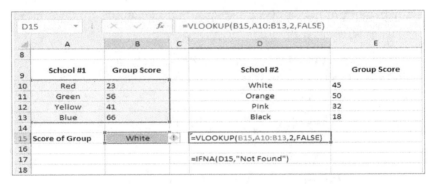

Figure 3.85 *Show Formulas example*

In case you want to see the formulas in one window and results in another window, then before using the Show Formulas option, open a new window by going to the View tab Window ➜ New Window option.

3.18.2 Trace Precedents, Trace Dependents, and Remove Trace Arrows

The precedents of any cell that contains a formula are all cells referenced by the formula in that cell. The dependents of any cell are all cells with formulas that reference that cell. Excel allows us to trace the cell relationships. Select the cell that has an error #N/A, D15 in the following example. Click on the Formula Auditing ➜ Trace Precedents and Formula Auditing ➜ Trace Dependents options. In our example, Excel draws blue colored arrows to show precedents and red colored arrow to show dependents of the selected cell with error value, D15. Note that D15 is been referenced in the formula in cell D17, hence, it becomes the dependent.

D15	▼	:	×	✓	*fx*	=VLOOKUP(B15,A10:B13,2,FALSE)

⬜	A	B	C	D	E	F	G	
8								
9	School #1	Group Score		School #2	Group Score			
10	Red	23		White	45			
11	Green	56		Orange	50			
12	Yellow	41		Pink	32			
13	Blue	66		Black	18			
14								
15	Score of Group	White	!	#N/A	=VLOOKUP(B15,A10:B13,2,FALSE)			
16								
17				Not Found	=IFNA(D15,"Not Found")			
18								

Figure 3.86 *Trace Precedents and Dependents*

Arrows can be removed by using the Remove Arrows option from Formulas ➜ Formula Auditing. You can remove both arrows or either of them representing the precedents or dependents.

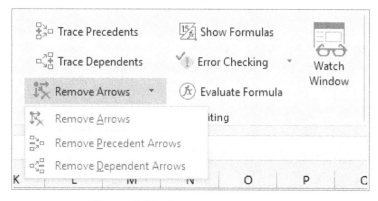

	Trace Precedents	Show Formulas	
	Trace Dependents	Error Checking ▾	Watch Window
	Remove Arrows ▾	Evaluate Formula	
	Remove Arrows	iting	
	Remove Precedent Arrows		
	Remove Dependent Arrows		

Figure 3.87 *Remove Trace Arrows*

3.18.3 Trace Error

The Formula Auditing ➜ Trace Error option helps in identifying the cell causing an error value to appear, activate the cell that contains the error, and then choose Formulas ➜ Formula Auditing ➜ Error Checking ➜ Trace Error. Excel draws arrows to indicate which cell is the source of the error.

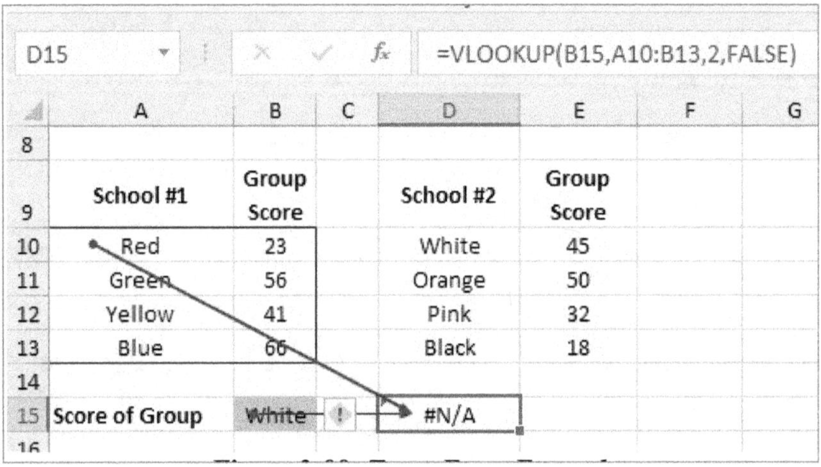

Figure 3.88 *Trace Error Example*

Arrows can be removed by using the Remove Arrows option from Formulas ➜ Formula Auditing.

3.18.4 Error Checking, Evaluate Formula

The Formula Auditing ➜ Error checking' dialog box gives an option to see help related to the error, step in the formula and see the calculation steps, ignore the error and edit the formula to make it correct.

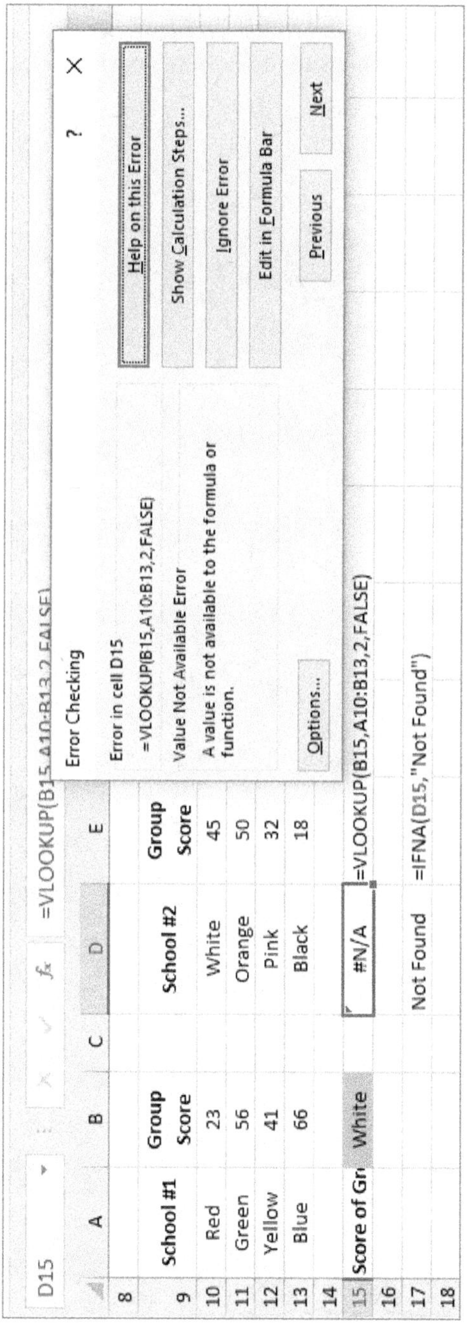

Figure 3.89 *Error Checking dialog box*

The Show Calculation Steps… option launches a window which allows you to step in the function and see the intermediate results. The same window is launched by using the Formula Auditing ➔ Evaluate Formula option.

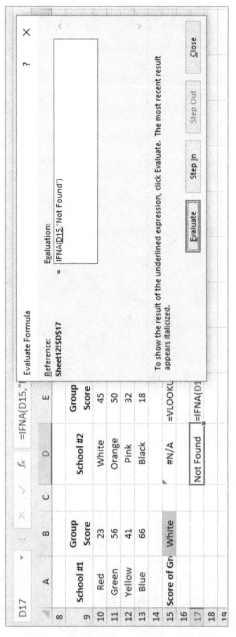

Figure 3.90 *Evaluate Formula window*

The Evaluate Formula helps you see the various parts of a nested formula evaluated in the order in which the formula is calculated. You can now use the Step In button at each step to go in and see the calculation.

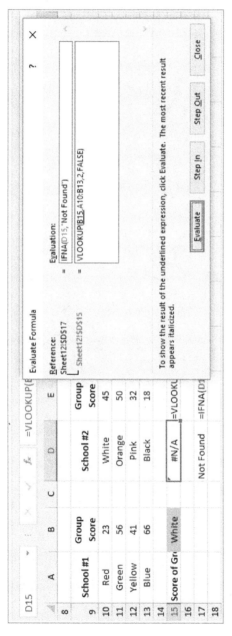

Figure 3.91 *Evaluate Formula window – Step-in level 1*

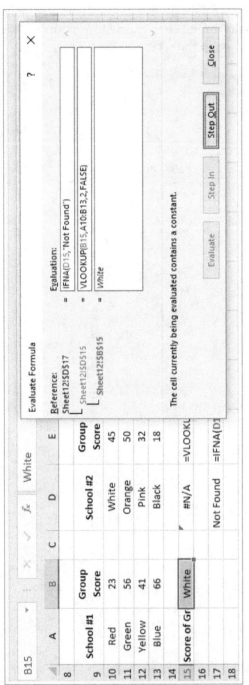

Figure 3.92 *Evaluate Formula window – Step-in level 2*

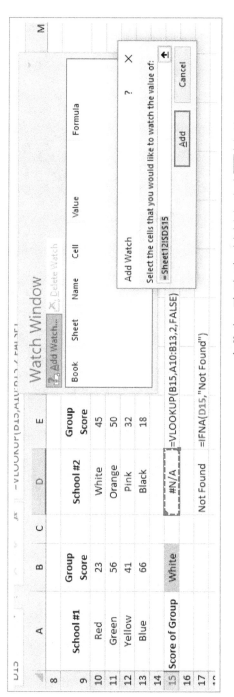

3.18.5 Watch Window

The Watch Window makes it easy to inspect, audit, or confirm formula calculations and results in large worksheets, avoiding repeatedly scroll or go to different parts of your worksheet.

Example #1: In this example, we want to watch the result of VLOOKUP in cell D15 and of IFNA in cell D17. Go to the Formula Auditing ➔ Watch Window option, launch the dialog box and click on the Add Watch... button to launch another dialog box to enter the cell D15 to watch. Again, click on Add Watch... and select cell D17 to add in the watch window.

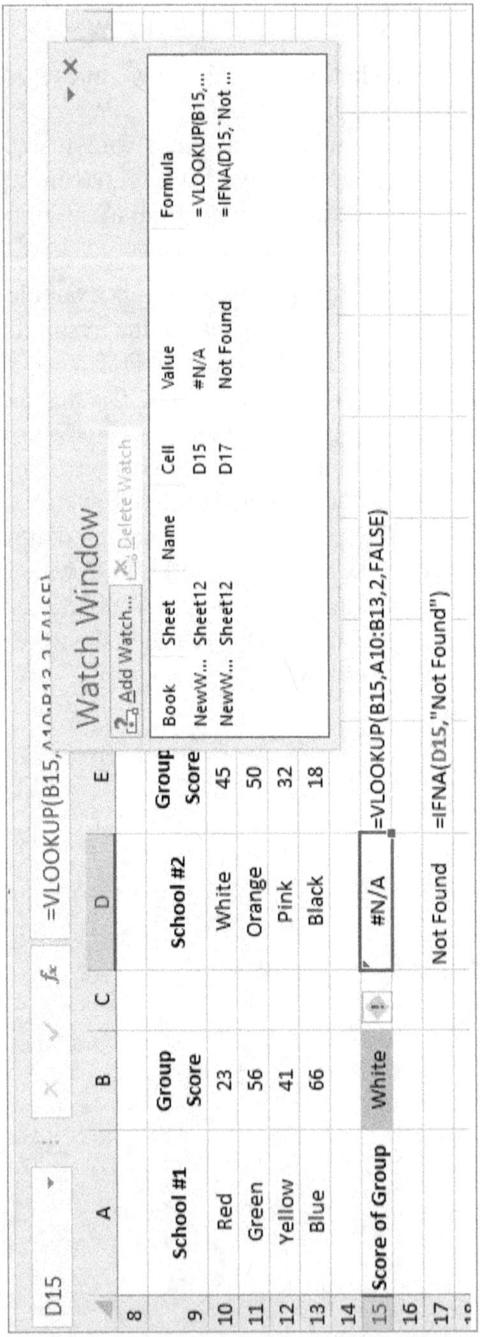

Figure 3.93 *Watch window – Add watch dialog*

Now we will change the look up value White in cell B15 to Green and see the change in values in the watch window.

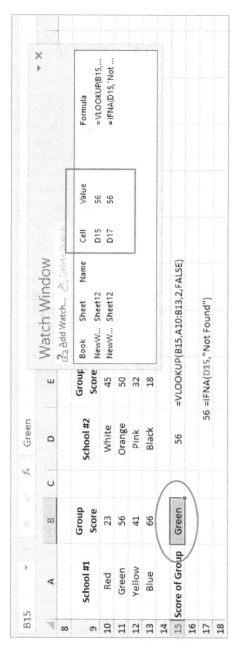

Note that when we entered **Green** in cell B15 the corresponding values for the D15 and D17 cells changed from '#N/A' and 'Not Found' to 56.

CHAPTER 4

Data Visualization with New Chart types

Excel has many built-in chart types that existed in previous versions before Excel 2016, like Column, Line, Pie, Doughnut, Bar, Area, Scatter, Bubble, Stock, Surface, Radar, and Combo chart types. In Excel 2016 six new built-in chart types were introduced – Waterfall, Histogram, Pareto, Box & Whisker, Treemap and Sunburst; powerful charts which help you quickly visualize common financial, statistical and hierarchical data. The 3D Maps that were previously used as Excel add-in *3-D geospatial visualization* has now been fully integrated in Excel 2016. In this section we will see an overview of the older build-in chart types and discuss new chart types in detail, including 3D Maps and Sparkline charts, which are not new but are very helpful.

4.1 Chart Types and When to Use Them

The following table gives an overview of different chart types and when to use which type.

Chart Type	When to Use
Column Chart	Compare values across a few categories, shown vertically.
Line Chart	Visualize trends over a period of time that is, months, days, years, and so on.
Pie Chart	Quantify items and display them as percentages.
Doughnut Chart	Show the relationship of parts as a whole. Similar to a Pie Chart, however with the difference that it can contain more than one data series.
Bar Chart	Comparing values across a few categories, shown horizontally.

Chart Type	When to Use
Area Chart	Illustrating the magnitude of change between two or more data points, using the sum of the plotted values to show the relationship of parts as a whole.
Scatter Chart	Show correlations between two sets of values.
Bubble Chart	Show correlations between two sets of values and also the relative impact of a quantitative data item. It's a variation of an XY scatter plot with the addition of a third dimension that is represented by the size of each bubble in the chart.
Stock Chart	Show fluctuations in stock prices or other data, such as daily rainfall or annual temperatures.
Surface Chart	To find the optimum combinations between two sets of data, colors, and patterns indicating areas that are in the same range of values.
Radar Chart	Compare the aggregate values of several data series.
Combo Chart	A visualization that combines two or more chart types into a single chart. Commonly used to show the difference between targets versus the actual results.
3D Map	Compare values and show categories across geographical regions.
Waterfall (*new*)	Visualize the impact of multiple data points (typically a series of positive and negative values) as a running total, commonly used when analyzing financial data.
Histogram (*new*)	A variation of the bar chart that shows the frequencies within a distribution.
Pareto (*new*)	Similar to Histogram but including a sorted histogram chart with a line representing the cumulative total percentage.
Box & Whisker (*new*)	Show the distribution of data into quartiles, highlighting the mean and any outliers. Commonly used in statistics.
Treemap (*new*)	A hierarchical view of data and a way to compare different levels of categorization. Also comparing proportions within the hierarchy.
Sunburst (*new*)	A hierarchical visualization of data, in the form of concentric circles and show how outer rings relate to inner rings

4.2 Waterfall Chart

Waterfall charts are helpful in visualizing the impact of multiple data points—series of positive and negative values—as a running total. Commonly used to the track monetary performance over time like analyzing financial data, for example an income statement. Waterfall charts are also helpful in scenarios like analyzing inventory or sales, comparing product earnings, showing product value over time and so on.

We will create a Waterfall chart for the data mentioned in the following screenshot:

Gross Revenue	3,45,621
Rev Adjustments	(3,050)
Net Revenue	**3,42,571**
Inventory	(1,24,900)
Merchandise	(16,700)
Other costs	(6,333)
Gross Income	**1,94,638**
Staff	(50,750)
Marketing	(12,579)
Facilities	(46,000)
Operating Income	**85,309**
Taxes	(5,400)
Net Income	**79,909**

Figure 4.1 *Waterfall chart example data*

Select the data cell range A1 to B13 and on the **Insert** tab select the **Waterfall** option from the **Charts** group. You can also select **Recommended Charts** and under the **Insert Chart** dialogue box go to the **All Charts** tab and select **Waterfall Chart** from the listed chart type options.

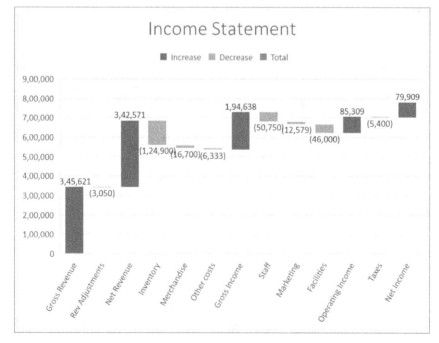

Figure 4.2 *Waterfall Chart*

It's useful for understanding how an initial value (for example, net income) is affected by a series of positive and negative values. The columns are color coded so you can quickly tell positive from negative numbers. The initial and final value columns often start on the horizontal axis, while the intermediate values are floating columns.

In the preceding example, we have values that are considered Subtotals or Totals, such as Net Revenue, Gross Income, Operating Income, and Net Income; and we want to set those values so they begin on the horizontal axis at zero and don't "float". For Excel to identify the bar as a total or sum value, right-click on the bar and select option **Set as Total**.

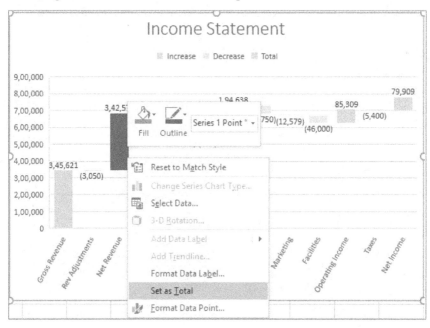

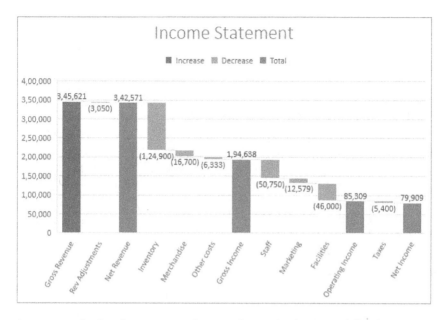

As you see in the above screenshot, each step in the waterfall takes you to the final result that is the net income and demonstrates how you got there.

4.3 Histogram

Commonly used in statistics, a Histogram automatically displays the frequencies within a distribution. Consider an example that a survey was done in a restaurant for knowing the popular age group in order to revise the menu card, ages being: 13, 10, 6, 22, 20, 13, 12, 25, 43, 29, 31, 23, 5, 6, 7, 15, 23, 47, 9, 50, 39, 40, 63, 5, 36, 57, 63.

To create a Histogram, copy these values in a column of a sheet. Select the cell range, go to the **Insert** tab and choose **Histogram** (the left-side chart type) from the **Charts** group.

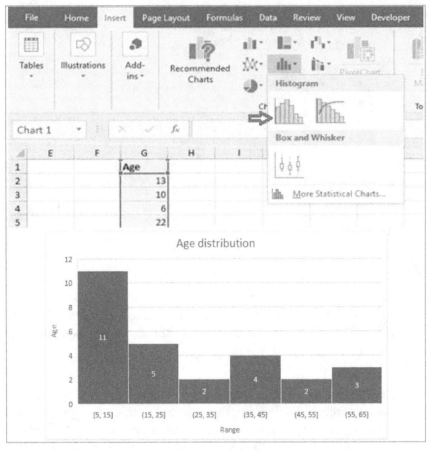

Figure 4.3 *Histogram Chart*

Histogram clearly shows that the most popular age group is 5-15.

4.4 Pareto Chart

The Pareto chart is used to find the largest impact. It is a variation of a bar chart with a combination of a line chart. The bars of the chart represent data values in a descending order while the line chart represents the progression of the cumulative percentage of the total. Using similar data as used while creating the Histogram, we will create a Pareto chart.

To create a Pareto, copy the age values as given in Histogram *sections* (4.3) in a column of a sheet. Select the cell range, go to the **Insert** tab and choose **Histogram** (the right-side chart type) from the **Charts** group.

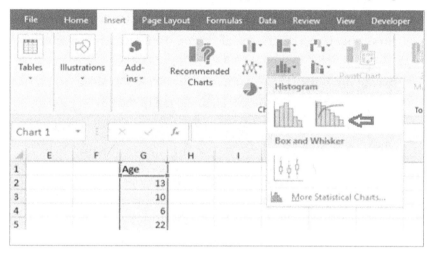

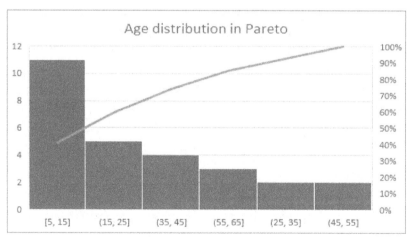

Figure 4.4 *Pareto Chart*

This chart shows the age groups in the order of its highest popularity to the lowest and shows that the top three age categories are 5-15, 15-25, and 35-45 that make up for around 75% of the population coming to the restaurant.

4.5 Box & Whisker Chart

The Box and Whisker chart show how your data is spread out. It is also used in statistics to show the distribution of data into quartiles, also highlighting the mean and outliers, if any. Quartiles are indicated as the following:

- **First quartile**: The horizontal line on the lower whisker (minimum value) up to the bottom line of the box.
- **Second quartile**: The lower line of the box to the Mean.
- **Third quartile**: From the Mean to the top of the box.
- **Last quartile**: The top of the box up to the length of the upper whisker (maximum value).
- **Outliers**: Are plotted as points above or below the length of either of the whiskers. They are suspected to be anomalies, that is, the values that are very high or very low and fall far outside the other values of the data set.

For creating the Box & Whisker chart we will use the data as seen in the following screenshot, with many more data points for plotting the graph.

Month	Date	Region	City	Order No	Category	Product	Price per	Quantity	Total Sale
July	01-07-2018	North	Delhi	1001	Beverages	Lemon Tea	330.00	200	66,000.00
July	01-07-2018	North	Delhi	1002	Beverages	Filter Coffee	257.00	75	19,275.00
July	01-07-2018	North	Delhi	1003	Beverages	Coconut Water	160.00	100	16,000.00
July	01-07-2018	North	Delhi	1004	Snacks	Biscuit	24.00	120	2,880.00
July	01-07-2018	North	Delhi	1005	Snacks	Roasted Almonds	445.00	20	8,900.00
July	06-07-2018	North	Delhi	1006	Snacks	Popcorn	22.00	165	3,630.00
July	07-07-2018	North	Delhi	1007	Sweets	Chocolate	420.00	120	50,400.00
July	08-07-2018	North	Delhi	1008	Sweets	Milk Cake	20.00	100	2,000.00
July	09-07-2018	North	Delhi	1009	Sweets	Candy	33.00	187	6,171.00
July	09-07-2018	North	Delhi	1010	Cooking	Salt	15.00	150	2,250.00
July	11-07-2018	North	Delhi	1011	Cooking	Lentil	63.00	112	7,056.00
July	12-07-2018	North	Delhi	1012	Cooking	Oil	108.00	50	5,400.00
July	13-07-2018	North	Lucknow	1013	Beverages	Lemon Tea	300.00	154	46,200.00
July	14-07-2018	North	Lucknow	1014	Beverages	Filter Coffee	250.00	50	12,500.00
July	15-07-2018	North	Lucknow	1015	Beverages	Coconut Water	112.00	175	19,600.00

Here we want to see the sales distribution for products by their **Category**, hence we will only consider the **Total Sales** values for the Categories. Select the data from the columns named **Category** and **Total Sale**, go to the **Insert** tab and select **Box and Whisker** from the **Charts** group.

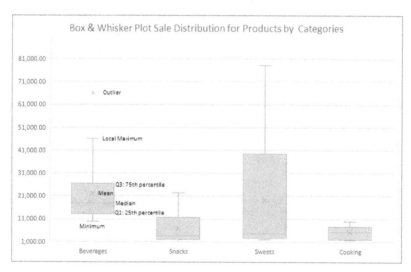

Figure 4.5 *Box & Whisker chart*

In our example, the **Box and Whisker** chart allows us to visualize the variation in sale for each product category as well as where details like the mean and any outliers fall in relation to that variation. There is one outlier for Beverages, whose value is very high and hence it is showing far away from the other values in the data set.

4.6 Treemap Chart

The Treemap Chart is great for visualizing hierarchical data within categories, as compared to other categories. For the data given in the following table, we will create the Treemap chart.

Category	Product	Total Sale
Beverages	Coconut Water	1,22,100.00
	Filter Coffee	1,29,250.00
	Lemon Tea	2,77,329.00
Cooking	Lentil	63,770.00
	Oil	48,268.00
	Salt	15,740.00
Snacks	Biscuit	26,146.00
	Popcorn	15,528.00
	Roasted Almonds	1,23,400.00
Sweets	Candy	34,378.00
	Chocolate	4,10,440.00
	Milk Cake	18,520.00

Looking at the data in the above table, even though grouped by category, the best or worst sales volume or trend is not evident at a glance. While if we create a Treemap chart for this data, we can clearly see that Beverages has the best sales at category level.

To create a Treemap, go to the **Insert** tab and select **Treemap** from the **Charts** group

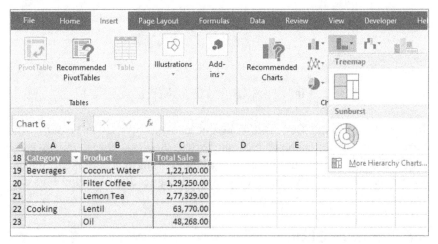

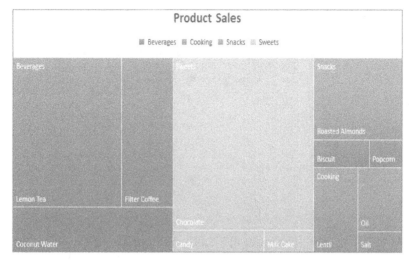

Figure 4.6 *Treemap Chart*

4.7 Sunburst Chart

The Sunburst Chart provides a hierarchical visualization of data which represents data in the form of concentric circles. When visualizing data that is organized into multiple levels of categories, the Sunburst chart shows how outer rings relate to inner rings.

We will create the Sunburst chart using the same data set used for the Treemap chart. To create, go to the **Insert** tab and select **Sunburst** from the **Charts** group.

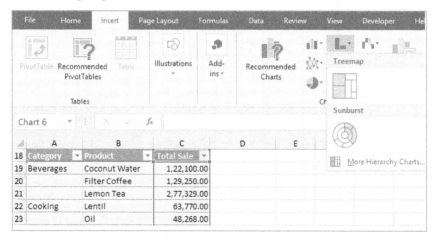

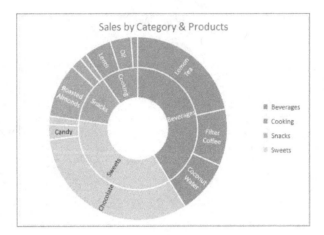

Figure 4.7 *Sunburst Chart*

4.8 Sparkline Chart

Sparklines are not new in Excel 2016 but are very helpful inline charts that we will discuss. They are tiny charts placed in single cells, each representing a row of data in your selection and provide a quick way to see trends. Sparklines are of three types; Line, Column, and Win/Loss.

Select the data for which the Sparklines are to be created. Preferably, position a sparkline near its data for greatest impact which is, in the next empty cell. A Quick Analysis button appears on the right bottom corner of the selected data, click on sparklines and then the type you want to create, for example Column in this case.

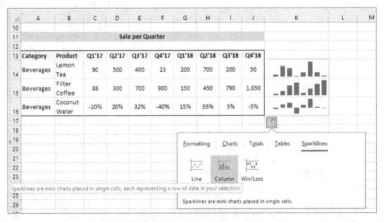

Figure 4.8 *Sparkline Chart*

You can change the sparkline design with existing styles by specifying what to show: **High Point / Low Point / First Point / Last Point / Negative Point** and also change the sparkline / marker colors.

In the Design tab, under the group **Show**, tick the checkboxes for **High Point, Low Point, First Point, Last Point** and **Negative Points** so that they are visible in the Sparkline chart.

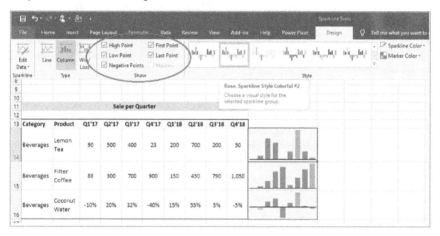

To change the Sparkline colors, in the Design tab go to group Style and for each marker point under **Marker Color** select the theme color of your choice.

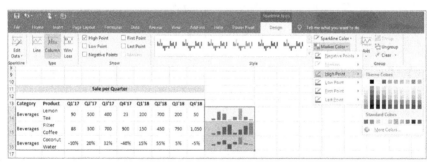

Figure 4.9 *Sparkline Designs*

Similarly, we can create Line and Win/Loss Sparklines. Each row can have a different type as shown below by selecting the row data and then inserting the required sparkline.

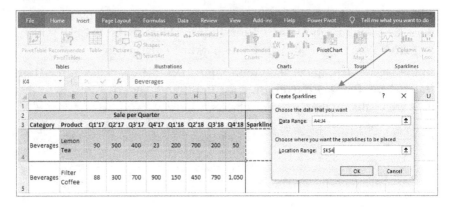

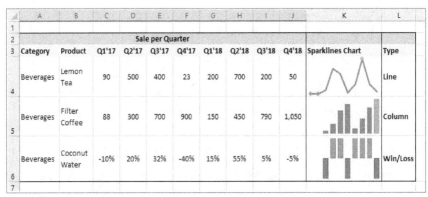

Figure 4.10 *Different Sparklines on each row*

4.9 3D Map

3D Map is a three-dimensional data visualization tool that lets you look at information in new ways. In earlier versions of Excel 2013, this was an add-in '3-D geospatial visualization' but it has been fully integrated now in Excel 2016. For creating a 3D map, your data should have geographic properties like the names of cities, countries, zip codes, longitude or latitude coordinates and so on. which can be mapped to the 3D map. It requires data to be in an Excel table format, where each row is a unique record and each column has a heading.

4.9.1 Create a Tour

We will create a 3D Map using sample data with a list of states and their estimated population. Note that the sample data we are using is in an Excel table format as required and has a column **State** that has a geographic property. To insert the 3D Maps, click on any cell within the table and go to the **Insert tab 3D Map** option under Tours. Click on **Open 3D Maps** and a new window is launched. 3D Maps uses Bing to geocode your data based on its geographic properties. After a few seconds, the globe will appear next to the first screen of the Layer Pane. When you start 3D Maps from a workbook that doesn't already contain a tour, a new tour with a single scene is automatically created. Tours and scenes are the basic way to save the 3D Maps visualizations of your data. You can have multiple Tours in a workbook and multiple Scenes in a Tour.

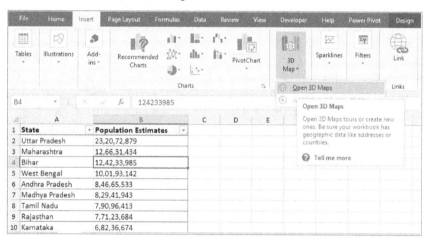

Figure 4.11 *3D Map sample data*

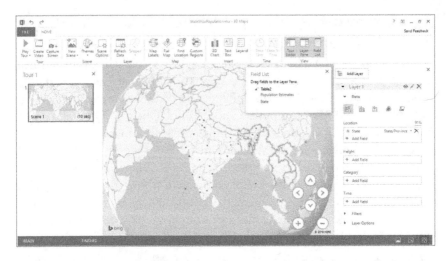

In the Layer pane, on the right-hand side, Layer 1 is shown by default. Since we want to depict the state wise population estimate, under **Location** select **State**. Now we will add fields in other parameters like **Population Estimates** for **Height** and **State** for **Category**. The data is plotted on the map that is, population estimates are shown as columns on the map region identified by the state name. Color legend is also shown for Layer 1.

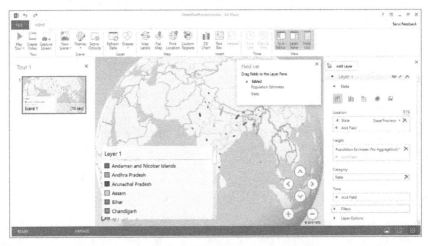

We can customize the look and feel of the map like; change the size or move the Layer 1 legend, Zoom in and out of the map using the plus and minus sign, Rotate left/right, tilt up and down using the arrows, change

Chart Type from column to a bubble chart using the option under Data in layer pane, change the Theme and add **Map Labels**.

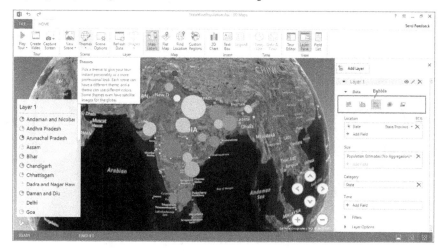

Figure 4.12 *3D Map - Tour*

Close the 3D Map window to Save. This is saved as a Tour named **Tour 1**, which can be opened again by going to **Insert ➔ 3D ➔ Map ➔ Open 3D Maps**.

4.9.2 Create a New Scene

We can add a **New Scene** to **Tour 1** by using the **New Scene** option in the 3D Maps window. Using the same process as before we created the 3D Map, except that here we are using columns for data and filtered this data (using the Add Filter option) to display only those states in a specified population range.

Multiple scenes can be created for different views of the same data. For each scene you can have a different setting, like the time duration for how long the scene will play, name of the scene preferable describing the data visualization, transition duration, effect and the speed of the effect, and the map type. **Scene Options** is available on the main menu's **Home** tab and also available on each Scene under the **Tour** pane on the left-hand side. The Tour name can also be changed by a single click on the name and typing the new name.

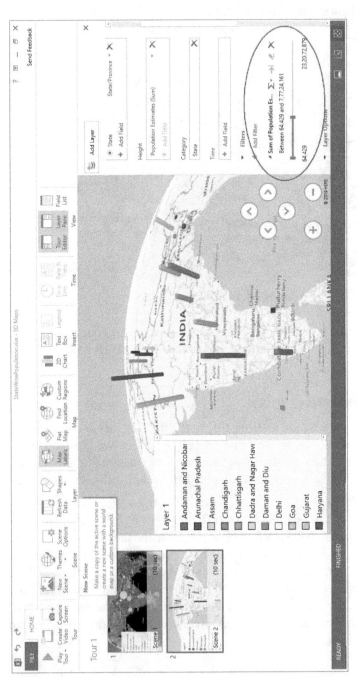

Figure 4.13 *3D Map - Scene*

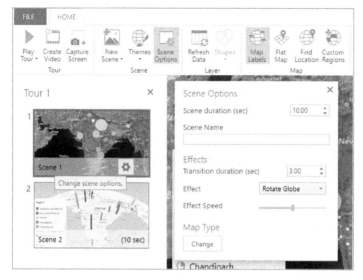

Figure 4.14 *3D Map – Scene options*

4.9.3 Play Tour/Scene, Create Video

After the Tours and Scenes are created, you can play them using **Play Tour** option or create a video for your presentations using the **Create Video** option in the 3D Map window.

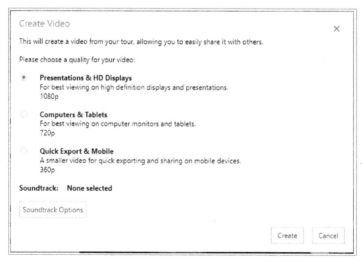

Figure 4.15 *3D Map: Create Video*

You can choose the quality of the video by selecting any of the available options. It also gives an option to add a Soundtrack with the Video.

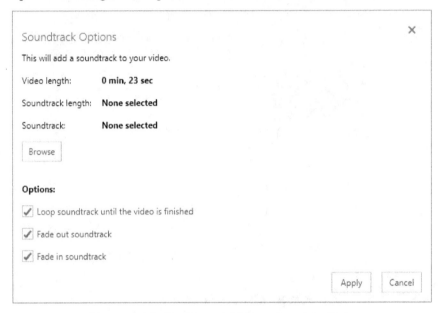

Figure 4.16 *3D Map: Add Soundtrack to Video*

Browse the audio file and click **Apply** to add the soundtrack. Then click **Create** on the **Create Video** dialog box to save the video in the selected location. The video is saved as an **.MP4** file. You can share your tour with people who don't have a version of Excel that supports 3D Maps, when you want to show it on the web through a media player or run it on a large monitor as a video file without using Excel.

CHAPTER 5

Gantt and Milestone Chart

A Gantt chart is a very important and popular tool of project management that helps you in planning and scheduling project activities or tasks required to achieve the project objective/goal and then helps in tracking its progress against time. Gantt includes details for each activity, like the duration of the activity, timeline of the activity, (which are its start and finish dates), resources attached to the activity (man power, hardware or software), relationship with other activities (dependencies), and so on.

You can create a Gantt to whatever detailed level required, it can have activities broken down to a 2-day duration or even less. It can thus have multiple line items, sometimes going up to 20, 50 or even a couple of hundred lines. Which is good for tracking details but not easy to monitor the overall project progress. Hence in project schedules, Milestones are identified. A Milestone is an activity with a fixed date but no duration, indicating a point in the project (noting down the start or finish of an activity or set of activities) marking the completion of a major phase of work or a branching decision point within a project. The Milestone Chart is a very helpful visual or graphical tool for monitoring the overall project health using milestones and good indicators or measures for reporting progress.

5.1 Creating a Gantt Chart in Excel

A Gantt Chart in Excel can be created either by typing data in a sheet, writing formulas, and creating bar charts and so on, or by using the existing templates. Using templates is not only easier, its faster and efficient. Launch Microsoft Excel, go to the **File** menu and click on **New**. On the right-hand pane a list of the existing templates is seen. Type **gantt** in the search box and you will see the available templates.

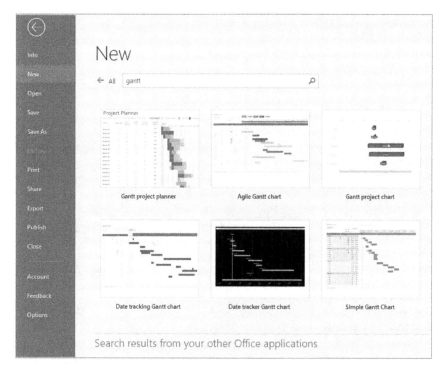

Select **Simple Gantt Chart** and click **Create** in the dialog box to start the process.

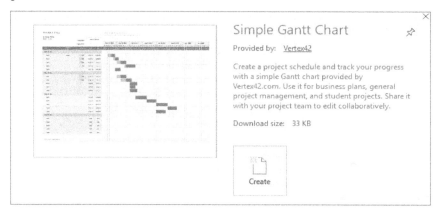

Excel will download the template and create a new workbook for you to use for your project.

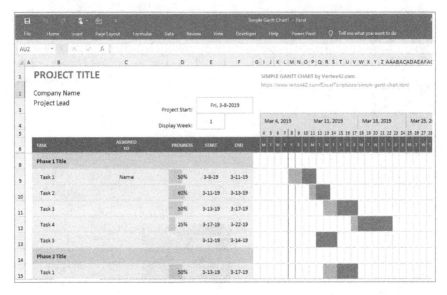

You can modify the project details like, **Company Name, Project Lead, Project Start date**, and **Display timeline**. Type your activities, owners of those activities, start and end date and percentage of completion of the activities. Based on the input data on the left-hand side the horizontal bars change on the right-hand side, as seen in the following screenshot. Save the file at the desired location for future tracking.

Figure 5.1 *Gantt Chart in Excel*

You can try the different templates available in Excel or via partners and modify them as per your requirements. Even complex Gantt charts can be created in Excel but it is not an easy task. Microsoft also has a standalone **Microsoft Project** software, a full fledge project management tool that is used by many organizations for project planning. Since both are from Microsoft, Gantt in Excel can be imported into Microsoft Project and the schedules made in Microsoft Project can be exported in Excel format.

5.2 Creating a Milestone Chart in Excel

We want to create a Milestone chart for a project in Excel as per the details given below, in the Project Milestones Table (including dates, name, and owners) and the desired output that is the Milestone Chart. X-Axis is the timeline and the different Milestones are plotted on the Y-axis.

Date	Activity	Owner
Mar-19	Inputs	Mktng
Mar-19	Kick-off Mtng	Engr
Apr-19	Final SRS	Engr
May-19	Final Design	Engr
Jul-19	Final Code	Engr
Aug-19	Final Testing	Val
Sep-19	Deliver	Val
Nov-19	Deploy	Field
Dec-19	Feedback	QA

Figure 5.2 *Project Milestones Table*

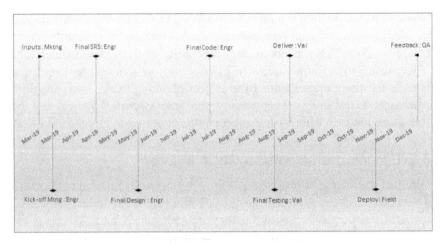

Figure 5.3 *Milestone Chart*

Following are the steps for creating the Milestones chart:

Step 1: Consolidate the Milestone data in a sheet and prepare data for creating the chart.

	A	B	C	D	E	F
1						
2		Date	Activity	Owner	Milestone + Owner	Text Placement
3		Mar-19	Inputs	Mktng	Inputs : Mktng	10
4		Mar-19	Kick-off Mtng	Engr	Kick-off Mtng : Engr	-10
5		Apr-19	Final SRS	Engr	Final SRS : Engr	10
6		May-19	Final Design	Engr	Final Design : Engr	-10
7		Jul-19	Final Code	Engr	Final Code : Engr	10
8		Aug-19	Final Testing	Val	Final Testing : Val	-10
9		Sep-19	Deliver	Val	Deliver : Val	10
10		Nov-19	Deploy	Field	Deploy : Field	-10
11		Dec-19	Feedback	QA	Feedback : QA	10
12						-10
13						10
14						-10
15						

Columns for **Date, Activity,** and **Owner** are as per the original data (as seen in *Figure 5.2*). The added two columns will be used later. Since we want to show **Activity** with its **Owner** in the chart, we have CONCATENATED the texts from both the columns in column E.

E3				f_x	=CONCATENATE(C3," : ",D3)	

	A	B	C	D	E	F
1						
2		Date	Activity	Owner	Milestone + Owner	Text Placement
3		Mar-19	Inputs	Mktng	Inputs : Mktng	10
4		Mar-19	Kick-off Mtng	Engr	Kick-off Mtng : Engr	-10

Column F which are the **Text Placement** values, will be used to plot the Milestones alternatively in the upper and lower halves of the timeline axis, for the display to be clear and neat.

Step 2: Go to the **Insert** tab and in the **Charts** group select **Line Chart with Markers**.

It will create a blank chart. Now to add data, go to the **Design** tab and click on **Select Data**.

Step 3: In the Select Data Source dialog box, click on **Add** to insert a series and enter the following:

Series Name = Date

Series Values = E3:E11 (i.e., *milestone + owner name*)

This inserts a line chart with its X-axis values as 1,2,3, …,9 and Y-axis values as 0.

Now in the Select Data Source dialog box, click on 'Edit' from the **Horizontal (Category) Axis Labels** and select the cell range B3:B11 that is the milestone dates.

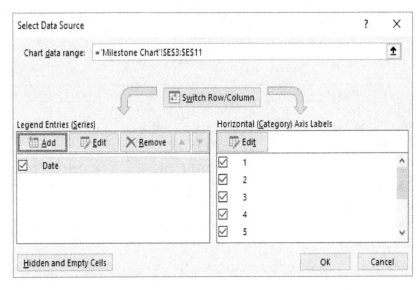

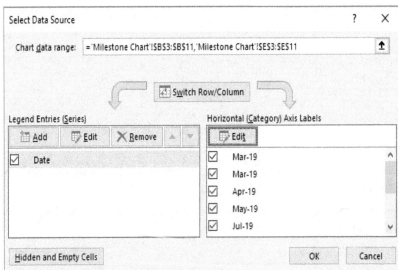

Now, the X-axis displays the dates instead of numbers 1,2,3 .... 9.

Step 4: In the **Select Data Source** dialog box, click on **Add** and in the **Edit Series** dialog box, enter the following:

Series Name = Activity

Series Values = F3:F11 (i.e., *text placement values*)

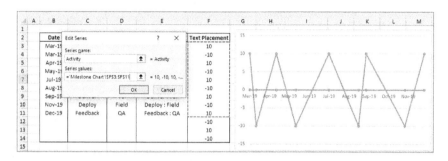

This creates a haphazard line chart.

Step 5: Now we will change the haphazard line to a column chart. Select the **Activity** series and right click on **Change Series chart type…** and select the **Column** chart.

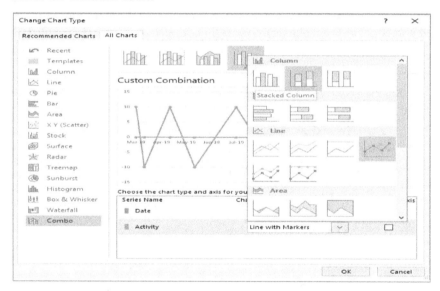

This creates a column chart.

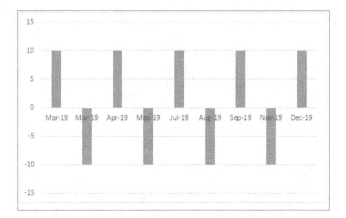

Step 6: Right click on the data bar and select **Format Data Series**. In the series option pane, select Secondary Axis in the **Plot Series on** option. A new secondary vertical axis on the right of the chart is inserted. But we do not want to see that, hence click on it and delete it.

Step 7: Go to the **Design** tab and click on **Select Data**. For the **Activity** series, click on **Edit** from the **Horizontal (Category) Axis Labels** and select the cell range E3:E11.

Now we will format the data bars. Select the data bars and right-click to select the option **Format Data Labels**. Uncheck all options and only select the **Category Name** check box and **Inside End** for the label position.

Step 8: Again, select the data bars. Go to the **Design** tab, in the **Chart Layouts** group select the option **Add Chart Element** and click on **Error Bars → More Error Bar Options**. In the **Error Bar Options** pane select the options; Vertical Error Bar: Minus, End Style: No Cap and Error Amount: Percentage – 100%

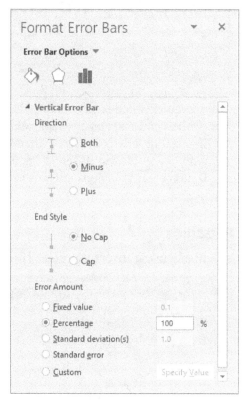

Right click on bars and select **Format Data Series**. In Format Data Series Pane (in Fill and Line) select **No Fill** and **No Border**.

There are many options on changing the look and feel that can be tried for example you can change the background of the chart area as gradient fill as in our example or solid fill, and so on.

CHAPTER 6
SmartArt and Organization Chart

SmartArt graphic helps to quickly and easily make a visual representation of your information as well as construct fancy graphical lists and diagrams in your worksheet. Organization charts are very often created using the SmartArt. In this section we will look at different SmartArt Layouts and create a simple Organization chart to understand how to insert a SmartArt graphic and then modify it.

6.1 SmartArt Graphics

SmartArt option is available in the **Insert** tab, in the **Illustrations** group.

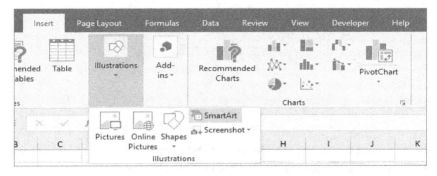

SmartArt has multiple layouts like **List, Hierarchy, Picture,** and so on, each having multiple graphics as seen in the following screenshot:

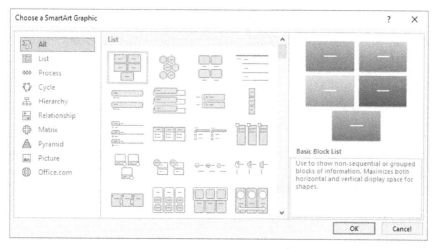

Figure 6.1 *SmartArt Graphic*

You can also view the different graphics based on the different types or categories. The following table has the list of different layouts along with some information to help choose which layout to consider for use.

SmartArt type	Used to
List	Show nonsequential information.
Process	Show steps in a process or timeline; creating a flow chart.
Cycle	Show a continual process.
Hierarchy	Create an organization chart.
Hierarchy	Show a decision tree.
Relationship	Illustrate connections.
Matrix	Show how various parts relate as a whole.
Pyramid	Show proportional relationships with the largest component on the top or bottom.
Picture	Use pictures prominently to convey or accent content.
Office.com	Show additional layouts available on Office.com

After you have inserted your SmartArt graphic, you will see contextual tabs **Design** and **Format** in **SmartArt Tools Ribbon**. Using the settings under these tabs you can modify the look and feel of the graphic added and also add information.

6.2 Organization Chart

Organization chart portrays the reporting structure or relationships in an organization, which can be easily represented using the graphics in the Hierarchy layout.

6.2.1 Insert Graphic

Select the worksheet in which you want to insert the SmartArt and go to the **Insert** tab, under the **Illustrations** group and select the **SmartArt** option. Under the layout **Hierarchy**, select any of the graphics that you think is a good representation as per your requirements.

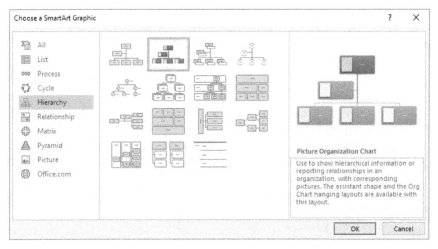

For our example we will use the Picture Organization chart and click **OK**. This inserts graphics in the sheet as seen in the following screenshot:

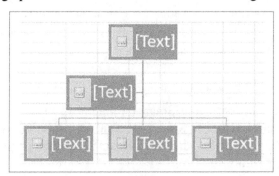

6.2.2 Change Layout, Color & Text

Click [Text] in the SmartArt Text pane, and then type your text. Click on the picture icon to insert pictures from either a file on your system, a Bing image search, or OneDrive.

Using the **SmartArt Tools** ➔ **Design** ➔ **Change Colors** option we changed the graphics to have different colors for the head of the organization and the team below.

We can also change the layout using any of the options available; we changed it from picture to **Name** and **Tile** organization. You will see that the text remains the same even on change.

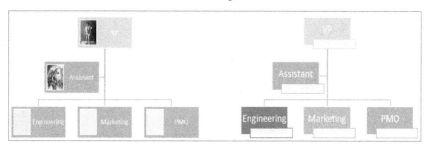

Figure 6.2 *Picture organization chart and Name and Title organization chart*

6.2.3 Add/Delete Boxes

You can add new boxes before, after, below, or above the selected box and also add an assistant to the selected box using the options under **Add Shape**.

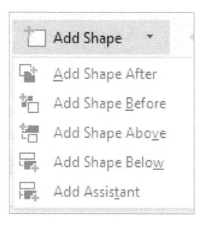

Select the VP box and go to **SmartArt Tools** ➔ **Design** ➔ **Add Shape** or right-click and select Add Shape and click on **Add Shape Above**. Similarly select the VP box each time and click on the other options to add the box before, above, and so on.

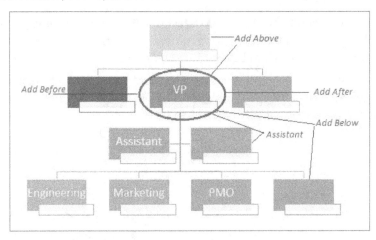

Figure 6.3 *Add boxes*

For the second assistant added, we will change the shape. Select the box, right-click and select the option **Change Shape** and click on the desired shape, we selected oval. Also, to change the color, right click and select **Format Shape** and use **Fill** to change the color to orange.

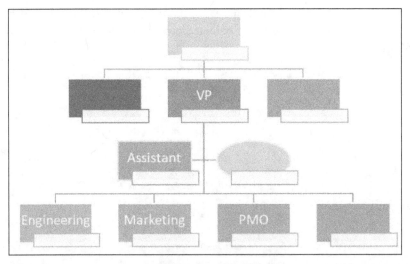

You can also Delete a box by selecting the new assistant box that was added, then right-click and click on Cut or press the *delete* button on keyboard.

6.2.4 Move Boxes

We can move the boxes within the chart using options **Promote, Demote, Move Up** and **Move Down** under the **SmartArt Tools → Design → Create Graphics** options. We have the organization chart as seen in the following screenshot and using this we will see how to use these options.

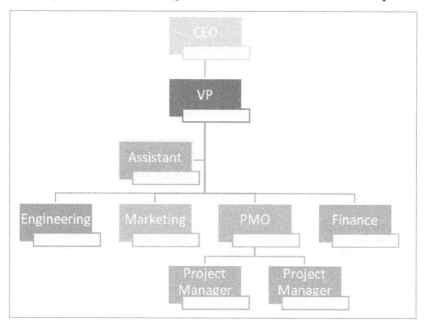

Following are the changes we want to make and the options we will use.

- Move the **Finance** box close to the **Marketing** box. Select the **Finance** box and use the **Move Up** option to move towards the left side. Similarly, **Move Down** moves the box to the right.
- There is a change in the organization and now PMO has to go under CEO. Select the PMO box and use the option **Promote**. PMO comes under the CEO, in alignment with the VP.

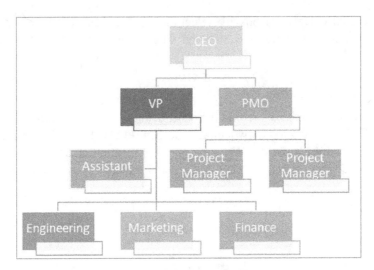

Figure 6.4 *Promote Box*

Note, when we promoted the PMO hierarchy the structure remained the same. But now if you want to bring the PMO structure down under VP again, you will need to select the PMO box as along with the two Project Manager boxes and click **Demote**.

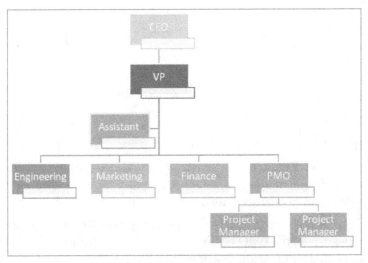

If we only select the PMO box as shown in Figure 6.4 and click **Demote**, all the three boxes that is the PMO and the two Project Managers will come under the VP box.

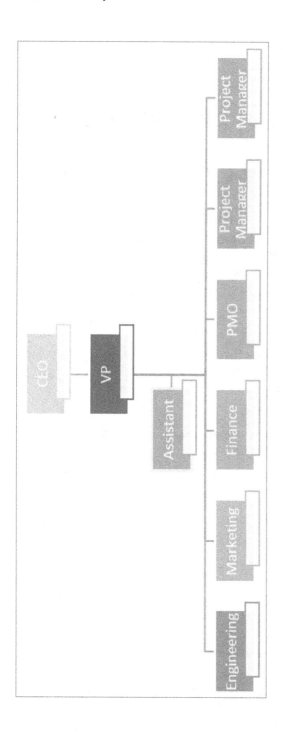

CHAPTER 7

Putting Data in perspective with Pivots

Pivot table is a simple but very powerful tool to summarize and analyze data and helps making decisions based on it. Generally, the problem is not the lack of data; instead, it's making sense out of the huge amount of data collected overtime. With the help of an example, this section will demonstrate the use of advanced Pivot table techniques.

7.1 Verify the Source

First step before starting to use a Pivot is to *scrub and organize your raw data* that will be the source for creating the Pivot. The source data should be verified for the following:

- no blank rows or columns.
- no missing data (preferably add an estimated value based on similar data in table if the actual is not available).
- unique column headers and only on one row.
- no duplicates.
- data organized in a tabular format that is into rows and columns.

7.2 Format Data for Sync

The best practice is to *format the data as Excel Table*, so that the data range becomes dynamic. A dynamic range will automatically expand and shrink the table as you add or remove data, and the corresponding Pivot table will always be in sync with your source data. Hence no data will get missed from your analysis and the changes will be reflected immediately in your Pivot.

To format data as Excel Table, select any cell in the dataset and use the shortcut key *CTRL+T* to create the table.

	A	B	C	D	E	F	G	H	I	J
1	Month	Date	Region	City	Category	Product	Price per	Quantity	Returned	Total Sale
2	July	01-07-2018	North	Delhi	Beverages	Lemon Tea	330.00	200	10	66,000.00
3	July	01-07-2018	North	Delhi	Beverages	Filter Coffe	257.00	75	4	19,275.00
4	July	01-07-2018	North	Delhi	Beverages	Coconu				16,000.00
5	July	01-07-2018	North	Delhi	Snacks	Biscuit				2,880.00
6	July	01-07-2018	North	Delhi	Snacks	Roaste				8,900.00
7	July	06-07-2018	North	Delhi	Snacks	Popcor				3,630.00
8	July	07-07-2018	North	Delhi	Sweets	Chocol				50,400.00
9	July	08-07-2018	North	Delhi	Sweets	Milk Ca				2,000.00
10	July	09-07-2018	North	Delhi	Sweets	Candy				6,171.00
11	July	09-07-2018	North	Delhi	Cooking	Salt				2,250.00
12	July	11-07-2018	North	Delhi	Cooking	Lentil	63.00	112	6	7,056.00
13	July	12-07-2018	North	Delhi	Cooking	Oil	108.00	50	3	5,400.00
14	July	13-07-2018	North	Lucknow	Beverages	Lemon Tea	300.00	154	8	46,200.00
15	July	14-07-2018	North	Lucknow	Beverages	Filter Coffe	250.00	50	3	12,500.00
16	July	15-07-2018	North	Lucknow	Beverages	Coconut Wa	112.00	175	9	19,600.00

Create Table dialog:
Where is the data for your table?
= $A$1:$J$97
☑ My table has headers
[OK] [Cancel]

Figure 7.1 *Format data as table*

7.3 Recommended Pivot Tables

Create the Pivot table using the option **Summarize with Pivot Table** from Table Tool's Design menu

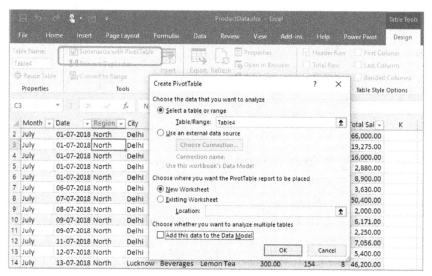

Figure 7.2 *Create Pivot*

Excel also gives the option of **Recommended Pivot Tables**. Based on the source data, Excel creates multiple Pivot Tables for you to choose from. This is a faster, time saving option and a good start point to work on Pivots.

You can start by selecting any one of the recommended Pivot tables and modify it. Or you can choose a Blank Pivot table and add columns, rows, and values as required.

Figure 7.3 *Recommended Pivot*

7.4 Adding Slicers & Timelines

Slicers, introduced in Excel 2010, are a powerful tool to filter and refine data included in the Pivot. To insert a Slicer, click anywhere within the Pivot table that you created and go to **PivotTable Tools** ➔ **Analyze tab** ➔ **Insert Slicers**.

Note that in case the **Insert Slicers / Timeline** options are greyed out, try the keyboard shortcut keys '*CTRL + 6*'.

With the help of different scenarios, we will understand the usefulness and usage of slicers and timelines.

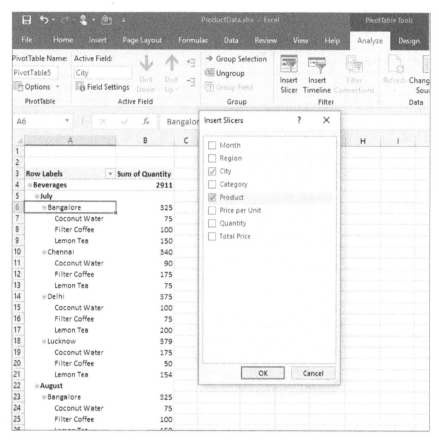

Figure 7.4 *Inserting Slicer*

Scenario Qs.: Without changing the Pivot table above, how can we view the total quantity for combination of Cities & Products on the click of a button?

Answer: Insert a Slicer and select the City and **Product** checkboxes and click **OK**. Now, assuming you want to see the total quantity of Lemon Tea sold in **Bangalore** and **Delhi** in different months, select **Bangalore** and **Delhi** in **City** slicer (hold the *CTRL* key for multiple selections) and **Lemon Tea** in **Product** slicer.

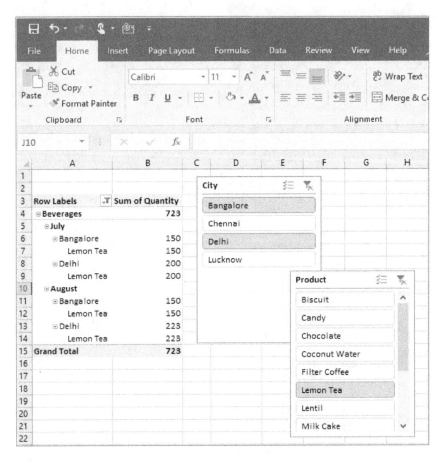

Scenario Qs.: Without changing the Pivot table, how can we view the total quantity of Products on a given date/dates with the click of a button?

Answer: Insert Timelines (go to **PivotTable Tools → Analyze tab → Insert Timeline**) and select the **Date** option. Timelines are special type of slicers, using which you can view information based on dates or for specific time periods. Note that you can use Timelines only if the original data has the date formatted as **Date** in the Excel.

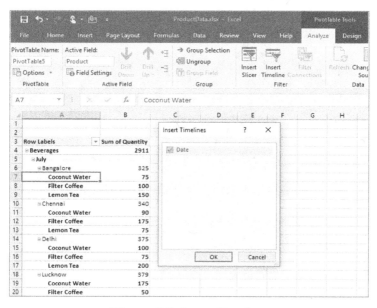

Figure 7.5 *Insert Timeline*

You can view data via Timelines for **YEARS, QUARTERS, MONTHS,** or **DAYS** based on the selection made.

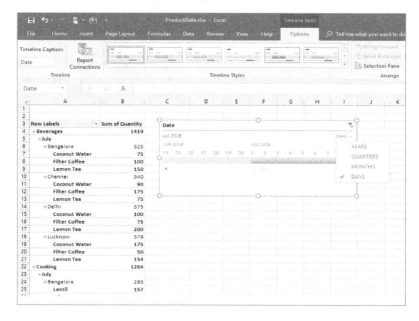

Now, if we want to view data for a duration, say from 6th Jul to 10th July, then we will select the month and the dates in the Timeline.

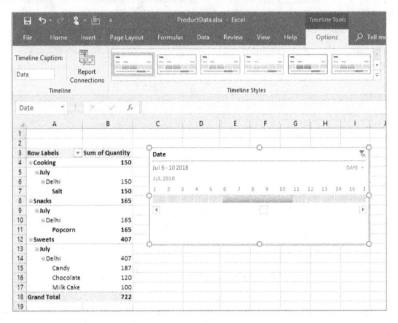

If we want to see the month total, then first select **MONTH** instead of **DAYS** from the upper right options and then select the desired month to view data.

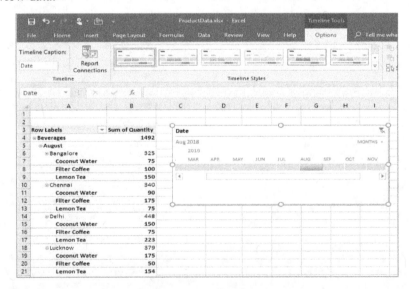

7.5 Adding Calculated Fields in Pivot

Calculated fields allow you to add additional information in your Pivot Table that was not in the original data but derived from it.

In the original data (see *Figure 7.1*) we have Product information related to the Price per Unit and number of Returned Units (could be due to a defect or some other reason) and now we want to know what is the **Return Loss** from the Pivot, which is not there in the original data.

We can create a Calculated field by navigating to **PivotTables Tools** ➔ **Analyze** ➔ **Fields, Items & Sets** ➔ **Calculated Fields**. Give a name to the new field, say **Return Loss** in our case, and in the Formula field add a formula constituting the existing fields by clicking the **Insert Field** button; then add the new calculated field in Pivot by clicking **Add** button.

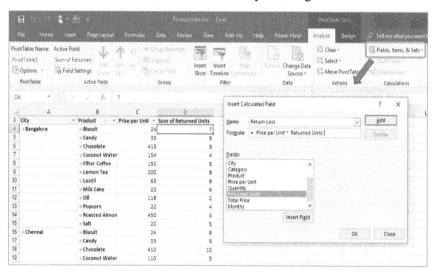

Figure 7.6 *Insert Calculated field in Pivot*

	A	B	C	D	E
2					
3	City ▾	Product ▾	Price per Unit ▾	Sum of Returned Units	Sum of Return Loss
4	⊟ Bangalore	⊟ Biscuit	24	7	168
5		⊟ Candy	33	5	165
6		⊟ Chocolate	415	5	2075
7		⊟ Coconut Water	154	4	616
8		⊟ Filter Coffee	150	5	750
9		⊟ Lemon Tea	200	8	1600
10		⊟ Lentil	63	8	504
11		⊟ Milk Cake	20	6	120
12		⊟ Oil	118	2	236
13		⊟ Popcorn	22	4	88
14		⊟ Roasted Almon	450	3	1350
15		⊟ Salt	20	5	100

7.6 Group Field in Pivot

We can group similar items in Pivot, without adding any new field in the original data, by using the Group field option from **PivotTable Tools →** **Analyse → Group field**. Grouping is another useful tool for analyzing data from perspectives by viewing data based on criteria, range, and so on.

Scenario Qs.: The following Pivot Table and chart depict the sale done on a specific date. We want to know in which price range products have the maximum sale. Currently it's not easy as both table and chart do not give us any meaningful information for any discussion or decision making.

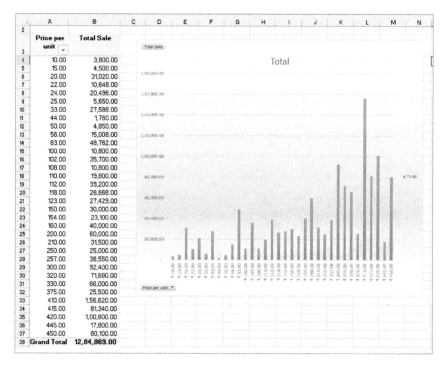

	A	B	C	D	E	F	G	H	I	J	K	L	M	N
2	Price per unit ▾	Total Sale												
3														
4	10.00	3,800.00												
5	15.00	4,500.00												
6	20.00	31,020.00												
7	22.00	10,648.00												
8	24.00	20,496.00												
9	25.00	5,650.00												
10	33.00	27,588.00												
11	44.00	1,760.00												
12	50.00	4,850.00												
13	56.00	15,008.00												
14	63.00	48,762.00												
15	100.00	10,800.00												
16	102.00	35,700.00												
17	108.00	10,800.00												
18	110.00	19,800.00												
19	112.00	39,200.00												
20	118.00	26,668.00												
21	123.00	27,429.00												
22	150.00	30,000.00												
23	154.00	23,100.00												
24	160.00	40,000.00												
25	200.00	60,000.00												
26	210.00	31,500.00												
27	250.00	25,000.00												
28	257.00	38,550.00												
29	300.00	92,400.00												
30	320.00	71,680.00												
31	330.00	66,000.00												
32	375.00	25,500.00												
33	410.00	1,56,620.00												
34	415.00	81,340.00												
35	420.00	1,00,800.00												
36	445.00	17,800.00												
37	450.00	80,100.00												
38	Grand Total	12,84,869.00												

Answer: Use the **Group Field** option for grouping the **Price per Unit** in a range, such that we get total sale for a range. The range can be decided by the user, although by default, based on the minimum and maximum values, Excel recommends a range.

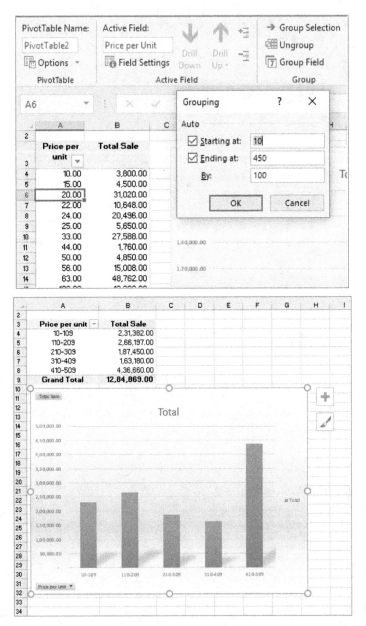

Figure 7.7 *Grouping in Pivot*

Note: What you have grouped can be ungrouped using the Ungroup option.

7.7 Interactive Dashboard with Pivot Tables, Charts and Slicers

In above sections we discussed the different Pivot features. In this section however we will discuss interactive dashboards that is, pivot tables and charts connected to slicers that give different perspectives based on selection. For the same data used in previous examples in this chapter, first we will create different Pivot Tables/Charts and Slicers, and then compile them in a dashboard.

Pivot Table/Chart #1 – City Wise - Total Sale (as percentage):

Create the Pivot table as explained in earlier sections, with City in Rows and **Total Sale** in the Values field. To convert your **Total Sale** to a percentage, click on any cell in Total Sale and right-click to select the option Show Value as ➜ % of Grand Total. Select the Pivot and add a Pie chart and Slicer for city and region as seen in the following screenshot.

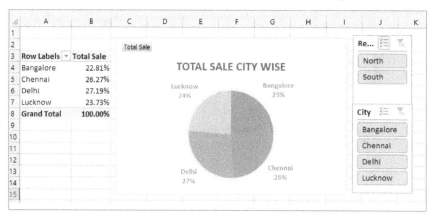

Pivot Table / Chart #2 – Product Wise - Total Sale:

Create a Pivot with Product in Rows and **Total Sale** in the **Value** fields. Then create a Column chart as seen in the following screenshot:

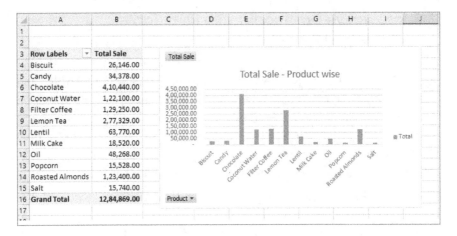

Create a new sheet and name it as **Dashboard**. Copy the Pivot charts and Slicers that we just created, in the new sheet as seen in the following screenshot:

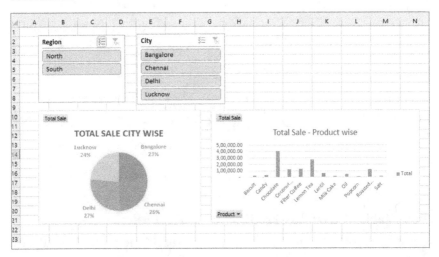

Now we also want a Slicer for month so that we can view data based on the month of sale. In the Dashboard sheet, we will create a Slicer by selecting the Pivot chart. Note that you can create a Slicer by selecting any one of the Pivot table or chart. Select the **Pivot chart Pivot Table / Chart #2** and select from the menu options **Pivot Chart Tools → Analyze → Insert Slicers** and click on **Month**.

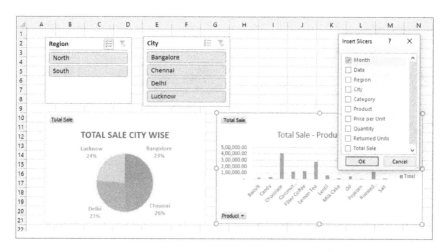

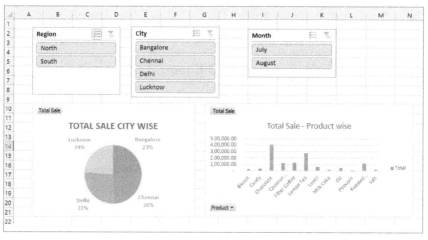

In above Dashboard, currently Slicers are associated with their respective graphs. Next step is to connect the Charts and the Slicers such that we can see the changes in both graphs based on a selection in any of the Slicers.

Firstly, note the Pivot tables names that are associated with the Slicers. In this case they are Pivot 1 and Pivot 4. On each Slicer, right-click and select the menu option **Report Connections** and check the Pivot names to connect.

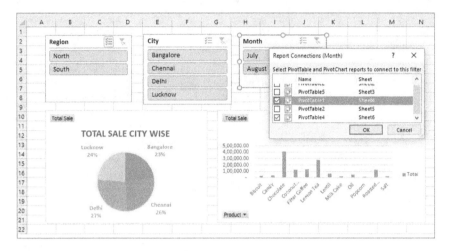

After the connections are made, the Dashboard has become interactive which means, the graphs will change based on the selection in the Slicers.

7.8 Consolidate Data from Different Sources in Pivot

7.8.1 Method #1: Data with Identical Column Structure using Pivot Wizard

Pivot Tables can be used to consolidate data from different sources, be it different sheets of the same workbook or sheets from different workbooks. Only condition is that the sheets should have identical column structure that is, the number and name of columns should be the same in all sheets to be consolidated, while the number of rows can be different.

In the previous sections the data used was for year 2018. Now we will also add similar data of year 2017 for consolidation and yearly comparison purposes. In the workbook we have two sheets named Yr 2017 and Yr 2018. We will use the Pivot Table and Pivot Chart Wizard for consolidating the data from these two sheets.

Note: There is no option available directly on the main menu so we will use the keyboard shortcut keys. Select any cell on a worksheet and press **ALT + D**, and then **press P** that will open the wizard. On the wizard select Multiple consolidation ranges and click **Next**.

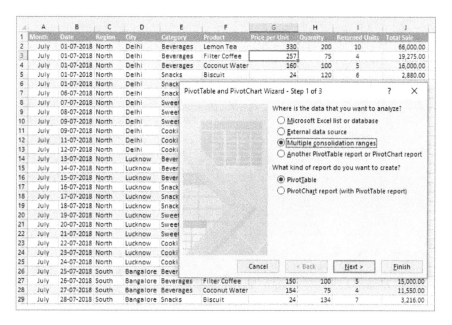

On the next screen select the option **I will create the page fields** and press **Next**.

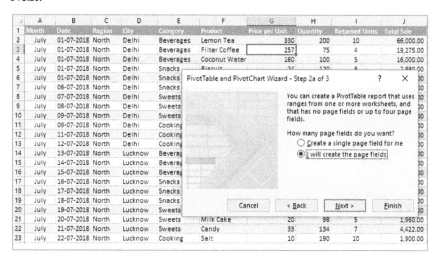

Select the ranges from the different sheets (Yr 2017 and Yr 2018) and press **Add**. Click 1 as the number of Page Fields, select each range, add the item labels, and then press **Next**.

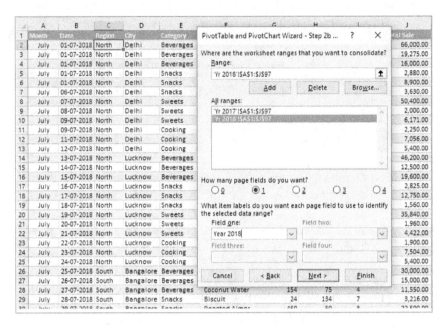

In the next window select the Pivot location and click on **Finish**. A pivot table is created on the worksheet, with the first field in the Row area, and all of the other fields from the source data in the Values area, showing a Count.

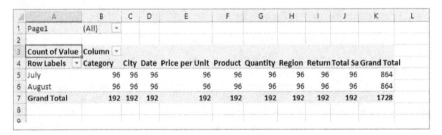

In the preceding format the Month is the first column in the data source and hence the Pivot table row heading shows the months (July, August) while remaining fields (Category, City and so on) are shown in the column area. In case the first column in the data source was the Product, the Pivot table would have made more sense as shown in the following screenshot:

	A	B	C	D	E
1	Page1	(All) ▾			
2					
3	Sum of Value	Column Labels ⊤	Page1	⅗≡	🏹
4	Row Labels ▾	Total Sale	Yr 2017		
5	Biscuit	39,624.04			
6	Candy	52,321.67	Yr 2018		
7	Chocolate	6,18,807.80			
8	Coconut Water	1,87,300.80			
9	Filter Coffee	1,97,401.09			
10	Lemon Tea	4,29,871.12			
11	Lentil	97,578.59			
12	Milk Cake	28,114.77			
13	Oil	72,594.81			
14	Popcorn	24,242.07			
15	Roasted Almonds	1,87,817.03			
16	Salt	24,126.49			
17					

To get the best results, rearrange your columns such that the most important column is to the far left. That column of data will become the Row values in the Pivot table. Columns that you don't want in the Pivot table, move those to the far right in the source data. Do not include those columns when selecting the data ranges for the Pivot table.

7.8.2 Method #2: Data with Identical Column Structure using Microsoft Query

There was a limitation in using the Pivot wizard, which is solved using the Microsoft Query method. Points to remember again are that the sheets should have identical column structure, the data should be in a table format and it's better to give a name to your tables such that they are clearly identifiable in the query. We will use the same data sheets as in previous example that is, sheets named **Yr 2018** and **Yr 2017**. Insert a new sheet for consolidating the data of the query. Click on any cell and go to option **Data → Get External Data → From Other Sources → From Microsoft Query**.

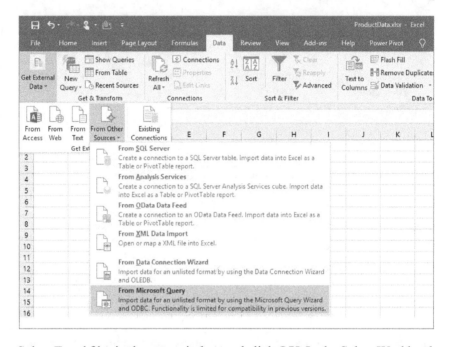

Select Excel files in the next window and click **OK**. In the Select Workbook window browse to your Excel file.

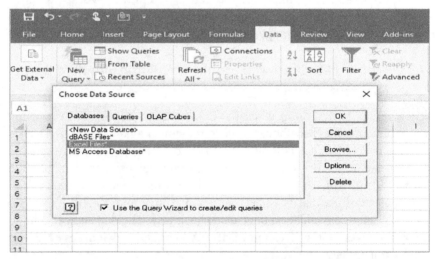

In the Query Wizard select the columns from one of the sheets that you want in the query, add them one by one and then click **Next**.

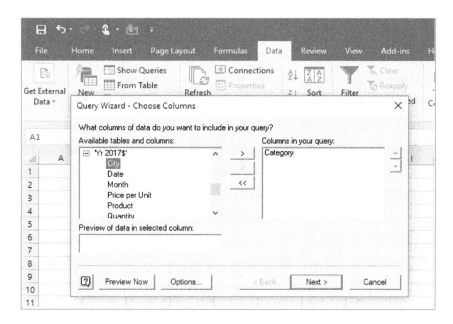

Click **Next** on the **Filter data** and **Sort by** windows. On the last window select the check box **View data** or **edit query in Microsoft query** and **click** on **Finish**.

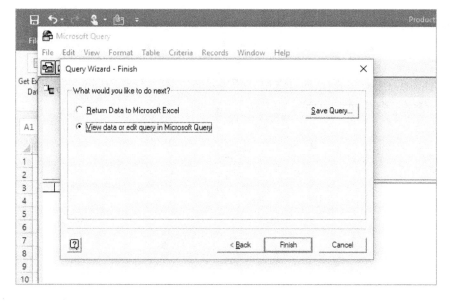

Select the **SQL** option and edit the SQL query to connect data from all the sheets, using the **UNION ALL** option. The format of the query will be as given as follows:

```
SELECT * FROM <<Sheet #1>>
UNION ALL
SELECT * FROM <<Sheet #2>>
```

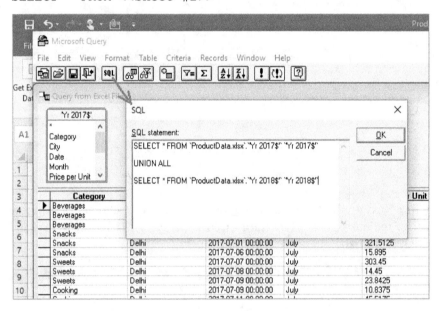

Click **OK** and now the Microsoft Query window will have data of all the sheets. Close the window and wait for few seconds for the next **Import Data** dialog box to come up.

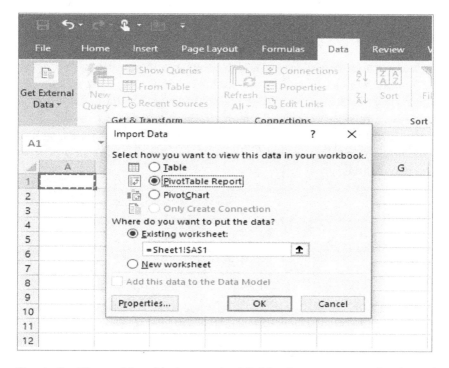

Create the Pivot table with the required fields. As we connect the data of the two sheets the Pivot shows the consolidated data.

	A	B	C	D	E	F	G	H
1	Row Labels ▾	Product	Years	City	Quantity	Price per Unit	Total Sale	
2	⊟Beverages	⊟Coconut Water	⊟2017	Bangalore	135	204.96	13,834.71	
3				Chennai	162	97.90	7,929.90	
4				Delhi	225	218.00	24,228.00	
5				Lucknow	315	121.96	19,208.20	
6			⊟2018	Bangalore	150	308.00	23,100.00	
7				Chennai	180	220.00	19,800.00	
8				Delhi	250	320.00	40,000.00	
9				Lucknow	350	224.00	39,200.00	
10		⊟Filter Coffee	⊟2017	Bangalore	180	199.64	17,967.15	
11				Chennai	315	90.78	14,297.85	
12				Delhi	135	350.16	23,635.97	
13				Lucknow	90	272.23	12,250.13	
14			⊟2018	Bangalore	200	300.00	30,000.00	
15				Chennai	350	204.00	35,700.00	
16				Delhi	150	514.00	38,550.00	
17				Lucknow	100	500.00	25,000.00	

7.8.3 Method #3: Data with Different Column Structure using Pivot

In this section we will combine data from two sheets that have different column structures but have some common columns to show the relationship between them. As in previous examples, modify the data in Table format and give a relevant name to the table. In this example the two data sheets have **SalesInfo** and **VendorInfo** tables and **Order No.** is the common column between the two that will help in creating a relationship between the two datasets.

	A	B	C	D	E	F	G	H	I	K
1	Month	Date	Region	City	Order N	Category	Product	Price per	Quantit	Total Sale
2	July	01-07-2018	North	Delhi	1001	Beverages	Lemon Tea	330.00	200	66,000.00
3	July	01-07-2018	North	Delhi	1002	Beverages	Filter Coffee	257.00	75	19,275.00
4	July	01-07-2018	North	Delhi	1003	Beverages	Coconut Water	160.00	100	16,000.00
5	July	01-07-2018	North	Delhi	1004	Snacks	Biscuit	24.00	120	2,880.00
6	July	01-07-2018	North	Delhi	1005	Snacks	Roasted Almonds	445.00	20	8,900.00
7	July	06-07-2018	North	Delhi	1006	Snacks	Popcorn	22.00	165	3,630.00
8	July	07-07-2018	North	Delhi	1007	Sweets	Chocolate	420.00	120	50,400.00
9	July	08-07-2018	North	Delhi	1008	Sweets	Milk Cake	20.00	100	2,000.00
10	July	09-07-2018	North	Delhi	1009	Sweets	Candy	33.00	187	6,171.00
11	July	09-07-2018	North	Delhi	1010	Cooking	Salt	15.00	150	2,250.00
12	July	11-07-2018	North	Delhi	1011	Cooking	Lentil	63.00	112	7,056.00
13	July	12-07-2018	North	Delhi	1012	Cooking	Oil	108.00	50	5,400.00
14	July	13-07-2018	North	Lucknow	1013	Beverages	Lemon Tea	300.00	154	46,200.00
15	July	14-07-2018	North	Lucknow	1014	Beverages	Filter Coffee	250.00	50	12,500.00
16	July	15-07-2018	North	Lucknow	1015	Beverages	Coconut Water	112.00	175	19,600.00
17	July	16-07-2018	North	Lucknow	1016	Snacks	Biscuit	25.00	113	2,825.00
18	July	17-07-2018	North	Lucknow	1017	Snacks	Roasted Almonds	375.00	34	12,750.00
19	July	18-07-2018	North	Lucknow	1018	Snacks	Popcorn	20.00	78	1,560.00
20	July	19-07-2018	North	Lucknow	1019	Sweets	Chocolate	320.00	112	35,840.00
21	July	20-07-2018	North	Lucknow	1020	Sweets	Milk Cake	20.00	98	1,960.00
22	July	21-07-2018	North	Lucknow	1021	Sweets	Candy	33.00	134	4,422.00

	A	B	C	D	E
1	Order N	City	Product	Vendor Info	
2	1001	Delhi	Lemon Tea	Taj Tea	
3	1002	Delhi	Filter Coffee	Narasus	
4	1003	Delhi	Coconut Water	Narasus	
5	1004	Delhi	Biscuit	Sunfeast	
6	1005	Delhi	Roasted Almonds	Kabila	
7	1006	Delhi	Popcorn	Kabila	
8	1007	Delhi	Chocolate	Dairy Milk	
9	1008	Delhi	Milk Cake	Kabila	
10	1009	Delhi	Candy	Dairy Milk	
11	1010	Delhi	Salt	Tata Sampann	
12	1011	Delhi	Lentil	Tata Sampann	
13	1012	Delhi	Oil	Tata Sampann	
14	1013	Lucknow	Lemon Tea	Taj Tea	
15	1014	Lucknow	Filter Coffee	Narasus	

Click on the first sheet that is, the **SalesInfo** sheet and create a Pivot Table, click the check box for **Add** this data to the **Data Model** and then click **OK**.

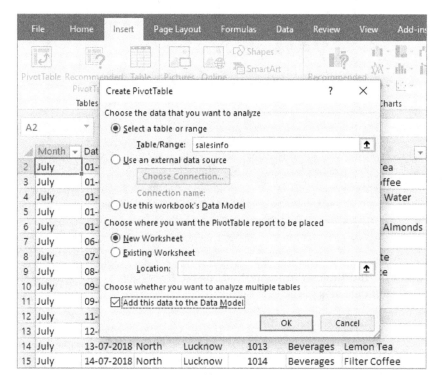

A new Pivot Table is created in a new sheet. In the PivotTable Fields task pane click **ALL** to see all existing tables. But at the moment the tables are not connected, which can be done by navigating to the option **PivotTable Tools → Analyze → Relationships**. On the **Manage Relationship** dialog click on **New**. In the **Create Relationship** dialog box, select the two tables that are to be combined and specify the Primary key which is the **Order No.** in this example.

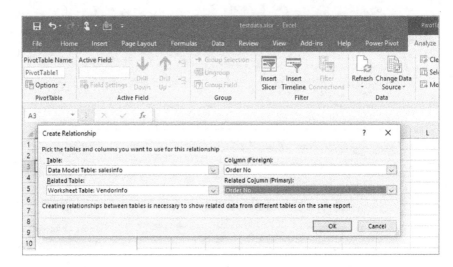

Now that the tables are connected, insert the required fields from the connected data sets in the Pivot table.

	A	B	C	D	E
1					
2					
3	Row Labels ▼	Product	Vendor Info	Total Sale	
4	⊟Bangalore	⊟Biscuit	Sunfeast	6,432.00	
5		⊟Candy	Dairy Milk	6,402.00	
6		⊟Chocolate	Dairy Milk	81,340.00	
7		⊟Coconut Water	Narasus	23,100.00	
8		⊟Filter Coffee	Narasus	30,000.00	
9		⊟Lemon Tea	Taj Tea	60,000.00	
10		⊟Lentil	Tata Sampann	19,782.00	
11		⊟Milk Cake	Kabila	4,920.00	
12		⊟Oil	Tata Sampann	8,732.00	
13		⊟Popcorn	Kabila	3,388.00	
14		⊟Roasted Almonds	Kabila	45,000.00	
15		⊟Salt	Tata Sampann	3,960.00	
16	⊟Chennai	⊟Biscuit	Sunfeast	8,304.00	
17		⊟Candy	Dairy Milk	6,790.00	
18		⊟Chocolate	Dairy Milk	1,56,620.00	

7.9 Using Power Pivot Add-in

Power Pivot is an Excel add-in for powerful data analysis and data modelling. As seen in previous section, in Excel we can also create a Data Model, a collection of tables with relationships. The basic difference between Power Pivot and Excel is that we can create a more sophisticated data model by working on it in the Power Pivot window. It has the ability to work on large volumes of data from various sources, perform information analysis rapidly, and share insights easily. The data model we see in a workbook in Excel is the same data model we see in the Power Pivot window. Any data we import into Excel is available in Power Pivot, and vice versa.

Power Pivot is an Excel add-in that can be installed by navigating to **File → Options → Add-Ins**. In the Manage box select COM Add-Ins and click on Go. Check the **Microsoft Power Pivot for Excel** box, and then click **OK**.

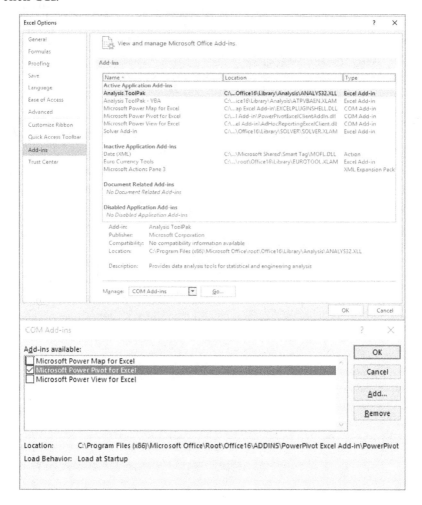

Power Pivot Tab with different options can be seen once the Power Pivot is enabled.

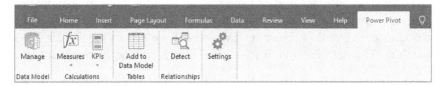

To demonstrate the usage of Power Pivot, we will use the same example as in the previous section where we had two data sheets having **SalesInfo** and **VendorInfo** tables; and the **Order No**. being the common column between the two will help in creating a relationship between the two data sets.

7.9.1 Add to Data Model

First, we will add the two tables into the data model. Select the range of data which is the **SalesInfo** and then navigate to the option **Power Pivot** → **Add to Data Model**. A new pop up window **Power Pivot** opens and you will notice it has several options to edit, modify, and update the data model. Notice that a new tab is created with the table name. Now close the window and select the range of data that is the **VendorInfo** and add it to the data model. In the **Power Pivot** tab, for each data added onto the Data Model, a new tab is created.

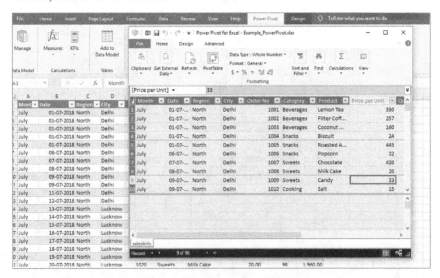

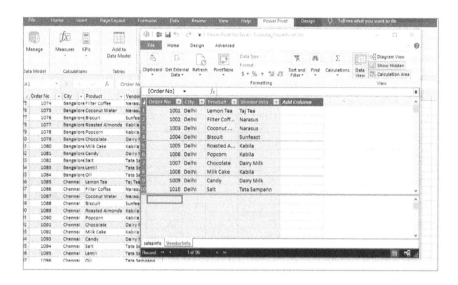

7.9.2 Create a Relationship between Datasets

The common field between the two datasets added to the data model (in this case the Order No.), will be used to create the relationship between them. To see the existing data models, navigate to the option **Power Pivot** ➔ **Manage** to launch the Power Pivot Window to continue working on the datasets.

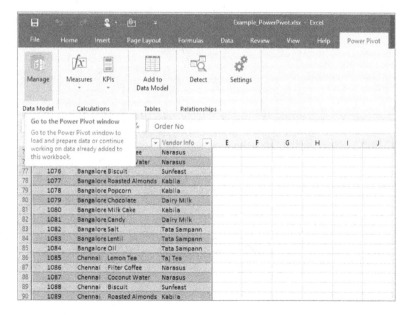

In the Power Pivot Window's Design tab select the **Create Relationship** option. Select the two tables and the common field for creating the relationship and click **OK**.

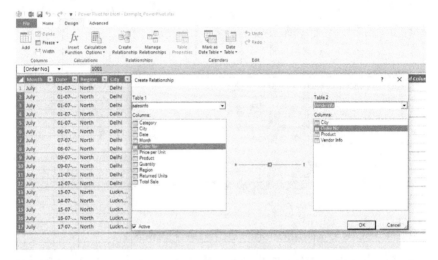

To verify that the relationship between the two datasets have been created correctly, go to the Power Pivot Window's **Home** tab and select the option **Diagram View**. Hover your mouse over the link and the common fields get highlighted in both tables.

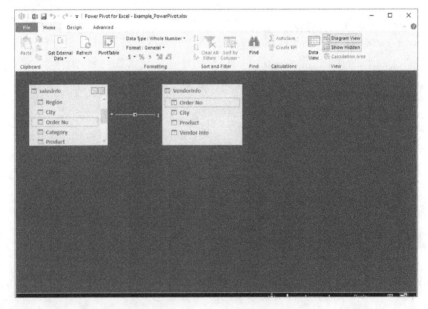

Now to go back to the columnar view and select **Data View**.

7.9.3 Adding Calculated Column

We can also add a calculated column in the Power Pivot data model. In the first cell of the column named **Add Column**, enter the formula. In this example we will calculate the cost of the returned units, which is the **Returned Unit** multiplied by the **Price per Unit**. Enter the formula in this column and press **Enter**.

fx =salesinfo[Returned Units]*salesinfo[Price per Unit]

M...	Date	Region	City	Orde...	Category	Product	Price per Unit	Quan...	Returned Units	Total Sale	Add Column
July	01-07-...	North	Delhi	1001	Beverages	Lemon Tea		330	200	10	66000
July	01-07-...	North	Delhi	1002	Beverages	Filter Coff...		257	75	4	19275
July	01-07-...	North	Delhi	1003	Beverages	Coconut...		160	100	5	16000
July	01-07-...	North	Delhi	1004	Snacks	Biscuit		24	120	6	2880
July	01-07-...	North	Delhi	1005	Snacks	Roasted A...		445	20	1	8900
July	06-07-...	North	Delhi	1006	Snacks	Popcorn		22	165	8	3630
July	07-07-...	North	Delhi	1007	Sweets	Chocolate		420	120	6	50400
July	08-07-...	North	Delhi	1008	Sweets	Milk Cake		20	100	5	2000
July	09-07-...	North	Delhi	1009	Sweets	Candy		33	187	9	6171
July	09-07-...	North	Delhi	1010	Cooking	Salt		15	150	8	2250
July	11-07-...	North	Delhi	1011	Cooking	Lentil		63	112	6	7056

A new column is created by the name of **Calculated Column 1** with the desired results for all rows, as shown in the following screenshot screenshot:

Date	Region	City	Order	Category	Product	Price per Unit	Quan...	Returned Units	Total Sale	Calculated Column 1
July 01-07...	North	Delhi	1001	Beverages	Lemon Tea	330	200	10	66000	3300
July 01-07...	North	Delhi	1002	Beverages	Filter Coff...	257	75	4	19275	1028
July 01-07...	North	Delhi	1003	Beverages	Coconut ...	160	100	5	16000	800
July 01-07...	North	Delhi	1004	Snacks	Biscuit	24	120	6	2880	144
July 01-07...	North	Delhi	1005	Snacks	Roasted A...	445	20	1	8900	445
July 06-07...	North	Delhi	1006	Snacks	Popcorn	22	165	8	3630	176
July 07-07...	North	Delhi	1007	Sweets	Chocolate	420	120	6	50400	2520
July 08-07...	North	Delhi	1008	Sweets	Milk Cake	20	100	5	2000	100
July 09-07...	North	Delhi	1009	Sweets	Candy	33	187	9	6171	297
July 09-07...	North	Delhi	1010	Cooking	Salt	15	150	8	2250	120
July 11-07...	North	Delhi	1011	Cooking	Lentl	63	112	6	7056	378
July 12-07...	North	Delhi	1012	Cooking	Oil	108	50	3	5400	324
July 13-07...	North	Luckn...	1013	Beverages	Lemon Tea	300	154	8	46200	2400
July 14-07...	North	Luckn...	1014	Beverages	Filter Coff...	250	50	3	12500	750
July 15-07...	North	Luckn...	1015	Beverages	Coconut ...	112	175	9	19600	1008
July 16-07...	North	Luckn...	1016	Snacks	Biscuit	25	113	6	2825	150
July 17-07...	North	Luckn...	1017	Snacks	Roasted A...	375	34	2	12750	750

*fx =salesinfo[Returned Units]*salesinfo[Price per Unit]*

We will rename this column to **Returned Unit Cost** by right-clicking and selecting the **Rename Column option**.

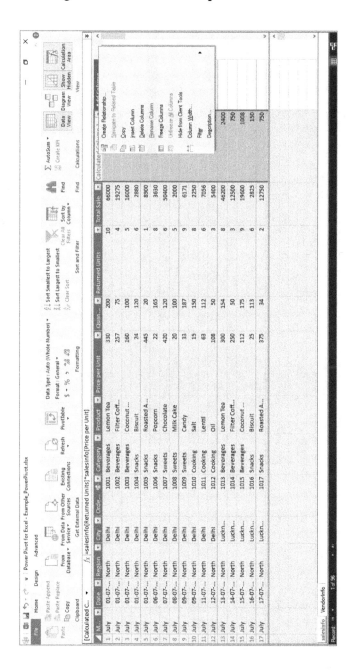

Paste Append | Paste Replace | Copy — Clipboard

From Database | From Data Service | From Other Sources — Get External Data

Existing Connections | Refresh | PivotTable

Data Type : - | Format : - | $ % , .00 .00 — Formatting

Sort A to Z | Sort Z to A | Clear Sort | Clear All Filters | Sort by Column — Sort and Filter

Find — Find

∑ AutoSum | Create KPI — Calculations

Data View | Diagram View | Show Hidden — View

Calculation Area

Date	Region	City	Orde...	Category	Product	Price per Unit	Quan...	Returned Units	Total Sale	Returned Unit Cost
01-07.... July	North	Delhi	1001	Beverages	Lemon Tea	330	200	10	66000	3300
01-07.... July	North	Delhi	1002	Beverages	Filter Coff...	257	75	4	19275	1028
01-07.... July	North	Delhi	1003	Beverages	Coconut. ...	160	100	5	16000	800
01-07.... July	North	Delhi	1004	Snacks	Biscuit	24	120	6	2880	144
01-07.... July	North	Delhi	1005	Snacks	Roasted A...	445	20	1	8900	445
06-07.... July	North	Delhi	1006	Snacks	Popcorn	22	165	8	3630	176
07-07.... July	North	Delhi	1007	Sweets	Chocolate	420	120	6	50400	2520
08-07.... July	North	Delhi	1008	Sweets	Milk Cake	20	100	5	2000	100
09-07.... July	North	Delhi	1009	Sweets	Candy	33	187	9	6171	297
09-07.... July	North	Delhi	1010	Cooking	Salt	15	150	8	2250	120
11-07.... July	North	Delhi	1011	Cooking	Lentil	63	112	6	7056	378
12-07.... July	North	Delhi	1012	Cooking	Oil	108	50	3	5400	324
13-07.... July	North	Luckn...	1013	Beverages	Lemon Tea	300	154	8	46200	2400
14-07.... July	North	Luckn...	1014	Beverages	Filter Coff...	250	50	3	12500	750
15-07.... July	North	Luckn...	1015	Beverages	Coconut. ...	112	175	9	19600	1008
16-07.... July	North	Luckn...	1016	Snacks	Biscuit	25	113	6	2825	150
17-07.... July	North	Luckn...	1017	Snacks	Roasted A...	375	34	2	12750	750

7.9.4 Creating Perspectives in Power Pivot

Using the Power Pivot add-in, we can add perspectives, which enable users to create custom views for a particular user group or business scenario; making it easier to navigate through large datasets. In the Advanced tab of the Power Pivot Window, select 'Create and Manage' under 'Perspectives'. All fields of the data model will be displayed. Click on 'New Perspective', that will add a new column with a check box against each field.

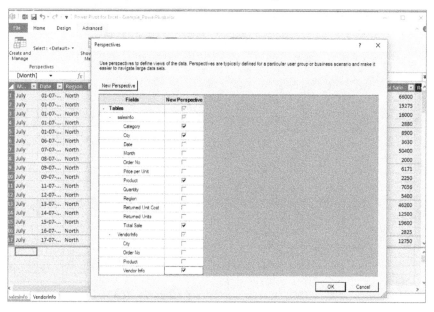

Select the check boxes to include the desired fields and click on **OK**. A new perspective gets created. In the Perspectives section the view selected is <Default>, change this to the **New Perspective** to view the same.

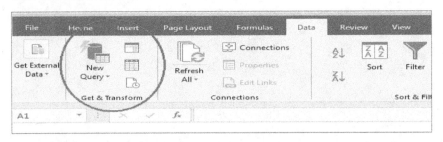

City	Category	Product	Total Sale	Add Column
1 Delhi	Beverages	Lemon Tea	66000	
2 Delhi	Beverages	Filter Coff...	19275	
3 Delhi	Beverages	Coconut ...	16000	
4 Delhi	Snacks	Biscuit	2880	
5 Delhi	Snacks	Roasted A...	8900	
6 Delhi	Snacks	Popcorn	3630	
7 Delhi	Sweets	Chocolate	50400	
8 Delhi	Sweets	Milk Cake	2000	
9 Delhi	Sweets	Candy	6171	
10 Delhi	Cooking	Salt	2250	
11 Delhi	Cooking	Lentil	7056	
12 Delhi	Cooking	Oil	5400	
13 Luckn...	Beverages	Lemon Tea	46200	
14 Luckn...	Beverages	Filter Coff...	12500	
15 Luckn...	Beverages	Coconut ...	19600	
16 Luckn...	Snacks	Biscuit	2825	
17 Luckn...	Snacks	Roasted A...	12750	

7.10 Get and Transform / Power Query tool

Get and Transform or Power Query tool in Excel enables you to connect, combine, and refine (that is remove a column, change a data type, or merge tables) data sources to meet analysis needs. It can link to external data from different sources, link them into an internal data model, or present data in form of tables.

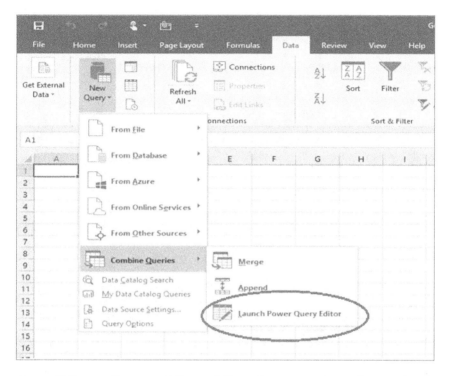

Query Editor, a feature of Get and Transform, records each step that is executed that is, whenever we connect to, transform, or combine data with other data sources and allow the user to undo, redo, change the order, or modify any step. The original data source remains unchanged after transformation, only the view changes.

The following options help in using the Get and Transform method in Excel:

- **Connect**: For making data connections using a Query. It could be a single data source or multiple files, databases, feeds, or websites.

- **Transform**: Also called Shaping data, which means we can remove a column, change a data type, or merge tables.

- **Combine**: To load transformed data into a table or into the built-in Data Model in Excel, and even refresh that data later on.

- **Share**: Created Query can be saved, shared and used for reports.

We will use a simple example to understand this feature. In a new workbook we will create a new query or import data from an existing Excel workbook that has the Sales data for the year 2018.

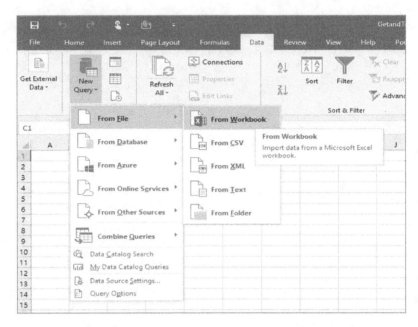

Select the workbook that has the source data and click **Import**. From the Navigator Window, select the sheet that has the Sales data for the year 2018 and click on the option **Load** or **Load To**, this gives an option to view data as a table or only a connection.

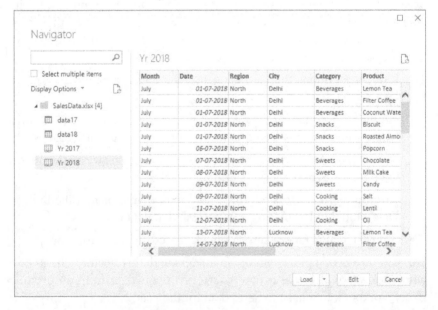

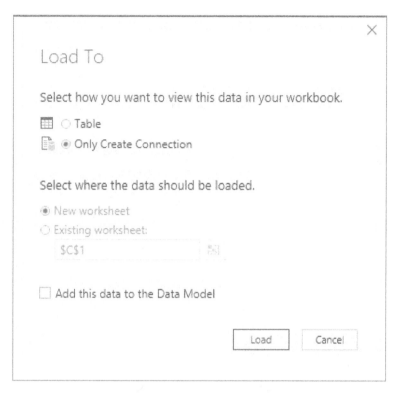

We will select **Load To** ➔ **Only Create Connection** and click **Load**. Similarly, we will again Load the Sales data for the year 2017. On right hand side the workbook queries are displayed. Now we will Launch the Power Query Editor and try to transform and merge the queries using the editor. Go to **Data** tab, under **Get & Transform** group, select **New Query** ➔ **Combine Queries** ➔ **Launch Power Query Editor**

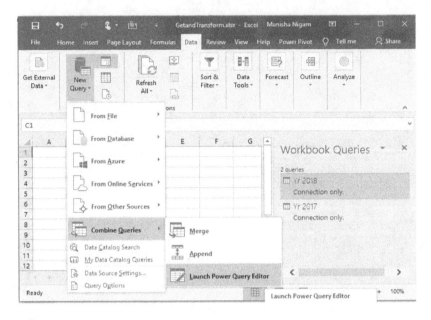

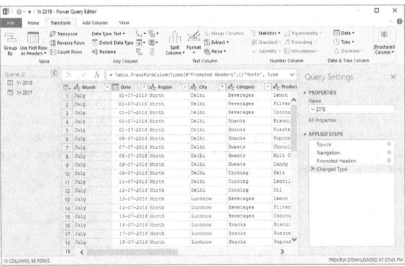

The Query Editor tracks each operation in the **Applied Steps** section of the Query Settings pane. There is a **Transform** tab that has different options to change the view and an **Add Column** tab that enables users to add new columns.

It's important to know that the actions we define in Query Editor don't change the original source data. Instead, Excel records each step and after we have finished shaping the data, takes a snapshot of the refined dataset and brings it into the workbook.

In the Power Query Editor, we will first remove columns that we do not want to see so that we have a clear view and then proceed with merging the queries.

Select the columns that you want to view that is, **Month, Date, Product,** and **Total Sales**; and go to option **Home → Remove Columns → Remove Other Columns**.

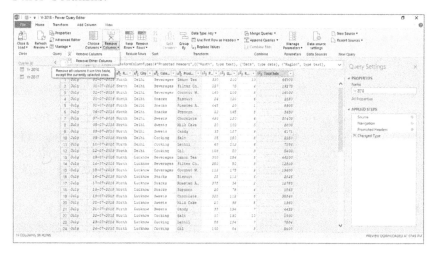

Note that in the **Applied Steps** this operation has been recorded and in case we want to go back we can either delete it (using the right-click option) or click on the previous step.

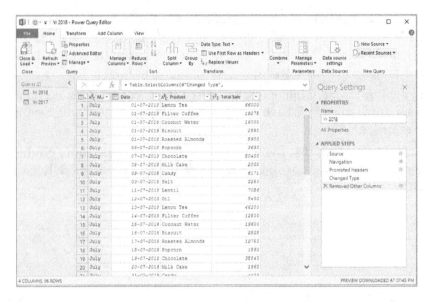

We will now merge the queries by using the option **Home | Merge Queries**. In the Merge window the current query is shown, now we will select the other query in the dropdown list for merge. Also highlight the matching columns for merge, say **Product** in this case and click **OK** with the default **Join Kind** selected.

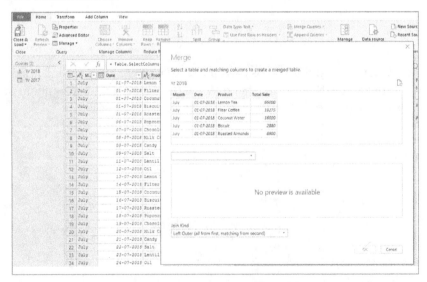

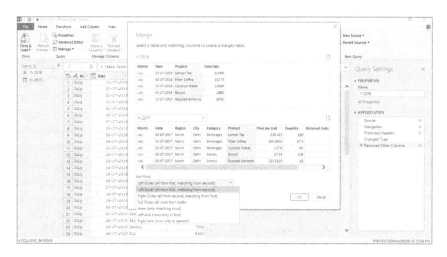

A new column is added, that contains the merged Sales data from the year 2017. This column has an expand icon and the rows say Table.

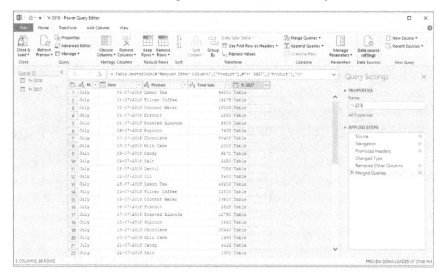

On clicking the expand icon on that column, we get a window in which we can again select the column we want to see. Select the check box of the desired columns and click **OK**.

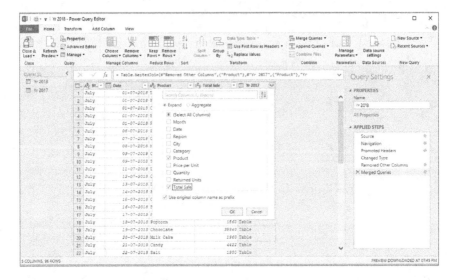

The column is expanded to show Yr 2017's Product information and their corresponding Total Sale values.

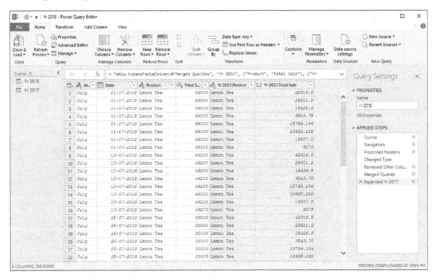

Use Close & Load to save the queries.

7.10.1 Different Merging Options

Before we close this topic, we will quickly look at the different Join Kind (Merge Types), which is very important as we can get a totally different result set when choosing a different type of merge. There are six different kinds as seen in the following screenshot:

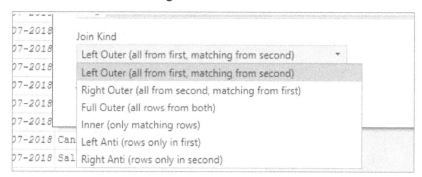

7.10.1.1 *Left and Right tables/queries*

Let's understand the concept of *Left and Right tables* (or queries). When we merge two datasets with each other, the first query is considered as LEFT and the second as RIGHT. In above example the Sales data of year 2018 is considered first and the data of year 2017 is second.

7.10.1.2 *Join Kind / Merge types*

Now we will look at the different Join Kind or Merge Type options available.

- **Left Outer (All from first, matching from second)**: This means the LEFT query is the important one. All records from this query (LEFT or FIRST) will be seen in the result set along with their matching rows in the right (or second table). In the LEFT Outer merge, only records from the Left table with matching rows from the right table will be selected.

- **Right Outer (all rows from second, matching from first)**: All rows from the RIGHT (or second) table will be seen with matching rows from the left (or first table).

- **Full Outer (all rows from both)**: As the name suggests, it will return all rows from both tables (matching and non-matching).

- **Inner (only matching rows)**: This method only selects matching rows. We will not have any record with null values (because these records are generated as a result of not matching)

- **Left Anti (rows only in first)**: This method only selects unmatched rows from the first table.

- **Right Anti (rows only in second)**: This method only selects unmatched rows from the second table.

CHAPTER 8
Complex Data Analysis using ToolPak

Analysis **ToolPak** helps in developing complex statistical or engineering analyses. Users have to only provide the data to be analyzed and its required parameters for each analysis, and the tool uses the appropriate functions to calculate and display results. This reduces the challenge users face with no prior knowledge of statistics.

8.1 Enabling Analysis ToolPak in Excel

First, we need to make sure that we have the **Analysis ToolPak** enabled or added. Go to menu '**File → Options → Add-ins**. The Excel options window will display all the add-ins grouped as per their status. Confirm that **Analysis ToolPak** is under the active add-ins.

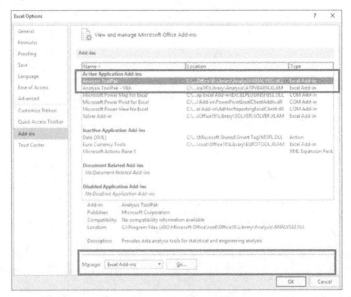

If not present, it can be added by selecting **Excel Add-ins** under **Options** → **Add-ins** → **Manage** and click **Go**.... In the next window select the checkbox for Analysis ToolPak and click **OK**. Data Analysis option under Data should appear and on clicking it, a window is launched displaying the list of analysis tools. In this section, we will discuss a few of these important tools.

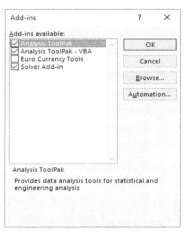

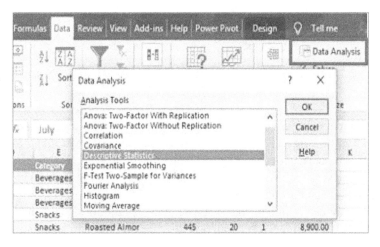

8.2 Descriptive Statistics in Excel

Descriptive statistics uses the data to provide a description of the population. Let us take a sample data of students age and use the **Descriptive Statistics** tool of Excel and see the details that it generates.

Age of Students: 3, 5, 7, 9, 4, 2, 2, 4, 6, 8, 15, 4, 20, 6, 10, 4, 5, 9, 11, 1, 6, 9, 4, 5, 13, 17, 7, 9, 6, 10

Put these figures in one column of Excel and select the option **Data | Data Analysis**, and in the Data analysis window select **Descriptive Statistics** and click **OK**. In the **Descriptive Statistics** dialog box, as shown in the following screenshot, select the **Input Range**, set the **Output Range** and click the Summary Statistics check box and click **OK**.

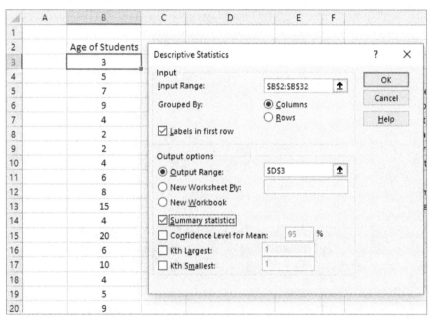

The summary is added in two columns, starting with the cell specified in the output range. The first column is the descriptive statistic and the second is its corresponding value. The result of the **Descriptive Statistics** tool can be seen in below screenshot, in the cells ranging from D3 to E17; thirteen statistics are calculated by default. For better understanding, the meaning of each statistic has been shown in column G and in column H the corresponding Excel function that can be used independently for calculation.

A	B	C	D	E	F	G	H
2	Age of Students						
3	3		*Age of Students*			Statistics Meaning	Excel function
4	5						
5	7		Mean	7.4		= average of the data values	=AVERAGE($B$3:$B$32)
6	9		Standard Error	0.8		= gives reliability of the mean	
7	4		Median	6.0		= middle value of the data set	=MEDIAN($B$3:$B$32)
8	2		Mode	4.0		= value that appears most often in the set	=MODE($B$3:$B$32)
9	2		Standard Deviation	4.5		= describes the spread of the data	=STDEV.P($B$3:$B$32)
10	4		Sample Variance	20.0		= deviation of a set of data from the mean value	=VAR.P($B$3:$B$32)
11	6		Kurtosis	1.3		= pointedness of a peak in the distribution	=KURT($B$3:$B$32)
12	8		Skewness	1.1		= measure of symmetry in distribution	=SKEW.P($B$3:$B$32)
13	15		Range	19.0		= difference between max and min value	
14	4		Minimum	1.0		= minimum value in the distribution	=MIN($B$3:$B$32)
15	20		Maximum	20.0		= maximum value in the distribution	=MAX($B$3:$B$32)
16	6		Sum	221.0		= total of the data values	=SUM($B$3:$B$32)
17	10		Count	30.0		= total number of values in the set	=Count($B$3:$B$32)
18	4						

For understanding the statistics in greater detail, please refer to the documentation or an expert related to the subject. This example is only intended to describe the capabilities of Excel and its usage for better data analysis.

8.3 ANOVA in Excel

Analysis of Variance (ANOVA) is a hypothesis testing technique; useful statistical function that lets you test different data sets to figure out the extent of difference among them. ANOVA analysis tools provide different types of variance analysis; Single Factor, Two Factor With/Without Replication.

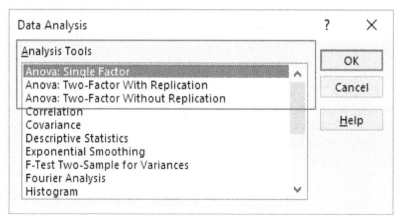

8.3.1 ANOVA: Single Factor

Single Factor or One-Way ANOVA is used to check whether there is any significant difference between the means of three or more unrelated groups.

First, we set up the hypothesis. ANOVA uses a Null hypothesis and an Alternate hypothesis.

$H0: \mu1 = \mu2 = \mu3 = ... = \mu N$ i.e., Null Hypothesis

$H1: \mu1 \neq \mu M$; at least one of the means is different. i.e., Alternate Hypothesis

where, $\mu1$, $\mu2$, μN are sample means and N is the number of samples.

The null hypothesis states that all the sample means are equal, or the factor did not have any significant effect on the results. Whereas, the alternate hypothesis states that at least one of the sample means is different from another. Let us understand this with the help of an example.

24 people were selected for testing weight loss methods. They were divided into 3 groups; 8 people who did only exercise, 8 people were put on a low-fat diet and 8 did exercise and also followed the diet. Weight loss per kg by using different methods was recorded, as in the following table:.

⊿	A	B	C	D	E	F	G	H	I	J
1										
2										
3						Weight Loss per kg				
4		Exercise	3	2	1	3	4	1	2	2
5		Low fat Diet	1	2	2	1	2	3	1	1
6		Exercise + Diet	3	5	4	2	3	5	2	2
7										

We can use ANOVA to compare these 3 weight loss methods and depict how different these samples are from one another. Here, weight is the only one factor. We will use the Excel ANOVA tools to generate the results. Go to **Data** ➔ **Data Analysis** and select **ANOVA Single Factor** and click **OK**. A window in launched, enter the **Input Range, Output Range** and click **OK**.

The result is displayed in the cells starting with the given **Output Range**.

	A	B	C	D	E	F	G	H	I
10									
11									
12		Anova: Single Factor							
13									
14		SUMMARY							
15		Groups	Count	Sum	Average	Variance			
16		Exercise	8	18	2.25	1.071428571			
17		Low fat Diet	8	13	1.625	0.553571429			
18		Exercise + Diet	8	26	3.25	1.642857143			
19									
20									
21		ANOVA							
22		Source of Variation	SS	df	MS	F	P-value	F crit	
23		Between Groups	10.75	2	5.375	4.93442623	0.017512071	3.466800112	
24		Within Groups	22.88	21	1.089285714				
25									
26		Total	33.63	23					
27									

where,

SS = Sum-of-Squares for between-group variability

df = degrees of freedom

MS = Measure of between-group variability i.e., SS / df

F = Between group variability / Within group variability

Between Group Variability refers to the difference between the grand mean/means of individual data samples. *Within-Group Variability* is an indication of the variability factor inside individual data samples owing to the dissimilarity of various constituting sample values.

P-value = Calculated probability, is the probability of finding the observed, or more extreme, results when the null hypothesis (H 0) of a study question is true

F crit = F-critical value, determined by looking at the F distribution tables corresponding to alternative right-tail probabilities (α) / alpha level

Alpha Levels / Significance Levels = It is the probability of making the wrong decision when the null hypothesis is true. Most commonly used alpha level is 0.05 that is 5%, that means the confidence level is 95%

Here we are concerned with *F-value*, which in this case is greater than the F-critical value for the alpha level selected (0.05). Therefore, we reject the null hypothesis and say that at least one of the three samples have significantly different means and thus belong to an entirely different population. Another measure is the *p-value*, which if it is less than the alpha level selected (0.05), we reject the null hypothesis.

ANOVA has a limitation that it does not tell us which groups are different. Hence, we need to drill down. A t-Test can be used here, to test each pair of mean to tell us exactly which groups have a difference in means.

8.3.2 t-Test following ANOVA

Two-Sample t-Test analysis tools test for equality of the population means that underlie each sample. In order to find which groups, have a difference in means in the above example, we will do the t-Test for the following group combinations; (i) Group 1 vs Group 2 (ii) Group 1 vs Group 3 (iii) Group 2 vs Group 3.

Go to **Data** ➔ **Data Analysis** and select **t-Test**: Two-Sample Assuming Equal Variances and click **OK**.

Enter the Cell Range for **Group 1** and **Group 2** in Variable 1 and Variable 2 Range respectively and specify the **Output Range**. The results are shown in three columns as seen in the following screenshot:

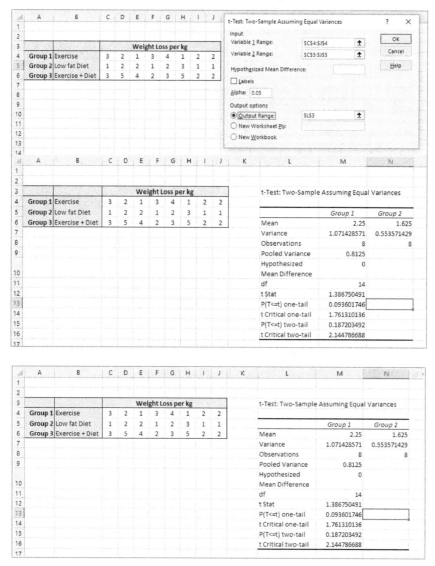

We will repeat the same process for the other two group combinations and compare the results.

K	L	M	N	O	P	Q	R	S	T	U	V
	t-Test: Two-Sample Assuming Equal Variances				t-Test: Two-Sample Assuming Equal Variances				t-Test: Two-Sample Assuming Equal Variances		
		Group 1	*Group 2*			*Group 1*	*Group 3*			*Group 2*	*Group 3*
	Mean	2.25	1.625		Mean	2.25	3.25		Mean	1.625	3.25
	Variance	1.071428571	0.553571429		Variance	1.07142857	1.6428571		Variance	0.553571429	1.642857143
	Observations	8	8		Observations	8	8		Observations	8	8
	Pooled Variance	0.8125			Pooled Variance	1.35714286			Pooled Variance	1.098214286	
	Hypothesized Mean Difference	0			Hypothesized Mean Difference	0			Hypothesized Mean Difference	0	
	df	14			df	14			df	14	
	t Stat	1.386750491			t Stat	-1.7167902			t Stat	-3.101271703	
	P(T<=t) one-tail	0.093601746			P(T<=t) one-tail	0.05402459			P(T<=t) one-tail	0.003906316	
	t Critical one-tail	1.761310136			t Critical one-tail	1.76131014			t Critical one-tail	1.761310136	
	P(T<=t) two-tail	0.187203492			**P(T<=t) two-tail**	0.10804918			**P(T<=t) two-tail**	0.007812632	
	t Critical two-tail	2.144786688			t Critical two-tail	2.14478669			t Critical two-tail	2.144786688	

We are interested in the p values, highlighted in yellow. P value for Group 2 and Group 3 is less than the alpha level selected (0.05), which means that Group 2 and Group 3 have less than 5% chance of belonging to the same population.

8.3.3 ANOVA: Two Factor with Replication

This analysis tool is useful when data can be classified along two different dimensions. Let us understand using the following example.

A children health drink company did a test on 16 students from two schools in 3 different age groups. Students of school A drank the health drink for over a year before the tests were conducted, while the students of school B did not. The following table shows the test scores.

		Age Group (yrs)		
	Group	2 to 5 yrs	5 to 8 yrs	8 to 12 yrs
	A (Health Drink)	6	4	8
		5	6	9
		2	9	7
		4	8	6
		5	5	9
		5	6	10
		2	9	7
		4	8	6
	B (No Drink)	1	5	6
		3	4	4
		2	5	6
		1	3	6
		1	4	8
		2	5	5
		1	6	8
		3	3	7

Now since we have 2 factors; Age and Health drink and have 8 observations for each combination, we will use Two Factor with Replication. Go to **Data → Data Analysis** and select **ANOVA: Two Factor with Replication** and click **OK**.

	Age Group (yrs)		
Group	2 to 5 yrs	5 to 8 yrs	8 to 12 yrs
A (Health Drink)	6	4	8
	5	6	9
	2	9	7
	4		
	5		
	5		
	2		
	4		
B (No Drink)	1		
	3		
	2		
	1		
	1		8
	2	5	5
	1	6	8
	3	3	7

Data Analysis dialog — Analysis Tools: Anova: Single Factor, Anova: Two-Factor With Replication, Anova: Two-Factor Without Replication, Correlation, Covariance, Descriptive Statistics, Exponential Smoothing, F-Test Two-Sample for Variances, Fourier Analysis, Histogram. Buttons: OK, Cancel, Help.

Enter the **Input Range** which is, the complete data set. Rows per Sample is 8 in this case as we have 8 observations each and enter the **Output Range** to the desired cell where you want the results to be displayed.

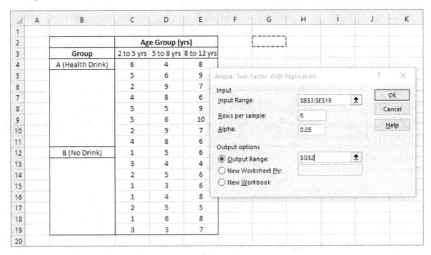

	Age Group (yrs)				Anova: Two-Factor With Replication				
Group	2 to 5 yrs	5 to 8 yrs	8 to 12 yrs						
A (Health Drink)	6	4	8		SUMMARY	2 to 5 yrs	5 to 8 yrs	8 to 12 yrs	Total
	5	6	9		*A (Health Drink)*				
	2	9	7		Count	8	8	8	24
	4	8	6		Sum	33	55	62	150
	5	5	9		Average	4.125	6.875	7.75	6.25
	5	6	10		Variance	2.125	3.55357	2.21428571	4.8913
	2	9	7						
	4	8	6		*B (No Drink)*				
B (No Drink)	1	5	6		Count	8	8	8	24
	3	4	4		Sum	14	35	50	99
	2	5	6		Average	1.75	4.375	6.25	4.125
	1	3	6		Variance	0.78571	1.125	1.92857143	4.72283
	1	4	8						
	2	5	5		*Total*				
	1	6	8		Count	16	16	16	
	3	3	7		Sum	47	90	112	
					Average	2.9375	5.625	7	
					Variance	2.8625	3.85	2.53333333	

ANOVA						
Source of Variation	*SS*	*df*	*MS*	*F*	*P-value*	*F crit*
Sample (Rows)	54.1875	1	54.1875	27.7123	4.5E-06	4.07265
Columns	136.625	2	68.3125	34.9361	1.2E-09	3.21994
Interaction	2.375	2	1.1875	0.60731	0.54953	3.21994
Within	82.125	42	1.95535714			
Total	275.313	47				

Based on the results we will determine if either of two categorical factors; that is Age and Health Drink and/or the interaction between these two factors, has had a significant effect on the data set.

The P-value of the two factors individually is less than the alpha level (0.05), so we can say that the effect of Age and Health Drink is statistically significant. P-value for interaction is greater than alpha level, so the interaction effect between Age and Health Drink is not statistically significant.

Check the F value against the F-crit value. If the F value is greater than the F critical value, it indicates that there is a significant difference between the test scores.

8.3.4 ANOVA: Two Factor without Replication

For this tool it is assumed that there is only a single observation for each pair.

		Age Group (yrs)		
	Group	2 to 5 yrs	5 to 8 yrs	8 to 12 yrs
	A (Health Drink)	6	4	8
	B (No Drink)	1	5	6

Go to **Data → Data Analysis** and select **ANOVA: Two Factor without Replication** and click OK.

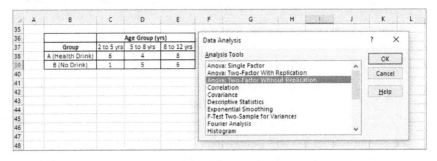

Specify the Input and Output Range and click OK.

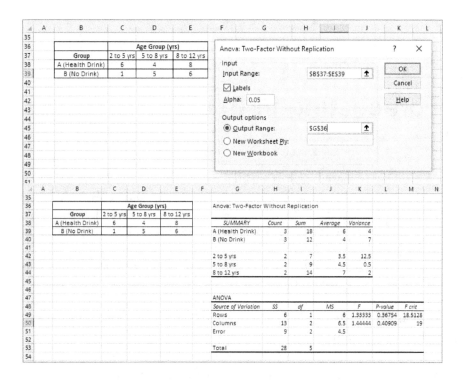

Interpretation of the results is the same as before. We again look at the p-Value and the F value against the F-crit.

CHAPTER 9
Forecasting in Excel

Forecasting is the process of making predictions of the future based on historical time-based data (past and present data), commonly by analysis of trends. The ability to forecast helps in effective and efficient planning, for example predicting things like future sales, inventory requirements, or consumer trends. In Excel 2016 the new one-click forecasting features, that is, the Forecast Sheet along with new forecasting sheet functions have been introduced for better and ease of forecasting. Excel also has analysis tools like What-if Analysis tools to help predict the future. **What-If Analysis** in Excel allows you to try out different scenarios for formulas/ data, even when the data is incomplete.

9.1 Forecast Sheet - One-Click Forecasting

Forecast Sheet option is available in Excel on the **Data** tab, under the Forecast group. We will create a Forecast Sheet for our existing Sales data (including timelines and sales values) to predict future sales. It has to be noted that in order to use this feature and get accurate results, the data set should have two data series that is, with date/time entries for timelines and corresponding values like sales and so on. And the timelines should have consistent intervals between its data points. For example, timelines can have monthly intervals (with values on the 1st of every month), yearly intervals, or numerical intervals. Forecasts will still be accurate if the timeline series is missing up to 30% of the data points or has several numbers with the same time stamp.

9.1.1 Create Forecast Worksheet

Open the Excel sheet with the time-based sales data for which forecast is to be created. To create a forecast, select any cell in the data series and go to the **Data** tab, in the **Forecast** group select **Forecast sheet** option.

Excel automatically selects the rest of the data and a **Create Forecast Worksheet** dialog box is launched.

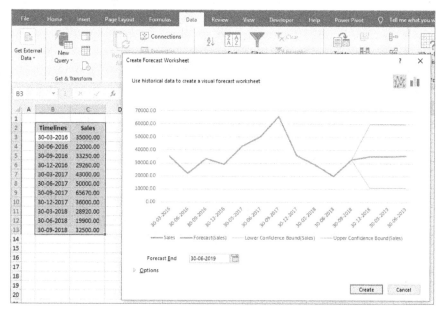

Figure 9.1 *Create Forecast Worksheet dialog box*

Click **Create** on the **Create Forecast Worksheet**. Excel creates a new worksheet that contains both a table of the historical and predicted values, and a chart that expresses this data.

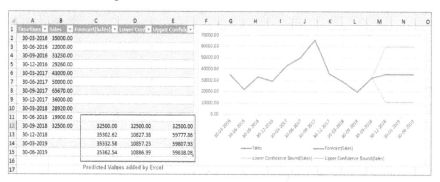

Figure 9.2 *New Forecast Sheet with table & graph*

9.1.2 Customize Forecast using Options

In the above section we created the forecast with default settings. Excel allows for various customizations, click on **Options** to change the Chart type, Forecast End/Start dates, and so on.

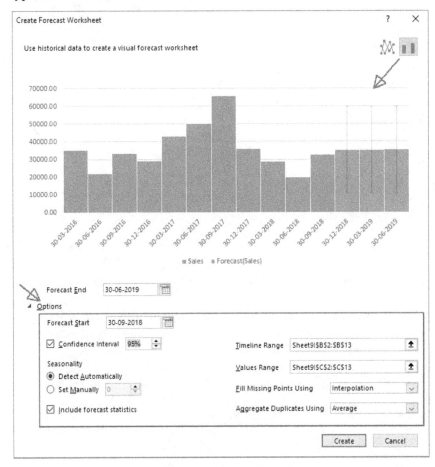

Figure 9.3 *Forecast Options*

- **Confidence Level**: The confidence interval helps to figure out the accuracy of the prediction. It is the range surrounding each predicted value —in which 95% (default value) of future points are expected to fall—based on the forecast (with normal distribution). A smaller interval implies more confidence in predicting a specific point.

- **Seasonality**: It is a number for the length (number of points) of the seasonal pattern and is automatically detected. By choosing **Set Manually** and picking a number, you can override the automatic detection. For example, in a yearly sales cycle, with each point representing a month, the seasonality is 12. For this to work properly it's better to have more repeating cycles in the historical data, at least 2–3 full seasonal cycles. **Timeline Range**: You can change the timeline range. Note that when changing the timeline range the corresponding values range also needs to be changed.

- **Values Range**: You can change the value range keeping in mind that both Timeline Range and Value Range need to be identical.

- **Fill Missing Points Using**: In case the data series have some missing points, Excel uses interpolation, meaning that a missing point will be completed as the weighted average of its neighboring points as long as fewer than 30% of the points are missing. To treat the missing points as zeros instead, click Zeros in the list.

- **Aggregate Duplicates Using**: In case the data contains multiple values with the same timestamp, Excel will average the values. You can use another calculation method from the list such as Median, Sum and so on.

- **Include Forecast Statistics**: If checked, additional statistical information on the forecast will be included in a new worksheet.

- **Forecast Start**: You can specify the date for the forecast to begin. To get an idea of the accuracy of the forecast, try changing the forecast start date to a date before the last historical point. This allows you to see how your prediction would have looked had it been calculated only over the earlier subset.

In our Sales example, we have changed the Forecast Start date to a date before the last historical data, seen in the following screenshot. Forecasted values or predictions are close to the actual values.

Figure 9.4 *Forecast Sheet with forecast statistics*

9.2 FORECAST Functions

Excel has new forecasting functions that are used for predicting future values. Even when we use the one-click forecasting feature for creating Forecast Sheets (see 9.1), Excel uses FORCAST functions for calculations.

Go to the Forecast Sheet created, as in example shown in *Figure 9.4*. Go to the **Formulas** tab and select **Show Formulas** from the **Formula Auditing** group. All the formulas used by Excel to predict the future values and the formulas used for showing forecast statistics are shown instead of values in the Excel worksheet.

Figure 9.5 *Forecast sheet with Formulas*

9.2.1 FORECAST.ETS

Calculates or predicts a future value based on existing (historical) values by using the AAA version of the **Exponential Smoothing (ETS)** algorithm. The predicted value is a continuation of the historical values in the specified target date, which should be a continuation of the timeline.

Syntax is

"=FORECAST.ETS(target date, values, timeline, [seasonality], [data completion], [aggregation])"

For predicting the value of A12 in example given in *Figure 9.5*, the formula used is

=FORECAST.ETS(A12, $B$2:$B$11, $A$2:$A$11, 1, 1) where,

Argument	Value	Description
target date	A12	***30-09-2018*** – The data point for which you want to predict a value
Values	$B$2:$B$11	***Sales values*** – The historical values, for which you want to forecast the next points
timeline	$A$2:$A$11	***Dates*** – The timelines corresponding to the values

Argument	Value	Description
seasonality	1	*Detect Automatically* was selected in Options, in the Forecast Sheet example (which Excel automatically calculates). Optional parameter, Default is 1. 0 indicates no seasonality, meaning the prediction will be linear. Positive whole numbers will indicate to the algorithm to use patterns of this length as the seasonality.
data completion	1	*Filling Missing Points Using – Interpolation* was selected in Options, in the Forecast Sheet example. Optional parameter, Default is 1. 0 will indicate the algorithm to account for missing points as zeros.
aggregation	omitted	*Aggregate Duplicates Using – Average* was selected in Options, in the Forecast Sheet example. Optional parameter, Default is 1. The default value of 1 will use AVERAGE, while other options are 2-COUNT, 3-COUNTA, 4-MAX, 5-MEDIAN, 6-MIN, 7-SUM

9.2.2 FORECAST.ETS.CONFINT

Returns a confidence interval for the forecast value at the specified target date. A confidence interval of 95% means that 95% of future points are expected to fall within this radius from the result **FORECAST.ETS** forecasted (with normal distribution). Using a confidence interval can help grasp the accuracy of the predicted model. A smaller interval would imply more confidence in the prediction for this specific point.

Syntax is

"=FORECAST.ETS.CONFINT(target date, values, timeline, [confidence level], [seasonality], [data completion], [aggregation])"

For calculating the Upper and Lower Confidence bounds of A12 in example given in Figure 9.5, the formulas used are

=C12+FORECAST.ETS.CONFINT(A12, $B$2:$B$11, $A$2:$A$11, 0.95, 1, 1) and

=C12-FORECAST.ETS.CONFINT(A12, $B$2:$B$11, $A$2:$A$11, 0.95, 1, 1)

Note that to calculate the Upper bound, the C12 value is added to the result of the **FORECAST.ETS.CONFINT** function, while it is subtracted in case of Lower bound calculation. **FORECAST.ETS.CONFINT** function is the same that is,

=FORECAST.ETS.CONFINT(A12, $B$2:$B$11, $A$2:$A$11, 0.95, 1, 1) where,

Argument	Value	Description
target date	A12	*30-09-2018* – The data point for which you want to predict a value
Values	$B$2:$B$11	*Sales values* – The historical values, for which you want to forecast the next points
timeline	$A$2:$A$11	*Dates* – The timelines corresponding to the values
confidence level	0.95	*Confidence Interval - 95%* was selected in Options, in the Forecast Sheet example. Optional parameter. A numerical value between 0 and 1 (exclusive), indicating a confidence level for the calculated confidence interval

Argument	Value	Description
seasonality	1	***Detect Automatically*** was selected in Options, in Forecast Sheet example (which Excel automatically calculates). Optional parameter, Default is 1. 0 indicates no seasonality, meaning the prediction will be linear. Positive whole numbers will indicate to the algorithm to use patterns of this length as the seasonality.
data completion	1	***Filling Missing Points Using – Interpolation*** was selected in Options, in Forecast Sheet example. Optional parameter, Default is 1. 0 will indicate the algorithm to account for missing points as zeros.
aggregation	omitted	***Aggregate Duplicates Using – Average*** was selected in Options, in Forecast Sheet example. Optional parameter, Default is 1. The default value of 1 will use AVERAGE, while other options are 2-COUNT, 3-COUNTA, 4-MAX, 5-MEDIAN, 6-MIN, 7-SUM

9.2.3 FORECAST.ETS.STAT

The Excel **FORECAST.ETS.STAT** function calculates a specified statistical value, relating to a time series forecasting. .

Syntax is

"=FORECAST.ETS.STAT(values, timeline, statistic type, [seasonality], [data completion], [aggregation])"

For displaying the Forecast Statistics in the example given in *Figure 9.5*, the formula used is *=FORECAST.ETS.STAT($B$2:$B$11, $A$2:$A$11, 1, 1, 1)* where the third parameter changes from 1 to 8 for different statistics.

Argument	Value	Description
Values	$B$2:$B$11	**Sales values:** The historical values, for which you want to forecast the next points
timeline	$A$2:$A$11	**Dates:** The timelines corresponding to the values
statistic type	1-8	See the following table
seasonality	1	**Detect Automatically** was selected in Options, in the Forecast Sheet example (which Excel automatically calculates). Optional parameter, Default is 1. 0 indicates no seasonality, meaning the prediction will be linear. Positive whole numbers will indicate to the algorithm to use patterns of this length as the seasonality.
data completion	1	**Filling Missing Points Using – Interpolation** was selected in Options, in the Forecast Sheet example. Optional parameter, Default is 1. 0 will indicate the algorithm to account for missing points as zeros.
aggregation	omitted	**Aggregate Duplicates Using – Average** was selected in Options, in the Forecast Sheet example. Optional parameter, Default is 1. The default value of 1 will use AVERAGE, while other options are 2-COUNT, 3-COUNTA, 4-MAX, 5-MEDIAN, 6-MIN, 7-SUM

Statistic Type

Alpha	Alpha parameters of ETS algorithm. Returns the **base value parameter**—a higher value gives more weight to recent data points.
Beta	Beta parameter of ETS algorithm. Returns the **trend value parameter**—a higher value gives more weight to the recent trend.
Gamma	Gamma parameter of ETS algorithm. Returns the **seasonality value parameter**—a higher value gives more weight to the recent seasonal period.
MASE metric	Returns the **mean absolute scaled error metric**—a measure of the accuracy of forecasts.
SMAPE metric	Returns the **symmetric mean absolute percentage error** metric—an accuracy measure based on percentage errors
MAE metric	Returns the **mean absolute percentage error** metric—an accuracy measure based on percentage errors
RMSE metric	Returns the **root mean squared error metric**—a measure of the differences between predicted and observed values.
Step size detected	Returns the *step size* detected in the historical timeline.

9.3 What-if Analysis Tools

What-If Analysis in Excel allows you to try out different values or scenarios for formulas. We will use an example to understand the different What-if analysis tools; **Scenario Manager, Goal Seek**, **Data Table**, and **Solver**. These tools are available on the **Data** tab, in **Forecast** and **Analyze** groups.

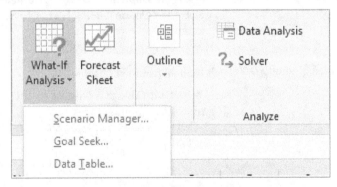

Figure 9.6 *What-if Analysis tools*

9.3.1 Scenario Manager

Using the **What-if Analysis** tool **Scenario Manager**, you can create and save different scenarios that is, different input values that create different results. For example, a vendor wants to know the profit that he could make from his sale of Mangos at different price units.

Currently the vendor is selling 50% of the total number at the highest price and 50% at the lowest price, as seen in the following screenshot:

⊿	A	B	C	D	E
1					
2		Vendor Item : Mango			
3		Total Number	150		
4					
5			%age	Unit Price	Num
6		Highest Price	50%	60	75
7		Lowest Price	50%	35	75
8					
9			Total Profit	7125.00	

Now he wants to know the profit if he sells different percentages (60%, 70%, 80%, 90%, and 100%) of Mangos at the highest price. One way is to create a table manually with different percentages like the one above and then calculate the total profits. Another easier way is to use the **Scenario Manager** wherein each different percentage is a different scenario.

Go to the **Data** tab, in the Forecast group, click on **What-if Analysis** and select **Scenario Manager** (see Figure 9.6). A **Scenario Manager** dialog box is launched.

Figure 9.7 *What-if Analysis: Scenario Manager*

Following are the steps to be followed to create Scenarios.

Step 1: Click on **Add…** in the **Scenario Manager** dialog box (Figure 9.7) and the **Edit Scenario** dialog box is launched. Type the name of the scenario, enter the cell C6 in the **Changing Cells** field that is, the highest percentage value. Add any comments you want and click **OK**.

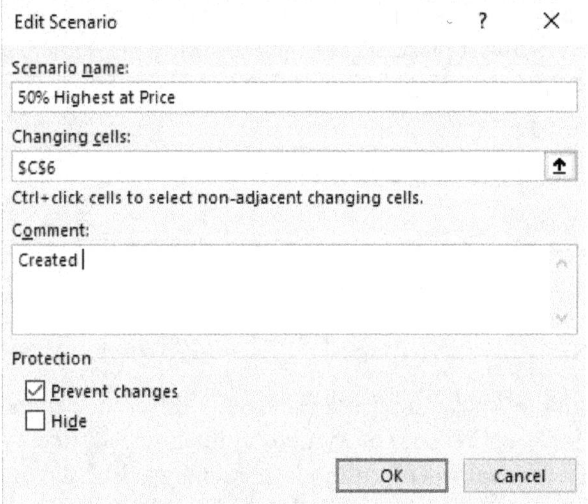

Figure 9.8 *Scenario manager – Step 1*

Step 2: Enter the corresponding value 0.5 (that is, for 50%) in the **Scenario Values**, and click **Add**.

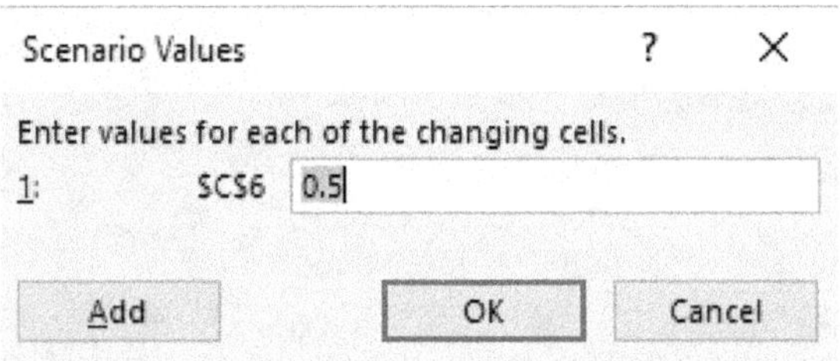

Step 3: Create/Add new scenarios for the percentages 60%, 70%, 80%, 90%, and 100%. Go to **Scenario Manager**, click **Add** and follow Step 1 & 2 to add the scenarios. The Scenario Manager dialog box will show all the scenarios as given as follows:

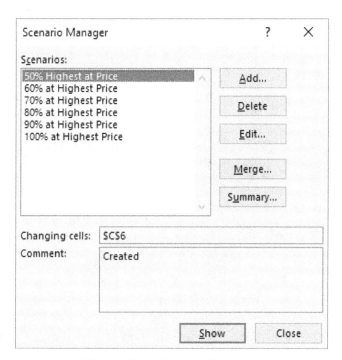

Figure 9.9 *Multiple Scenarios*

Step 4: To see the result, select the scenario you want to view and click **Show**. The value in C6 cell will change that is, if you select scenario named **80% at Highest Price** the value of C6 will be 80% and the total profit gets calculated accordingly.

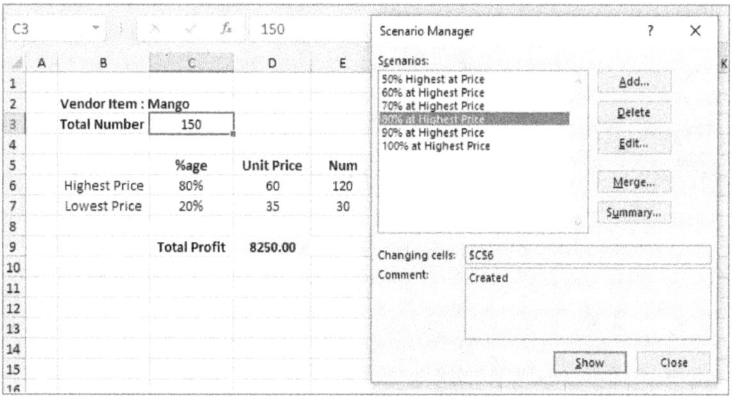

Figure 9.10 *Scenario Manager: Show*

In this case, you see the result of one scenario at a time. To see results for all the different scenarios, click on **Summary**…. In the **Scenario Summary** dialog box, select the report type and enter D9 in the result cells that is, the **Total Profit** value cell in the sheet and click **OK**.

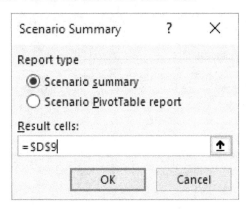

Figure 9.11 *Scenario summary*

A new worksheet named **Scenario Summary** is created by Excel with the consolidated results of all the scenarios created.

Scenario Summary							
	Current Values:	50% Highest at Price	60% at Highest Price	70% at Highest Price	80% at Highest Price	90% at Highest Price	100% at Highest Price
Changing Cells:							
$C$6	80%	50%	60%	70%	80%	90%	100%
Result Cells:							
$D$9	8250.00	7125.00	7500.00	7875.00	8250.00	8625.00	9000.00
Notes: Current Values column represents values of changing cells at time Scenario Summary Report was created. Changing cells for each scenario are highlighted in gray.							

Figure 9.12 *Scenario Summary sheet*

If the **Report Type'** was selected as **Scenario PivotTable Report** then a new worksheet named **Scenario PivotTable** is created by Excel.

	A	B	C
1	$C$6 by	(All) ▼	
2			
3	Row Labels ▼	$D$9	
4	100% at Highest Price	9000	
5	50% Highest at Price	7125	
6	60% at Highest Price	7500	
7	70% at Highest Price	7875	
8	80% at Highest Price	8250	
9	90% at Highest Price	8625	
10			

Figure 9.13 *Scenario PivotTable Report*

9.3.2 Goal Seek

Scenario manager is good for known variables, however, sometimes it is desirable to work backwards. Goal Seek is in a way opposite to the Scenario Manager that is, you start with the desired result, and it calculates the input value that will give you that result.

Using the same example of selling Mangos, now the vendor wants to know how many will have to be sold at the highest price to make a profit of say 8500. Go to the 'Data' tab, in the 'Forecast' group select **What-if Analysis** and click on **Goal Seek** (see *Figure 9.6*).

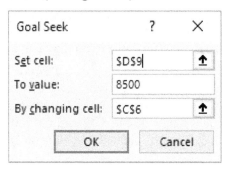

Figure 9.14 *Goal Seek*

In the **Goal Seek** dialog box, select D9 in **Set Cell** field (the Total Profit cell), in the **To value** enter 8500 (the goal to achieve) and select C6 in the

By changing cell and click **OK**. The **Goal Seek Status** dialog is opened and the worksheet is updated to show that the vendor will have to sell 87% Mangos at the Highest price to make a profit of 8500. Click **OK** to close the Goal Seek Status dialog box.

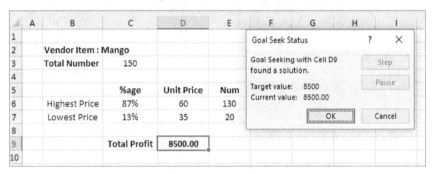

Figure 9.15 *Goal Seek Status*

9.3.3 Data Table

Data Table lets you see how changing one or two values will affect the bottom line, by creating one variable data table or a two variable data table respectively.

9.3.3.1 One Variable Data Table

In previous section we created different scenarios using **Scenario Manager**, to know the total profits that vendor will make on selling different numbers (%) of Mangos at the highest price (see 9.3.1) and also created the Scenario Summary (see Figure 912). Instead of creating scenarios, we can also use Data Table to do the same thing.

In cell C12 type the formula '=D9' to get the **Total Profit** value and in the column B that is, cell range B13-B17, enter the different percentages (Mangos to be sold at highest price) for which we want to find the **Total Profits**. Select the cell range B12 to C17 and go to the **Data** tab, in the **Forecast** group select What-if Analysis and click on **Data Table**.

▲	A	B	C	D	E	F	G
1							
2		Vendor Item : Mango					
3		Total Number	150				
4							
5			%age	Unit Price	Num		
6		Highest Price	50%	60	75		
7		Lowest Price	50%	35	75		
8							
9			Total Profit	7125.00			
10							
11				Data Table	?	✕	
12			7125.00				
13		60%		Row input cell:		↑	
14		70%		Column input cell: $C$6		↑	
15		80%					
16		90%		OK	Cancel		
17		100%					
18							

Figure 9.16 *Data Table dialog box – one variable*

Click on the **Column input cell** box (as the percentages are in a column) and select cell C6 because the percentages refer to cell C6 (% sold for the highest price). With the formula in cell C12, Excel knows that it should replace cell C6 with 60% to calculate the total profit, replace cell C6 with 70% to calculate the total profit, and so on. Click **OK** and the corresponding total profit values are inserted against the percentages.

▲	A	B	C	D	E
4					
5			%age	Unit Price	Num
6		Highest Price	50%	60	75
7		Lowest Price	50%	35	75
8					
9			Total Profit	7125.00	
10					
11					
12			7125.00		
13		60%	7500		
14		70%	7875		
15		80%	8250		
16		90%	8625		
17		100%	9000		
18					

Figure 9.17 *One Variable Data Table Result*

9.3.3.2 Two Variable Data Table

Now, if we want to also see what the profits will be if the unit price is also changed along with the percentage, we can make use of the two variable data table.

In cell B12 type the formula '=D9', type the different percentages in column B in cells B13 to B17 and type the different unit price in row 12 in cells C12 to E12. Select the cell range B12 to E17, go to the **Data** tab, in the **Forecast** group select **What-if Analysis**, and then click on **Data Table**....

▲	A	B	C	D	E	F	G	H	I
4									
5			%age	Unit Price	Num				
6		Highest Price	50%	60	75				
7		Lowest Price	50%	35	75				
8									
9			Total Profit	7125.00					
10									
11									
12		7125.00	60	75	85	Data Table		?	X
13		60%				Row input cell:	SDS6		↑
14		70%				Column input cell:	SCS6		↑
15		80%					OK		Cancel
16		90%							
17		100%							
18									

Figure 9.18 *Data Table dialog box – two variables*

Click on the **Row input cell** box (the unit prices are in a row) and select cell D6. And in the **Column input cell** box (the percentages are in a column) select cell C6. Together with the formula in cell B12, Excel knows that it should replace cell D6 with 60 and cell C6 with 60% to calculate the total profit, replace cell D6 with 60 and cell C4 with 70% to calculate the total profit, and so on. Click **OK** and the corresponding total profit values are inserted in the two-dimensional table.

◢	A	B	C	D	E	F
4						
5			%age	Unit Price	Num	
6		Highest Price	50%	60	75	
7		Lowest Price	50%	35	75	
8						
9			Total Profit	7125.00		
10						
11						
12		7125.00	60	75	85	
13		60%	7500	8850	9750	
14		70%	7875	9450	10500	
15		80%	8250	10050	11250	
16		90%	8625	10650	12000	
17		100%	9000	11250	12750	
18						

Figure 9.19 *Two Variable Data Table Result*

Results show that if 60% of the Mangos are sold at the highest price of 60, the total profit is 7500 and if they are sold at the highest price of 85, the total profit is 9750, and so on.

9.3.4 Solver Add-In

Solver is a Microsoft Excel add-in program you can use for what-if analysis. Solver can be used to find an optimal (maximum or minimum) value for a formula in one cell (called the objective cell) subject to constraints, or limits, on the values of other formula cells on a worksheet.

Make sure that Solver Add-in is active. Go to the **File** menu and select **Options**. In the **Excel Options** dialog box, go to Add-Ins and ensure that Solver Add-in is active.

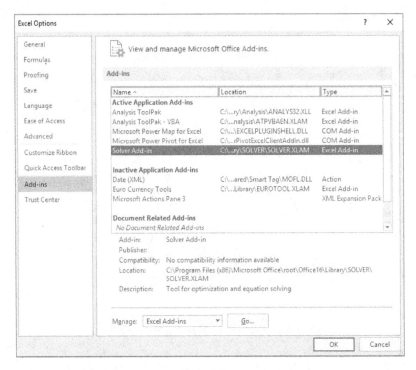

If not active, then for **Manage** select **Excel Add-Ins** and click **Go**….

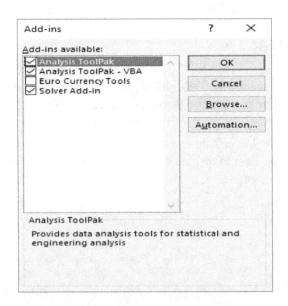

Select the checkbox for **Solver Add-In** and click **OK**. Solver Add-In will now be shown under the Active Application Add-Ins and also in the 'Data' tab under the **Analyse** group (see *Figure 9.6*).

To see how Solver helps in solving a problem, we will use the following example:

A vendor sells three types of fruits; Mangos, Apples, and Strawberries; and makes a unit profit of 300,150, and 80 respectively. The total capital available to him is 50000 and the total space is 250. Also known is the amount of space and capital that each unit of fruit requires. All the information has been put in a worksheet as given below. In order to maximize his profits, the vendor wants to know the optimal order (that is, how many to order of each fruit type), taking into consideration the space and capital constraints he has.

◢ A	B	C	D	E	F	G
1						
2		Unit Profit	Space Req per unit	Capital Req per unit	Order	
3	Mangos	300	3	85	0	
4	Apples	150	2	120	0	
5	Strawberries	80	5	74	0	
6						
7	Space Available	250		Space Utilized	0	
8	Capital Available	50000		Capital Utilized	0	
9						
10				**Total Profit**	0	

Now let us understand the problem we want to solve and the information we know which will help us in using the Solver tool.

Objective: Vendor needs to know optimal number of fruits to order of each type (Mangos, Apples and Strawberries) so as to maximize the Total Profit.

Constraints: Vendor has a limited amount of space (250) and capital (50000). So, order should be such that it is within these limits, knowing that each Mango uses 3 units of space and 85 units of capital, Apples uses 2 and 120, and Strawberries uses 5 and 74 units respectively.

To ease our calculations, we defined names for cell ranges and added formulas in the sheet. Defined names are as shown in the **Names Manager** dialog box. Go to **Formulas** tab, select **Name Manager**, where you will see the existing or defined names in the dialog box. You can create new defined names or named ranges by clicking on **New** (see 3.3).

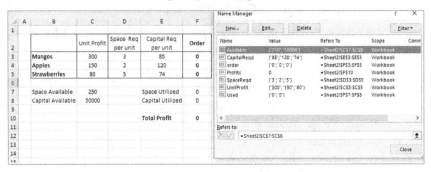

These defined names are used in the formulas using the **SUMPRODUCT** function (see function details in section 3.10.5) to calculate the utilization and total profits, as given in the following screenshot:

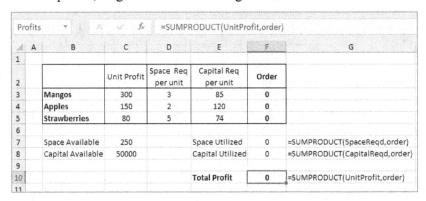

Now using this sheet, we can manually put values in Order and try out some permutations and combinations to find the optimal values. Below are two such combinations, wherein first the storage used is 241 that is, within the limit 250 and total profit is 10360, while in the second the storage utilization is maximum 250 but the total profit is less 7850 than first one.

⊿ A	B	C	D	E	F
1					⬇
2		Unit Profit	Space Req per unit	Capital Req per unit	Order
3	Mangos	300	3	85	23
4	Apples	150	2	120	6
5	Strawberries	80	5	74	32
6					⬇
7	Space Available	250		Space Utilized	241
8	Capital Available	50000		Capital Utilized	5043
9					
10				Total Profit	10360

⊿ A	B	C	D	E	F
1					⬇
2		Unit Profit	Space Req per unit	Capital Req per unit	Order
3	Mangos	300	3	85	12
4	Apples	150	2	120	7
5	Strawberries	80	5	74	40
6					⬇
7	Space Available	250		Space Utilized	250
8	Capital Available	50000		Capital Utilized	4820
9					
10				Total Profit	7850

Here is where Solver helps us in getting an optimal solution without manually trying out different combinations. Go to the **Data** tab, in the **Analyze** group click on **Solver** and the Solver Parameters window gets launched. Enter **Profits** that is, the defined name for cell F10, for Objective, click on **Max**, enter **order** that is, F3:F5 for Changing Variable cells, and select the **Simplex LP** solving method. For adding a constraint, click on **Add** and enter the values in the dialog box which are, F7:F8 (Used) <= C7:C8 (Available). Click on **OK** to go back to the Solver Parameters window.

Figure 9.20 *Solver: Add Constraints dialog box*

Figure 9.21 *Solver Parameters*

Click on **Solve** and it launches a **Solver Results** dialog box.

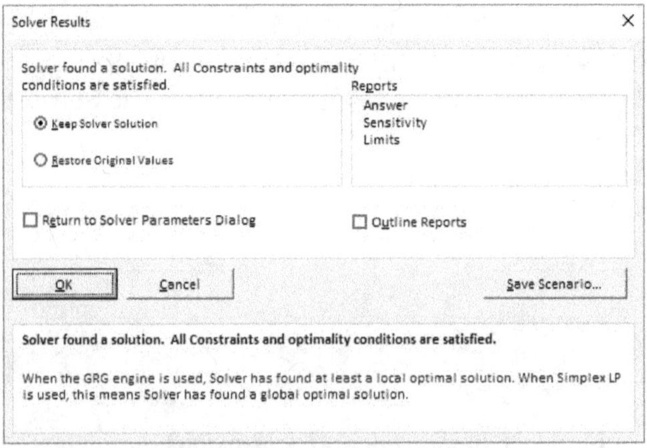

Figure 9.22 *Solver Results*

Click **OK** to see the results in the sheet.

	A	B	C	D	E	F
1						
2			Unit Profit	Space Req per unit	Capital Req per unit	Order
3		Mangos	300	3	85	83.33333
4		Apples	150	2	90	0
5		Strawberries	80	5	74	0
6						
7		Space Available	250		Space Utilized	250
8		Capital Available	50000		Capital Utilized	7083.333
9						
10					Total Profit	25000

So, the optimal solution is to order only 84 units of Mangos to get the maximum profit that is, 25000. Now add another constraint such that not more than 55 Mangos and 30 Apples can be ordered.

Click on **Solve** and in the **Solver Results** dialog box click on **OK**.

	A	B	C	D	E	F
1						
2			Unit Profit	Space Req per unit	Capital Req per unit	Order
3		Mangos	300	3	85	55
4		Apples	150	2	90	30
5		Strawberries	80	5	74	5
6						
7		Space Available	250		Space Utilized	250
8		Capital Available	50000		Capital Utilized	7745
9						
10					Total Profit	21400

With new constraints on the maximum number of Mangos and Apples that can be ordered, the maximum profit of 21400 can be reached by ordering 55 Mangos, 30 Apples, and 5 Strawberries units. Space utilization in this case is 250, that is complete utilization.

You can also save this as a scenario, click on **Save Scenario** in the **Solver Results** window (see Figure 9.22). It opens a **Save Scenario** dialog box where you enter the name and then click **OK**.

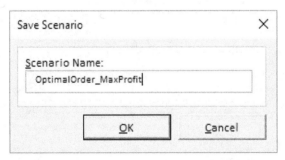

This scenario is saved by the given name and can be viewed in the Scenario Manager (see *Figure 9.7*)

CHAPTER 10
Mail Merge using Excel

Mail Merge is a feature that helps in creating multiple documents at once, which are identical with respect to layout, text, formatting, graphics and so on, except for some sections that vary and are personalized.

Mail Merge is a supported feature in the Microsoft Office suite, and you can utilize it to create bulk labels, letters, envelopes, or send out multiple emails from Microsoft Word using an Excel workbook. Excel in this case becomes the data source or database from where the specific information is picked for customizing or personalizing the document. We can also perform Mail Merge from Excel itself without using Word. This would require writing some formulas and a Macro (VBA) in the Excel.

In this chapter we will explain both the methods of Mail Merge with the help of examples.

10.1 Mail Merge from Word using Excel

This is the most commonly used method of using Mail Merge feature. We will take an example for generating pay slips and sending emails to employees. Companies generally have a single payslip template that is used for each employee. Hence in the payslip layout, the formatting remains the same but for each employee the contents or data values differ. Mail Merge involves three documents; the data source or database, document template, and the resultant Mail Merged document. We will create each of them one by one for our example.

10.1.1 Preparing the Database

Excel is our data source or the database from where the employee specific information will be picked to generate individual pay slips. Add all the information in the Excel database that you want to use in the generated document. The first row is the header row, with descriptive and unique

	A	B	C	D	E	F	G	H	I	J	K
1	Name	Employee ID	Email	Designation	Basic	Allowance	Others	Tax	Net Payable	Salary Month	Salary Year
2	Karthik G S	10011	kgs@abs.com	Strategy Lead	47000.00	9400.00	4700.00	3915.10	57184.90	June	2018
3	Neelakshi S	10012	ns@abc.com	Architecture Lead	56000.00	11200.00	6720.00	4664.80	69255.20	June	2018
4	Puja N	10013	pn@abc.com	Quality Lead	46200.00	9240.00	3696.00	3848.46	55287.54	June	2018
5	Avinash P	10015	ap@abc.com	Analytics Lead	46200.00	9240.00	4158.00	3848.46	55749.54	June	2018
6	Karthik G S	10011	kgs@abs.com	Strategy Lead	43000.00	8600.00	4300.00	3581.90	52318.10	April	2018
7											

Figure 10.1 *Mail Merge: Excel database example*

labels to identify the data in the columns or cells beneath. These labels will be used as tags in the template to correlate the Excel database and the template while generating payslips using Mail Merge. We have created our sample database in a new Excel file, in a worksheet named **Sheet 1**. The following screenshot shows the example that we will use.

In above database, first row is the header row that has descriptive labels such as **Name, Employee ID, Email** and so on, and subsequent rows have information. For each of the four employees we have given their unique employee id, email, designation, salary break up that is, earnings: basic, allowance, others and deductions: tax and then the total net payable. The last two columns specify the month and year for which the payslip is to be generated. After completing the data entry in the Excel file, save it for later use.

Using this information, we will generate the payslip of all four employees for June 2018 and the payslip of one employee for the month of April 2018, just to show how data changes based on row information. Each row corresponds to one payslip (one record) and each column corresponds to a field that will be inserted in the document generated.

10.1.2 Creating the Template

Next step is to create the payslip template in Microsoft Word. This template will have some common text and some text will vary that is, enclosed within "<>", denoting them as tags to be mapped with the data source. Open a new Word document and insert the text, similar to our example as seen in the following screenshot and save the document.

COMPANY – ABC LTD			
PAYSLIP FOR << Salary Month>> << Salary Year>>			
Employee Name: <<Name>> Designation: <<Designation>>		Employee Id: << Employee ID>>	
Earnings		Deductions	
Basic Salary	<<Basic>>	Taxes	<<Tax>>
Spl. Allowance	<<Allowance>>		
Others	<<Others>>		
		Net Payable: <<Net Payable>>	

Figure 10.2 *Mail Merge: Word template*

Note that the text within "<<>>" have the same name as the column labels in the header row for the Excel database, which makes it easier to correlate or map the template and database.

10.1.3 Generating the Merged document

Open the Word template created for payslip generation and go to menu **Mailings**. Select the option **Start Mail Merge | Step-by-Step Mail Merge Wizard**....

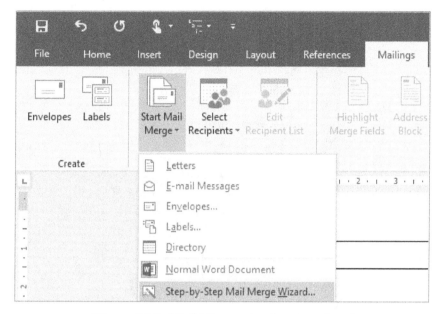

Figure 10.3 *Mail Merge: step by step wizard*

We will use the **Step-by-Step Mail Merge Wizard** to create the Mail Merge document and explain each step as we go.

On clicking the **Step-by-Step Mail Merge Wizard** option, you can see the Mail Merge option on the right-hand side pane. You can move, size, or close this pane as per your convenience, using the options that are given. We will keep it as is for our example.

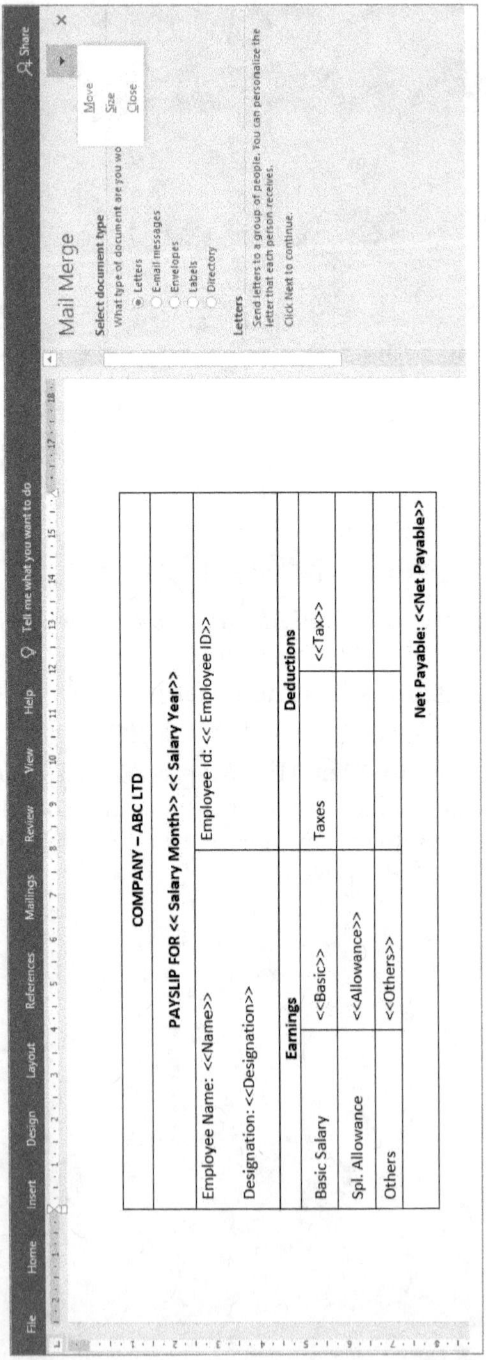

File Home Insert Design Layout References Mailings Review View Help ♀ Tell me what you want to do

Mail Merge

Select document type
What type of document are you wo

- ● Letters
- ○ E-mail messages
- ○ Envelopes
- ○ Labels
- ○ Directory

Letters

Send letters to a group of people. You can personalize the letter that each person receives.

Click Next to continue.

Move
Size
Close

COMPANY – ABC LTD		
PAYSLIP FOR << Salary Month>> << Salary Year>>		
Employee Name: <<Name>>	Employee Id: << Employee ID>>	
Designation: <<Designation>>		
Earnings		**Deductions**
Basic Salary	<<Basic>>	Taxes	<<Tax>>
Spl. Allowance	<<Allowance>>		
Others	<<Others>>		
		Net Payable: <<Net Payable>>

In Step 1, we will select the document type as 'Letters, and click on the **Next: Starting document**. In Step 2, select **Use the current document**, as this is our payslip template that we want to use for Mail Merge and click on **Next | Select recipients**.

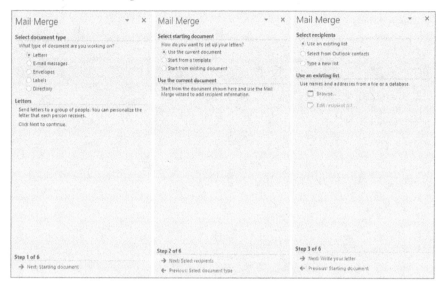

Figure 10.4 *Mail Merge: Steps 1-3*

In Step 3, we will connect the Word with the Excel database to get the recipients. Click on **Browse…** and select the Excel file in which we created the employee info database for payslips and click **OK**. Another window is launched showing all the sheets of the workbook; select **Sheet1** as we have the data in there. Click the checkbox indicating that the first row of data contains column headers, this way Excel will know the names to pick for merge.

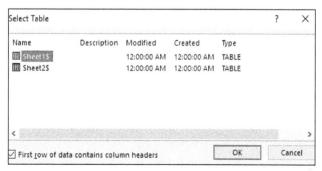

Click **OK** and it launches another window displaying the records from the Excel database that is, information from the selected **Sheet 1**. You can select/deselect the rows that you want to use for Mail Merge. We will select all and click **OK** to go to the next step.

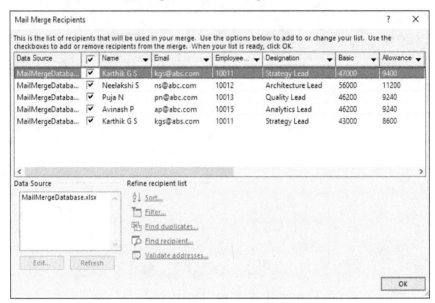

Figure 10.5 *Mail Merge: Select recipients window*

On clicking **OK** it moves back to the **Mail Merge** pain and displays our selection.

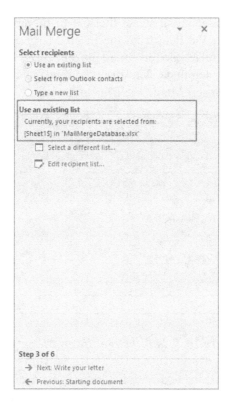

Again, click on **Next: Write your letter** and select **More Items…** to launch a dialog box to insert merged fields.

Figure 10.6 *Mail Merge: Insert Merge Field dialog*

Now, in the word document select the text to be replaced for example, <<Name>>, choose the field from the Insert Merge field dialog 'Name' and click Insert. Similarly do this for all the other texts that we had inserted with '<<>>' in our template. The Insert Merge Field option also comes from 'Mailings ➜Insert Merge Field' as given below.

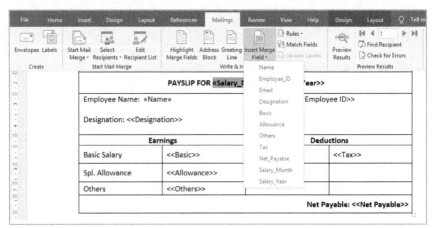

Figure 10.7 *Mail Merge: Insert Merge Field*

After you replace all the text with fields from the database, click on **Next ➜ Preview your letters** and see how it replaces the tags with actual values.

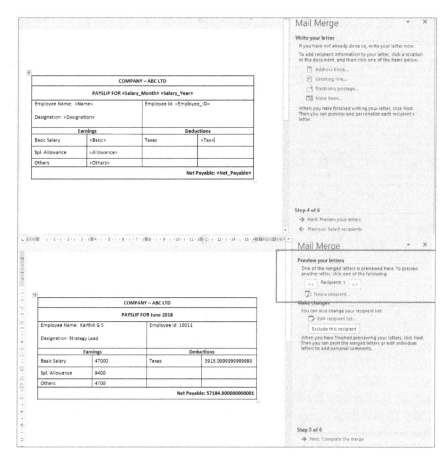

Figure 10.8 *Mail Merge: Preview letters*

It displays the first record and you can traverse through all the records and see the preview that is, preview all the payslips using the Next and Previous arrows.

If you perform a Mail Merge in Microsoft Word and use a Microsoft Excel worksheet as the data source for the recipient list, some of the numeric data may not retain its formatting when it is merged. For example, in the above preview the **Base Salary** does not have any decimals while **Taxes** shows multiple decimal places. We can format the merged field codes in Word to display a specific consistent format.

Select the merged field for **Taxes**, right-click and select **Toggle Field Codes** or press the *SHIFT +F9* shortcut key.

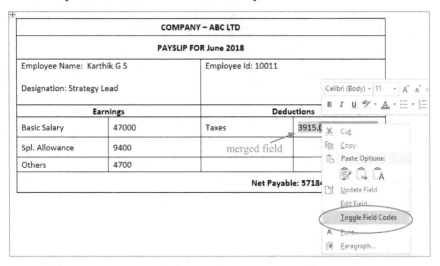

It will display the merged field code as {MERGEFIELD Tax} instead of the value 3915.0999999999999. Modify the merged field code to {MERGEFIELD Tax \# 0.00} and again click **Toggle Field Codes**. You will see that now it displays the value as 3915.10 for Taxes. You can also use the option **Update Field** in the right-click menu to reflect the changes. The Merged field codes are explained in more detail with examples later in this chapter.

After you have corrected the formatting and other aspects, and previewed all payslips, it's time to click **Complete the merge** option as given in *Figure 10.9*.

Figure 10.9 *Mail merge: Complete the merge*

In the next step, you get the option to either Print the documents, send email messages, or edit the individual documents.

10.1.3.1 Print Documents

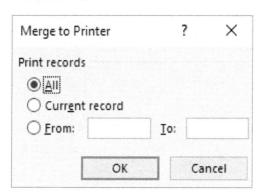

Figure 10.10 *Merge to Printer*

In the **Merge to Printer** dialog box you can choose to either print **All** the records that get generated, only **Current record**, or some specific records by giving the record numbers in **From** and **To** fields. On clicking **OK** the print dialog is launched for printing.

10.1.3.2 Send Email Messages

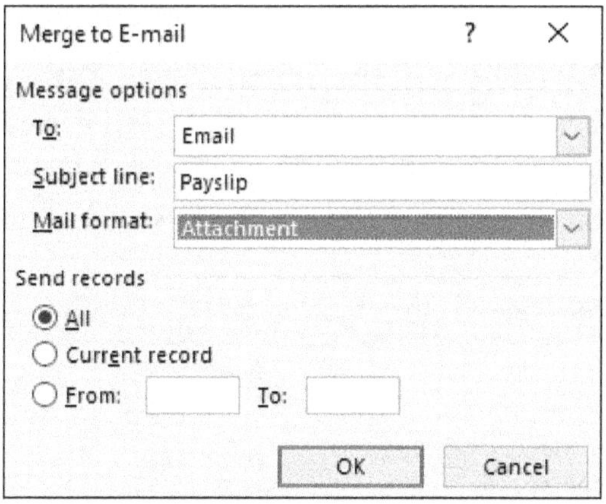

Figure 10.11 *Merge to E-mail*

In the **Merge to E-mail** dialog box, the **To** message options field shows the list of database fields to select, which is, Email in our case. You can also specify the Subject line, Mail format (attachment, text or html), and the records to send. Click **OK** to send email to recipients. By default, it tries to connect with Microsoft Outlook.

10.1.3.3 Edit Individual Documents

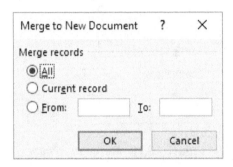

Figure 10.12 *Merge to Edit*

Edit Individual Documents option allows you to edit the generated documents and save them. It opens a new merged document for editing, with the selected records. Preferably, personalization's like special notes should be handled in the data source itself by adding a notes column to enter comments and so on; that is a better and easier way to handle.

10.1.4 Merged Field Codes

Field codes can be formatted in Word. In this section we will see how to format numbers, date and time with help of some examples.

To format a numeric merge field, use the \# switches mentioned in the following table:

Switch	Description	Example
\# 0	For rounded whole numbers	NUM = 4.5 {NUM \# 0} displayed as 5 (roundup) NUM = 3.1 {NUM \# 0} displayed as 3

Switch	Description	Example
\# ,0	For rounded whole numbers with a thousand separator	NUM = 3500 {NUM \# ,0} displayed as 3,500
# ,0.00	For numbers accurate to two decimal places, with a thousand separator	NUM = 3500 {NUM \# ,0.00} displayed as 3,500.00
\# $,0	For rounded whole dollar with a thousand separator	NUM = 3500 {NUM \# $,0} displayed as $3,500
\# 0%	For percentage	NUM = 8 {NUM \# 0%} displayed as 8%

To format a date and time merge field, use the \@ switches mentioned in the following table:

Switch	Example
\@ dd-MMM-yy	Formats as: 13-Mar-18
\@ dd/MM/yyyy	Formats as: 13/03/2018
\@ dd MMMM yyyy	Formats as: 13 March 2018
\@ dddd, dd MMMM yyyy	Formats as: Tuesday, 13 March 2018
\@ HH:mm	Formats as: 14:45
\@ HH:mm:ss	Formats as: 14:45:30
\@ h:mm:ss AM\PM	Formats as: 2:45:30 PM

Mailings Ribbon

On the Mailings tab of a Word document, we have some useful options that can also be used directly from the Ribbon apart from been accessed via the wizard pane like:

- 'Preview Results', which helps to toggle between actual values and Mail Merge template, using the Navigation arrows to traverse and preview the records.
- 'Find Recipient' to find records based on the different fields like Employee Id, Name and so on.

- 'Check for Errors' that gives multiple options for example simulate merge and report errors, complete merge and report errors as encountered, or report at the end in a new document,
- 'Highlight Merge Fields' under the Write & Insert Fields group, is a toggle button to select/deselect all the merged fields in the document. You can also use the *alt+F9* shortcut key.
- 'Select Recipients' and 'Edit Recipients List' under the 'Start Mail Merge' groups help to select new recipients / data source and modify the existing recipients list respectively.

10.2 Mail Merge from Excel (without Word)

We will use the same payslip generation example to show how to do Mail Merge from within the Excel without using Word. In case of a small letter, email, and so on, this method might be easier but as you will see, generating a payslip via this method is tedious and not that easy as compared to using Word Mail Merge. This method involves preparing a Mail Merge template in Excel, using Excel as the data source or the database and then generating the merged document.

In our example we will make use of the function INDIRECT, Named Ranges, and one simple Macro. Macros are discussed in more details in *Chapter 11*, *Macros in Excel* and for our example here you can just go and copy paste the code as described.

Note that the Excel file should have Macros enabled. If not then save the existing Excel as Macro enabled Excel that is, it will get saved with file extension **.xlsm**.

10.2.1 Prepare Database in Excel

We will use the same Excel database for the payslip generation that we created for Mail Merge with Word, (see *section 10.1.1*). Open the Excel file and rename the sheet in which we have the employee information as **Data**.

	A	B	C	D	E	F	G	H	I	J	K
1	Name	Employee ID	Email	Designation	Basic	Allowance	Others	Tax	Net Payable	Salary Month	Salary Year
2	Karthik G S	10011	kgs@abs.com	Strategy Lead	47000.00	9400.00	4700.00	3915.10	57184.90	June	2018
3	Neelakshi S	10012	ns@abc.com	Architecture Lead	56000.00	11200.00	6720.00	4664.80	69255.20	June	2018
4	Puja N	10013	pn@abc.com	Quality Lead	46200.00	9240.00	3696.00	3848.46	55287.54	June	2018
5	Avinash P	10015	ap@abc.com	Analytics Lead	46200.00	9240.00	4158.00	3848.46	55749.54	June	2018
6	Karthik G S	10011	kgs@abs.com	Strategy Lead	43000.00	8600.00	4300.00	3581.90	52318.10	April	2018
7											

10.2.2 Prepare Mail Merge Template in Excel

We will create the Mail Merge template in the same Excel workbook or file that has the Excel database. Create a new sheet in the workbook and name it as **Form**. Now add the payslip entries (see *section 10.1.2*) in the sheet as given in the following screenshot. In addition, we will add three more entries; **Current Record** – for displaying the corresponding values in the payslip fields, 'From & To' – for specifying the records for **Print Preview**.

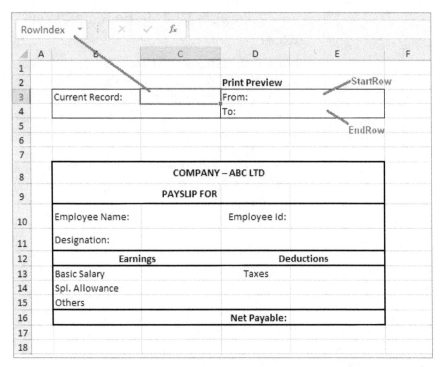

Figure 10.13 *Mail Merge template in Excel*

We will also use Named Ranges (see *section 3.3*) and name the cells; C3 as **RowIndex**, E3 as **StartRow** and E4 as **EndRow**. These will be used later in the Macro that will be used in this example.

In the Print Preview, we only want the payslip entries to be shown. To do that we will set the Print Area by selecting the cell range A6 to F18 and go to menu **Page Layout** ➜ **Print Area** ➜ **Set Print Area**.

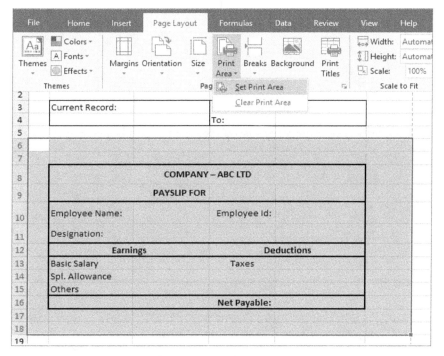

Figure 10.14 *Mail Merge template in Excel: Set Print Area*

Again, select the cell range A6 to F18 and go to menu option **Home →
Font → Fill Color**. Select the fill color as white, so that the print area
background is all white and we do not see the row and column lines. It will
look like text on a plain white sheet.

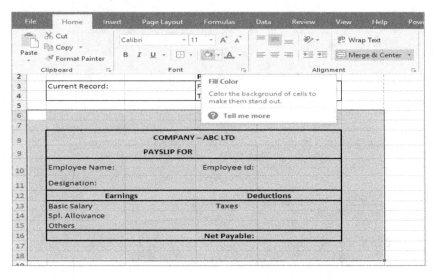

Figure 10.15 *Mail Merge template in Excel: Set background color*

Next step is to add some formulas and new named ranges that will be used in displaying the employee information in the template created.

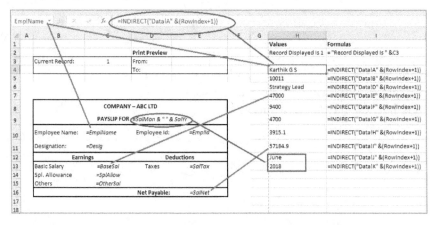

We have linked the employee information in column H, with help of the INDIRECT function (see formula in column I, for function help see *section 3.12.4*), which is in the same workbook or file but in a different sheet named *Data* (see 10.2.1 & 10.1.1). Each cell in column H, from H4 to H13 has been given a name. And these defined names are used in the formulas in the payslip template area to fill the values.

Note that in formulas for example, *=INDIRECT("Data!A"* *&(RowIndex+1))* we are adding 1 to the RowIndex (defined name for cell C3). The reason being that the first row in the employee database sheet **Data** is the header row, so we want to skip that. Hence, when we specify 1 for the Current Record field, in the formulas the first actual record in row 2 is picked, and so on.

For example, cell H4 is named **EmplName** that is used in cell C10 formula (=EmplName) to specify the value of the current record (which is 1), against the **Employee Name:** field. Similarly, cell H7 is named BaseSal indicating the Base Salary value in cell C13. And cells H12 & H13 are named **SalMon** & **SalYr** to print the Salary Month and Year of the Payslip that is, used in formula in cell D9 (=SalMon & " " & SalYr).

Now that all the formulas are set, we can view the different payslips of employees by changing the number in the 'Current Record' field (cell C3).

First Record - Current Record =1

	A	B	C	D	E	F	G	H
1								
2				Print Preview				Record Displayed is 1
3		Current Record:	1	From:				
4				To:				Karthik G S
5								10011
6								Strategy Lead
7								47000
8			COMPANY – ABC LTD					9400
9			PAYSLIP FOR	June 2018				4700
10		Employee Name:	Karthik G S	Employee Id:	10011			3915.1
11		Designation:	Strategy Lead					57184.9
12		Earnings		Deductions				June
13		Basic Salary	47000	Taxes	3915.1			2018
14		Spl. Allowance	9400					
15		Others	4700					
16				Net Payable:	57184.9			
17								
18								

Third Record - Current Record =3

	A	B	C	D	E	F	G	H
1								
2				Print Preview				Record Displayed is 3
3		Current Record:		3	From:			
4					To:			Puja N
5								10013
6								Quality Lead
7								46200
8				COMPANY – ABC LTD				9240
9				PAYSLIP FOR June 2018				3696
10		Employee Name:	Puja N		Employee Id:	10013		3848.46
11		Designation:	Quality Lead					55287.54
12			Earnings			Deductions		June
13		Basic Salary		46200	Taxes	3848.46		2018
14		Spl. Allowance		9240				
15		Others		3696				
16					Net Payable:	55287.54		
17								
18								

10.2.3 Print Preview the merged documents

In order to see the Print Preview of each record, we will write a small Macro and attach it to a control. To add a control in the sheet, insert a rectangular shape via the menu option **Insert → Illustrations → Shapes**, with the text **Print Preview** in cell E2 of the sheet **Form** as seen in the following screenshot. Select the inserted shape and format it as you like by using the **Drawing Tools → Format option**.

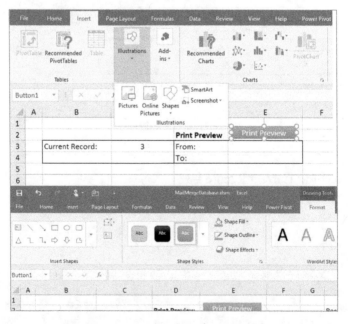

Select the inserted rectangular shape and select the **Assign Macro** option in the right-click menu. **Assign a Macro** dialog box will be launched, click on **New** to add the Macro code.

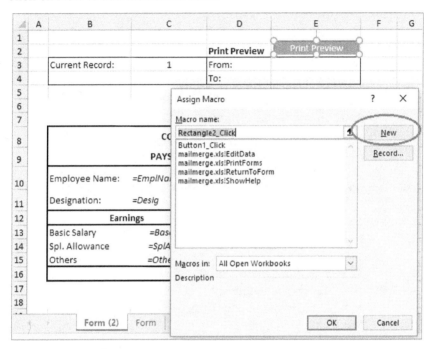

Figure 10.16 *Add new macro for control*

This will open the Microsoft **Visual Basic Application (VBA)** editor. Copy the code in the editor and save the file.

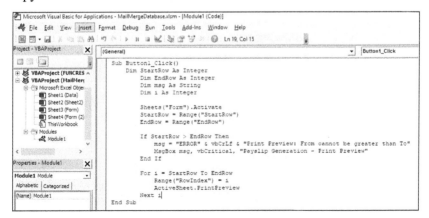

Code sample:

```
Sub Button1_Click()
    Dim StartRow As Integer
        Dim EndRow As Integer
        Dim msg As String
        Dim i As Integer

        Sheets("Form").Activate
        StartRow = Range("StartRow")
        EndRow = Range("EndRow")

        If StartRow > EndRow Then
            msg = "ERROR" & vbCrLf & "Print Preview:
From cannot be greater than To"
            MsgBox msg, vbCritical, "Payslip
Generation - Print Preview"
        End If

        For i = StartRow To EndRow
            Range("RowIndex") = i
            ActiveSheet.PrintPreview
        Next i
End Sub
```

Now everything is set for **Print Preview**. To see the **Print Preview** of records 1 to 3, enter the numbers 1 and 3 in the sheet in cells E3 and E4 respectively and then click on the **Print Preview** control (which we just added a Macro to). Excel will launch 3 print preview windows similar to the following screenshot:

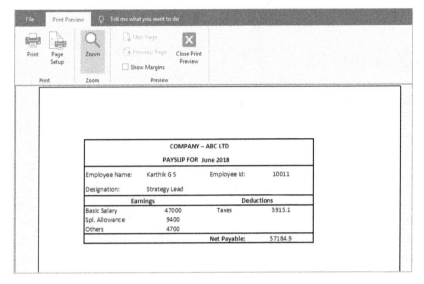

Figure 10.17 *Print Preview of Merged document*

CHAPTER 11

Macros in Excel

A Macro is a piece of programming code in VBA that runs in Excel and helps in automating routine tasks. It is an action or a set of actions that you can run as many times as you want. VBA is an acronym for Visual Basic for Applications, a programming language that is used to create or record Macros in Excel. In this chapter we will give an overview of VBA language, Recording & Writing Macros, and their usage with the help of examples.

Note that in order to use the Macros, the Excel workbook or file should be Macro enabled that is, saved as a Macro enabled file with extension **.xlsm**. Open Microsoft Excel and create a new file using the 'Blank Workbook' template. Go to **File → Save As** and select the destination folder by double-clicking on the folder name. In the **Save As** dialog box, specify the file name in the **File Name** field and select the **Save as type** as **Excel Macro-Enabled Workbook (*.xlsm)**.

11.1 VBA Quick Overview

Visual Basic for Applications (VBA) is a subset of the powerful Visual Basic programming language and is included with most MS Office applications. Although VBA gives you the ability to automate processes within and between MS Office applications, it is not necessary to know VBA code or computer programming if the Macro Recorder does what you want.

VBA uses English like statements to write instructions and has a short learning curve. The **user interface (UI)** is like the paint program, where you can drag, drop, and align controls.

11.1.1 Basic Language Constructs

In this section we will discuss the basic constructs of the language that will help in writing simple Macros.

- **Variables**: Are descriptive names for an integer, string, date, and so on, that are stored in a computer memory or storage system. They can be assigned a value to be used later in the code to execute.

- **Constant**: Is like a variable that once assigned cannot be modified by code. Keyword 'Const' is used to declare constant variables. The scope can be private or public, by default it is private.

- **Operators**: Similar to operators used in Excel formulas, arithmetic operators like '+' (addition), '- '(subtraction), '*' (multiplication) and '/' (division) can be used here as well.

- **Logical operators**: OR, AND, NOT can be used in conditional IF statements.

11.2 Enabling Developer Tab

Macros are one of the developer features, available on the **Developer** tab. By default, the **Developer** tab is hidden in Excel but we can enable it from the **File** menu by going to **File → Options → Customize Ribbon**. Click on the checkbox for **Developer** under **Main Tabs** and then click **OK**.

Figure 11.1 *Enable Developer Tab*

The **Developer** tab is added in Excel as a main tab with the following options for recording Macros, writing Macro code in VBA, and so on.

Figure 11.2 *Developer tab Ribbon*

11.3 Create Macro

We will create a simple Macro that will display *Hello Name* on clicking a button, where *Name* will be picked from a cell in the Excel sheet. First, we will add a button control in the Excel and then assign a new Macro to it. Open a Macro enabled Excel file, go to the Developer tab and click **Insert** to select 'Command button' under ActiveX Controls. Click anywhere in the Excel sheet to insert the Command button.

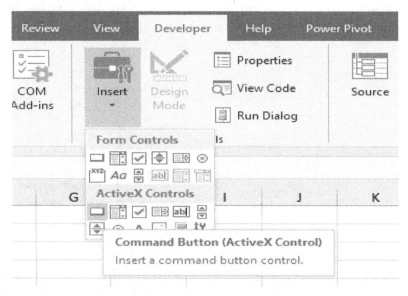

Right-click on the **Command Button** and click **View Code** to go to VBA editor. We will write our code in the editor.

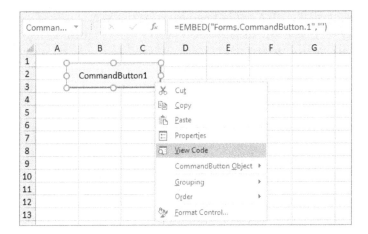

On clicking **View Code**, the VBA editor displays the default method or function for the command button. It is an empty method, where we will write the code.

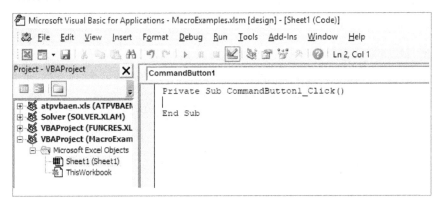

We will insert the code in the **CommandButton1_Click** method, code and the explanation of the code (in red) is given in the following screenshot:.

```
CommandButton1

    Private Sub CommandButton1_Click()

        Dim name As String ————————————————— Variable "name" declared as String

        name = Range("B5").Value ——————————— "name" assigned value in cell B5

        Range("D2").Value = "Hello " & name ——— "Hello" and "name" variable value are concatenated
                                                  and assigned to cell D2
    End Sub
```

Figure 11.3 *Macro code*

Save and close the VBA editor to go back to the Excel sheet. In the cell B5 enter any text, say **World** and then click on the command button. **Hello World** will be inserted in cell D2, as per the Macro code. Now change the text in cell B5 to **Children** and again click on the command button. **Hello Children** is inserted in D2, without changing anything in the Macro code and by just entering a new text in B5.

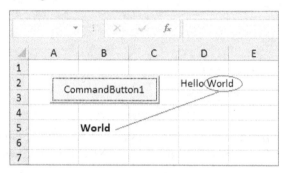

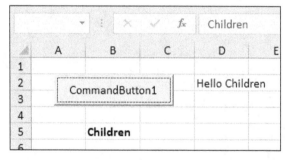

Figure 11.4 *Macro assigned to command button*

Another example of Macro code has been given in the mail merge payslip generation example in Chapter 10.2.3

11.4 Record Macro

In Excel we can also record a Macro, where it basically records and saves every mouse click and keystroke, we make. After recording when the Macro is run it performs the same steps. We will now record a Macro to export a .csv file into Excel and run the Macro to see the results. Identify a **.csv** file to import, in our case we have a file name **capitals.csv**.

Open a Macro enabled Excel file, go to the **Developer** tab and click on the **Record Macro** option. It opens a **Record Macro** dialog box. Enter the **Macro name**, shortcut key you want to assign with this Macro, scope of the Macro—this workbook, new workbooks, all open workbooks, and so on—and a description of what the Macro is intended to do.

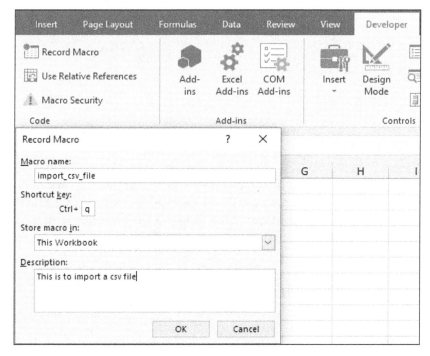

Click on OK to start recoding the Macro. We will do the following steps,

- Select cell A1

- Go to the **Data** tab and select **Get External Data** ➔ **From text**

- In the **Import Text File** dialog, browse and select the file **capitals. csv**

- Click **Import** in the dialog box

- Follow the **Import from Text** process as described in Chapter 1.10.1 so that the CSV file data will be imported in the Excel file

- Go to the **Developer** tab and select **Stop Recording**

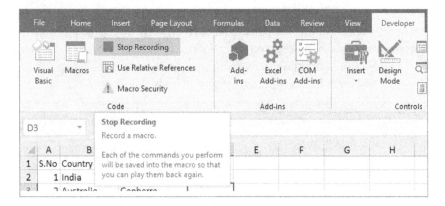

- Delete the imported data and save the file as a macro enabled Excel file.

When we record a Macro, Excel generates the code automatically based on the recorded actions that is, mouse clicks and keystrokes. We can go and see the code by going to the **Developer** tab. Go to the option **Macros** and select the recorded Macro name from the list and click **Edit**. VBA editor will be opened with the code generated for the Macro.

Figure 11.5 *Recorded Macro code*

Now we will check if the recorded Macro works.

- Open the saved Macro enabled Excel file, which has the recorded Macro.
- Go to the **Developer** tab and click on **Macros** to view the existing Macros in the file.

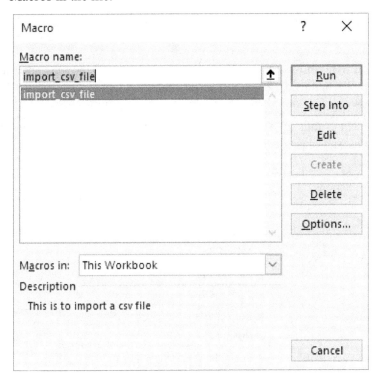

- Select the Macro **import_csv_file** that we had recorded earlier and click **Run**
- Once the Macro executes, it follows the same steps and import the data from csv to Excel

CHAPTER 12
What's in Excel 2019

General availability Office 2019 for Windows and Mac was announced in Sep 2018. Office 2019 is the on-premises version of Word, Excel, PowerPoint, Outlook, Project, Visio, Access, and Publisher.

Excel 2019 adds powerful new data analysis features, including new formulas and charts and enhancements to PowerPivot for both Windows and Mac.

New Functions	• CONCAT
	• IFS
	• MAXIFS
	• MINIFS
	• SWITCH
	• TEXTJOIN
New Maps	• Map charts
	• Funnel charts
Enhanced Visuals	• Scalable Vector Graphics (SVG)
	• Convert SVG icons to shapes
	• Insert 3D models to see all the angles
PivotTable Enhancements	• Personalize the default PivotTable layout
	• Automatic relationship detection
	• Creating, editing, and deleting custom measures
	• Automatic time grouping
	• PivotChart drill-down buttons
	• Search in the PivotTable
	• Smart rename
	• Multiple usability improvements
	• Multi-select Slicer
	• Faster OLAP PivotTables!

Power Pivot Updates	• Save the relationship diagram view as picture • Enhanced Edit Relationship dialog, creates faster and more accurate data relationships • Table selection using keyboard navigation • Column selection using column navigation • Auto column suggestion for same column name in both tables • Fixes that improve your overall modelling user experience

Get & Transform (Power Query)	• New and improved connectors
	• Improved transformations
	• General improvements
	  – New Queries & Connections side pane
	  – Improvements to the Power Query Editor including "select-as-you-type" drop-down menus, date picker support for date filters and conditional columns
	  – The ability to reorder query steps via drag-and-drop
	  – The ability to keep the layout in Excel when refreshing.

Sharing is easier	• Insert recent links • View and restore changes in workbooks that are shared • Quickly save to recent folders

Other new features included are related to Ink Improvements, Better Accessibility, Publish to Power BI and multiple General improvements like new themes, improved autocomplete, CSV(UTF-8) support, DLP support, and so on. Please refer to Microsoft's official support web site for further details on the new features.

www.ingramcontent.com/pod-product-compliance
Lightning Source LLC
La Vergne TN
LVHW022334060326
832902LV00022B/4025